JESUS: THE INCARNATION OF THE WORD

By the same author

The Message of the Psalter
An Eschatological Programme in the Book of Psalms

The Songs of Ascents
Psalms 120 to 134 in the Worship of Jerusalem's Temples

Messiah ben Joseph

Jesus

The Incarnation of the Word

DAVID C. MITCHELL

CAMPBELL
PUBLISHERS
GLASGOW SCOTLAND

CAMPBELL
PUBLISHERS

CampbellPublishers.com

First published in paperback (May 2021)

Paperback ISBN: 978-1-916619-13-5

Front cover: *Head of Christ* by Rembrandt van Rijn.
Back cover: A fifth-century Syriac text of Romans 6.

Brightmorningstar.org

To the people of
Holy Trinity Pro-Cathedral Brussels

Contents

Preface

ONE DAY, Leonard Bernstein was discussing American music with his students.

"What", they asked him, "do you think of Aaron Copland?"

The maestro replied, "He's the best we've got."

Lots of things are the best we've got. This is especially true of books about Jesus. Falling short is guaranteed. The subject inevitably dwarfs the writer. For Jesus is the colossus of history, striding the globe with one foot in the future and one in the past. In 2014, Cambridge University Press published *Who's Bigger? Where Historical Figures Really Rank* by two quantitative analysts, Steve Skiena and Charles Ward. They ranked the most influential people in history by aggregating the traces of millions of online opinions, and concluded that Jesus is by far the most influential person ever to have lived. He is more searched, more sought, more cited, more known, more discussed, than anyone else who ever passed through this poor vale of tears. Millions have written about him, in billions of books and homilies and films and songs and blogs, comprising trillions of words. What can one add to what has been said?

Well, if one must add, it's best to add only a little. And so this book speaks only of Jesus's coming into the world. It is, in fact, a sibling volume to my *Messiah ben Joseph* (2016). As *Messiah ben Joseph* dealt with ancient Israelite and rabbinic teaching on the Passion of the Messiah, so this book covers what these sources say on the Messiah's Incarnation. As *Messiah ben Joseph* looked at the paradigm of the Josephite Messiah, so this book looks at the paradigm of the priestly Messiah. As *Messiah ben Joseph* raised questions about the Messiah's lineage, so this book answers them.

I ask what Jesus was doing before he was born in Bethlehem, and how he was known by the patriarchs and prophets. What did the mysterious priest Melchizedek have to do with this revelation? I examine the lines of his genetic descent. I give a full explanation for his divergent genealogies, as found in Matthew and Luke, showing that they are not only credible, but necessary to bypass the prophets' curses on Josiah's sons. I uncover information about his mother's background and youth that will be new to many readers. I discuss the evidence for his paternity. I ask whether the ubiquitous assertion of the 'Jewishness of Jesus' is not a great over-simplification. Yes, Jesus was an Israelite. That is clear enough. But simply to call him Judahite or 'Jewish' seems a step too far. The first-century Judeans did not think he was Judahite. Then, last of all, I look at the name he received at birth, and how it sums up his being and his mission.

I have tried to make the book clear to the reader with no theological training. That is always my goal. But there are moments when my case requires analysis of the source texts. I have tried to keep these discussions as lucid as possible. If you are not familiar with the biblical languages, then read these sections slowly and carefully, in first gear, and you will get there. Unfamiliar words will be found at the end of the book, in the Glossary.

I am grateful to all who have helped or advised with this book in any way, to Robert Gordon and Hector Patmore for their thoughts on the name of Jesus and the targum to Psalm 110 respectively, and to Seth Postell, who has been most generous in sharing his thoughts on many passages, not least Genesis 49:10 and Isaiah 7:14. I warmly thank Michael Heiser and Adam Hensley for their back-cover reviews and their most helpful comments. An earlier version of chapter four appears in 'Psalm 110, Jesus, and Melchizedek' in D.M. Howard and A. Schmutzer, *Reading the Psalms Theologically* (Lexham Press), and I am grateful to be able to republish it here.

There are plenty books on Jesus, and plenty on his Incarnation. But if you want to know about his deeds before Bethlehem, about his link with Melchizedek, about how he spoke to the prophets, about his lineage and background, and about his Jewishness and non-Jewishness, then this may just be the best you've got.

Brussels
Christmas 2020

Before Abraham was, I am.

Jesus

1

The Visible God

DEEP is the well of the past. The Holy One, blessed be he, called Avram from Ur of the Chaldees to the land of Canaan.

On arriving there, he met a mysterious figure called Malki-Tsedeq, now better known to us as Melchizedek. He seems, at first glance, like a minor figure. He appears, in Genesis, for only three verses, and is named there only once. Nor did Avram seem in any hurry to meet him. He had been all around the land, and up and down to Egypt, before they met. But, after Avram defeats a coalition of Mesopotamian kings against overwhelming odds, the enigmatic Melchizedek steps forth from his equally enigmatic background and blesses him.

> [18]And Melchizedek king of Shalem brought out bread and wine, and he was *kohen* of El Elyon. [19]And he blessed him and said. "Blessed be Avram by El Elyon, possessor of heaven and earth. [20]And blessed be El Elyon who has delivered your enemies into your hand"; and he gave him a tenth of all.

That's it. Just three verses. Yet over the ages they have aroused much curiosity. For a start, they contain a lot of firsts. Melchizedek is the first *kohen* or 'priest' in the Bible. He is the first man in the Bible to bless another. He is the first to speak of El Elyon—God Most High—a name later given to Israel's God.[1] He is the first to offer bread and wine. He is the first linked with an offering of a tenth or 'tithe'. And he is one of

[1] Ps. 78:35, 56; Num. 24:16; Deut. 32:8; 2 Sam. 22:14; Isa. 14:14; Ps. 9:2; 87:5; 97:9.

only two people in the Bible to be both king and priest, and to be called 'King of Peace', the other being, of course, the promised Messiah (Isa. 9:7, Zech. 9:10).

Yet these three verses contain further details that flag up just how unusual Melchizedek is.

For a start, he blesses Avram. Remember, Avram is the man called and blessed by God himself. Avram is to father the kings and *kohanim* of Israel. He is the one appointed to be a blessing for all the nations of the earth. Who is this priest who appears from nowhere to bless the man blessed by the Almighty?

Figure 1. Abraham and Melchizedek by Charles Foster (1897).

Next, this *kohen* of El Elyon blesses Avram first and El Elyon second. In the Bible, order of names is usually significant. And here it is striking. Why would the priest of El Elyon place his heavenly master after Avram, whom he seems to be meeting only for the first time? Rabbinic sages, as we shall see, found this quite contrary to protocol. They said Melchizedek got his wrist slapped for it. So was he an uppety priest? Was he so exalted that he could dispense with proprieties? Or did he know something about the Holy One's decree to Avram in Genesis 12:2–3? Did he have a private line to heaven?

Then there's the question of the 'tenth' or tithe-offering. For it's not said in the text who gives it to whom. Since Avram has the booty of all the plundered kings, it very much looks like the 'tenth of all' goes from Avram to Melchizedek. But, on the other hand, since the tithe directly follows Melchizedek's speech, one might just argue that it is the other way round. The oldest Bible translations preserve the ambiguity.[2] Other early texts say it was indeed Avram who paid the tithe.[3]

> The patriarch Abraham gave him a tithe of the plunder. (Heb. 7:4)
>
> And he gave him a tithe of all he had brought back. (Tg Yerushalmi)
>
> And he gave him a tithe of all the flocks of the king of Elam and his confederates. (1QApGen 22:17)
>
> Avram then offered him the tithe of the spoil. (Josephus, Ant. 1:10:2)

But later Jewish texts say Melchizedek paid up. In fact, it became a hot topic in Jewish-Christian debate. For, since the tithe goes from the lesser to the greater, it shows the relative rank of the two figures. Was Melchizedek greater than Avram? That was not an idea the Jews liked at all. Or was it the other way round?

But, admitting the obvious sense, that Avram tithes the plunder of the kings to Melchizedek, one must ask why. Here comes Avram with the plunder of four conquered kings—vast quantities of gold and booty. Did he give a tenth to everyone he met on the road? If not, then why to Melchizedek? Was it because he was a king? But Avram knew other local potentates, and he did not tithe to them. He did not tithe to the King of Sodom, one verse later. Avram must have thought that Melchizedek deserved the tithe.

In the Bible, the tithe is a return for a blessing bestowed. In later times, the Israelites brought their harvest-tithe to God as the author of their bounty. In the same way, Avram gives the tithe of the fruit of his conquest to Melchizedek. It suggests that Avram saw Melchizedek and El Elyon as the author of his victory. So Avram and Melchizedek at least worship the same deity.

[2] LXX; Syriac; Targums Onq. & Neof.; Vulgate. Cf. Jerome, Epis. 73:6 (App. 2).
[3] Jub. 13:25–26 preserves enough to show the same view (Charles, *Apocrypha*, 2:33).

Then there's Melchizedek's anonymity. Nothing at all is said of his origins. This leads the Epistle to the Hebrews famously to say that Melchizedek is *without father, without mother, without genealogy, without beginning of days or end of life* (Heb. 7:3). Many say that the author of Hebrews deduces too much from silence. But I'm not so sure. Most ancient priesthoods depended on genealogy. Israel's totally did. So the silence on this priest's lineage is very strange.

Then there's the question whether Melchizedek is a name or a title. It comes from the Hebrew nouns *melekh* (king) and *tsedeq* ('justice' or 'righteousness'). So it means 'King of Righteousness' or 'Righteous King'.[4] It could be simply a description, meaning 'just' and 'lawful' king, one legally entitled to royal office. But most interpreters, from Psalm 110 on, see it as a name, reflecting the character of its bearer.[5]

Likewise, there's the question of whether Shalem is a place or an aspect of the man. Some take *shalem*—that is, perfection, peace, or completeness—to be part of his title: *melekh shalem,* that is, King of Peace. Others take it to mean Jerusalem which, in ancient times, was called Shalem, being named, perhaps, after the Canaanite god of sunset and completion.[6] In other words, Melchizedek's credits include being the first king of Jerusalem. But most interpreters hold the two views together: he is the King of Peace who rules in Shalem.[7]

Then there's a textual issue. In verse 22 of the Masoretic text—the Hebrew text from medieval Palestine—Avram says to the king of Sodom, *I have raised my hand to YHVH El Elyon.*[8] Yet the name YHVH is absent from the early texts. They simply say, *I have raised my hand to El Elyon.*[9] The name YHVH is found only in the Targums and the Masoretic text. So it looks like a later addition. But why was it added?

All in all, it does seem strange that Melchizedek should be such a minor figure and that Avram should take so long to meet him. After all, Melchizedek is not like the Canaanites. Their moral corruption was

[4] Philo, *De legum allegoria* 3:79; Josephus, *Ant.* 1:10:2; *War* 6:10:1; Heb. 7:2; Tg Y. *ad loc*, take the *yodh* of *malki* as the old semitic genitive (cf. Sáenz-Badillos, *History*, 23). It does not mean 'my king is righteous' (*pace* Wilson, 'King Messiah', 400).

[5] Philo, *De legum allegoria* 3:82; Josephus, *Ant.* 1:10:1; Heb. 7:2.

[6] Ps; 76:2; Josephus, *Ant.* 1:10:2; *War* 6:10:1; Tg Onq. and Tg Y. to Gen. 14:18. Jub. 30:1 records a town called Shalem near Shechem; cf. Jerome, Epis. 73:7 (Appendix 2).

[7] E.g. Tgs Y. & Neof. on Gen. 14.18.

[8] YHVH is a transcription of the Hebrew sacred name of God. See the Glossary.

[9] LXX, Genesis Apoc. (1Q20:22), Peshitta, Philo (Abr. 235), Josephus (Ant. 1:10).

plain even in Avram's time (Gen. 18:20; 19:13). Avram's clan held them in contempt.[10] But Melchizedek is the righteous king, *kohen* of El Elyon, a monotheist in a polytheistic world. And Avram is the founder of the world's first monotheistic faith. They obviously worship the same God, for Avram humbly accepts Melchizedek's blessing in the name of El Elyon, swears an oath in that name, and gives him the tithe. Melchizedek brings out food for him—bread and wine, the makings of a feast—and they eat together. There they sit, two monotheist fellow-believers, all alone in a world of Amorite, Hurrian, Egyptian, and Canaanite polytheistic idolatry. They have everything in common. You would think they might have more to do with one another than this one chance meeting.

And perhaps they had. Let's see what light we can shine on this priest Melchizedek. Who was he? What were his dealings with Avram?

A Mortal Melchizedek

Over the centuries, many answers have been proposed to the question, 'Who was Melchizedek?' But they boil down to only two views: He was either a mortal or an immortal.

Let's begin with those who thought Melchizedek was a mortal. Here are some of the options suggested.

Melchizedek a Canaanite king. Josephus calls Melchizedek a 'Canaanite chief' and the idea appears in some modern writers too.[11] This view need not detain us. As I said, the writer of Genesis tells how Avram's clan held the Canaanites in disdain. He tells too how the Canaanites, for the sin of Ham, were cursed with perpetual servitude to Shem and Japheth (Gen. 9:25–27). It is unlikely that the same author, on the very next column of his scroll, would allow a Canaanite to bless Avram and receive the tithe from him.

Melchizedek an unknown antediluvian. A unique view is found in 2 Enoch 64–73, where Melchizedek is the virgin-born son of Sopanima, the wife of Nir, the brother of Noah. His mother dies before his birth

[10] Gen. 24:3; 27:46. The biblical Hittites, of whom Rebecca speaks at Gen. 27:46, were Canaanites (Gen. 10.15). The later Hittites of Anatolia perhaps took their name from the Canaanite group, but are thought to have been Indo-European.

[11] Josephus, *War* 6:10:1. Cf. also Simon, 'Melchisédech', 60; Kaiser, *Christian and the "Old" Testament*, 48; Cargill, *Melchizedek*, thinks he was king of Sodom.

and he emerges from her body of his own accord. Gabriel takes him to 'the paradise Eden' that he might become priest after the Flood. This view is unknown by later writers, and not found again.

Melchizedek a righteous man. Most church fathers stress the humanity of Melchizedek without specifying his ancestry. Epiphanius, Cyril of Alexandria, Ephrem of Syria, and Jerome all held some form of this view.[12] Jerome ascribes it also to Irenaeus, Hippolytus, Eusebius of Caesarea, Eusebius of Emesa, Apollinaris, and Eustathius. (Since Jerome's letter will become important to our discussion, I have reproduced it in full in Appendix 2.) The early Ambrose agreed—Melchizedek was no angel, but a holy man who was a type, and only a type, of Christ—though Ambrose later changed his mind.[13]

The fathers tell how Melchizedek was an uncircumcised priest whose priesthood was superior to that of Levi.[14] The implication, of course, is that the uncircumcised Christian priesthood is superior to the Jewish. Yet, except for Jerome and Ephrem, they leave aside the issue of ancestry, always less important to Christians than to Jews. In this they were perhaps encouraged by the letter to the Hebrews which describes Melchizedek as *without father or mother, without genealogy, without beginning of days or end of life* (Heb. 7:3). But, as we shall see, they failed to grasp that text properly.

Melchizedek is Shem the son of Noah. The standard Jewish view—found throughout Rabbinic literature—is that Melchizedek was Shem ben Noah, also known as Shem Rabba, that is, 'Shem the Great'. Since Shem was Avram's ancestor, this neatly solved the Jewish problem of Avram's obeisance to him. (This view was also held by Christians who followed the Hebrew text, like Jerome, Ephrem, and, later, Luther.[15]) After the flood, they said, Shem became *kohen* in Shalem-Jerusalem.[16]

> And Melchizedek, king of Jerusalem—he is Shem Rabba—brought out bread and wine, for he was the priest who ministered in the high priesthood before El Elyon. (Tg Neofiti on Gen 14.18)

[12] Epiphanius, *Panarion* 55; Cyril, *Glaphyra on Genesis* 2; Jerome, Epis. 73.

[13] Ambrose, *On Faith* 3:11.

[14] E.g. Tertullian, *Adv. Jud.* 2–3; Justin, *Dial.* 19, 33; Aphrahat, Hom. 2:4.

[15] Jerome (Epistle 73 [see App. 2]; Hebrew Ques. on Gen., 14:18–19) defends the Hebrew chronology of Genesis and the view that Melchizedek was Shem. Ephrem cites Ned. 32b verbatim in his commentary on Genesis 14:18–20; Luther on Gen. 14.

[16] Tg Y. Gen. 14:18; Gen. R. 46:7; 56:10; Lev. R. 25:6; Num. R. 4:8; Ned. 32b.

> And Melchizedek—he is Shem bar Noah, king of Jerusalem—came forth to meet Avram, and brought him bread and wine. At that time he ministered before El Elyon. (Tg Yerushalmi on Gen. 14.18)

In answer to Christian claims about his uncircumcision, the rabbis said he was born circumcised.

> *King of Shalem* [perfection]. Rabbi Yitzhak the Babylonian said: '[This is because] he was born circumcised. (Genesis Rabbah 43:6)

He had a *medrasha* or school in Jerusalem where Isaac studied for three years after being spared as a sacrifice.

> And the angels of the height took Isaac and brought him into the *medrasha* of Shem Rabba; and he was there three years. And in the same day Abraham returned to his young men; and they arose and went together to Beersheba, and Abraham dwelt at Beersheba. (Targum Yerushalmi 22:19)

It was after he returned from Shem's *medrasha* that Isaac met Rebekah.

> And Isaac came from the *medrasha* of Shem Rabba, by way of the well [Be'er LaḤai Ro'i] where was revealed to him the Living and Eternal One, who sees and is not seen. And he dwelt in the land of the south. And Isaac went out to pray in the open field at evening time. And he raised his eyes and saw and, behold, camels were approaching. (Tg Yerushalmi Gen. 24:62–63)

It was to Shem's school in Jerusalem that Rebekah went to enquire when her pregnancy was difficult, as the Targum again relates:

> *And the children pressed in her womb like men doing battle* (Gen. 25:22) And she said, If this is the anguish of a mother, then what are children to me? And she went into the *medrasha* of Shem Rabba to beseech mercy before the Lord. (Tg Yerushalmi; cf. Tg Neofiti)

The Talmud tells us that Shem also had a *bet-din* or courthouse in Shalem-Jerusalem. There the Holy Spirit spoke in a heavenly voice to adjudge the paternity of Tamar's child by Judah.

> Rabbi Eleazar says: In three places the Divine Spirit appeared [to endorse a righteous judgement]: In the court of Shem, in the court of Samuel the Ramathite, and in the court of Solomon.
>
> In the court of Shem, as it is written: *And Judah acknowledged them and said: She is more righteous than I* [*mimmenni*] (Gen. 38:26). How did he know [that Tamar's child was indeed his]? Perhaps, just as he

> went to her, another person went to her as well [and so Judah was not the father]. [But] A heavenly voice came forth and said: From Me [*mimmenni*] these secrets emerged. (B. Mak. 23b)[17]

Yet the Talmud relates that, despite all his great eminence, Shem-Melchizedek lost the *k'hunah* or priesthood to Avram because he blessed Avram before blessing El Elyon.

> R. Zechariah said in the name of R. Yishmael: The Holy One, blessed be he, wished to derive the *k'hunah* from Shem, as it is said: *And he was kohen to El Elyon* (Gen. 14:18). [But] since he [Shem-Melchizedek] prefaced the blessing of Avram to the blessing of ha-Maqom [the Omnipresent], he [God] derived it from Avram, as it is said: *And he blessed him and said, 'Blessed be Avram by El Elyon possessor of the heavens and earth, and blessed be El Elyon.'* (Gen. 14:19b–20a)
>
> Avraham said to him, 'And does one preface the blessing of the slave to the blessing of his master?'
>
> Immediately he [God] gave it [the *k'hunah*] to Avraham, as it is said, *HaShem said to my Lord, 'Sit on my right hand until I set your enemies as a stool for your feet.'* (Ps. 110:1) And after this it is written, *The Lord has sworn and will not repent. You are a priest forever* 'al-dib̲rati *Malki-zedeq,* (Ps. 110:4) that is, on account of that which Melchizedek had said [*l'dib̲oro shel malki-tsedeq*]. This corresponds to what is written, *And he was kohen to El Elyon.* [Which means] he [Melchizedek] was a *kohen*, but his sons were not *kohanim* [i.e., Melchizedek lost the hereditary *k'hunah* to Avram]. (B. Ned. 32b).[18]

So the Jewish tradition presents quite a coup. Melchizedek-Shem was in line to receive the hereditary *k'hunah.* But, because he flouted blessing protocol, the *k'hunah* went to Avraham and his seed, and so ultimately to Levi and Aaron.

Now there's no question that Shem could have been Melchizedek, at least according to the Hebrew text. According to Gen. 11.10–26, Shem lived 600 years, and was 390 years old when Avram was born. He was 465 years old when Avram arrived in the promised land, and he outlived Avram by 35 years. For Jews—and Christians like Jerome, Ephrem, and Luther who knew the Hebrew text—Shem could indeed have been *kohen* in Jerusalem in Avram's time.

But in the genealogy of the Greek Septuagint Bible, with its longer antediluvian time-periods, that is not possible at all. In the Septuagint,

[17] The same judgement is alluded to in B. Avodah Zarah 36a.

[18] Cited also in Lev. R. 25:6; alluded to in B. Sanh. 108b; Midr. Ps. 76 §3; 110 §4.

Shem was dead long before Avram arrived in the promised land.[19] That is why the Greek fathers never accepted the view that Melchizedek was Shem. Epiphanius, for instance, totally rejects it.[20]

But perhaps some details have been overlooked in the Hebrew view. First, if Melchizedek were Shem, then Avraham and Levi were his seed. And so, if Melchizedek lost the hereditary *k'hunah* to Avram, then Avram and Levi lost it too, since they were Melchizedek's sons. It's a bit like when Marty McFly travels back in time from 1985 to 1955, and his mother starts crushing on Marty and not his father, Marty finds that he disappears in the future. Of course, one could reply that the *k'hunah* removed from Melchizedek could have been reassigned to his descendant. But in that case, Melchizedek was not really disqualified from the hereditary *k'hunah* after all. It's a strange argument altogether. One wonders if Rav Zechariah ever thought about that.

Second, for Christians, the view that Shem was Melchizedek is at odds with the argument of the book of Hebrews that Melchizedek's priesthood was greater than Levi's, since Levi paid the tithe-tribute to Melchizedek through Avraham (Heb. 7:10). If Melchizedek were the ancestor of Levi, then their priesthood was one and the same. Melchizedek's priesthood, though older, was no different in essence. One wonders if Jerome, Ephrem, and Luther ever thought about that.

In fact, it is honestly puzzling why so many of the Fathers, with the letter to the Hebrews in their hand, make so little of its statement that Melchizedek is *without father or mother, without genealogy, without beginning of days or end of life* (Heb. 7:3). This leads to our next point.

An Immortal Melchizedek

In the first centuries of the Christian period, some took Melchizedek to be a heavenly figure. Hippolytus of Rome (175–235) opposes one Theodotus who claimed that Melchizedek was 'the very greatest power, greater than Christ, and that Christ existed in his image'.[21] Origen and his disciples, according to Jerome, took Melchizedek to be an angel; and Jerome wrote a refutation of a work which claimed that

[19] See Appendix 1: The Genesis Genealogies and the Second Cainan.
[20] Epiphanius, *Panarion* 55.
[21] Hippolytus, *Refutation of All Heresies* 7:24.

Melchizedek was the Holy Spirit.[22] Epiphanius and Marcus Eremita, in the fourth and fifth centuries, opposed a group called the Melchizedekites, who believed Melchizedek was an incarnation of the Logos and the son of God.[23] Timotheus of Constantinople, in *On the Receiving of Heretics*, mentions a sect of Phrygian Melchizedekites called Untouchables, who do not touch others or accept food from their hand; neither Jews nor pagans, they keep the Sabbath, but are uncircumcised. Of course, these devotees of Melchizedek were all fringe groups. But, strangest of all, the great Ambrose, only a few years after asserting that Melchizedek was only a man, later came to call him the 'son of God' and 'God'.[24] Clearly, Melchizedek was a subject of no small interest in the early church.

Now, this idea of an immortal Melchizedek arose in communities which knew the Epistle to the Hebrews. Their views were influenced by Hebrews 7:3. But is there anything to suggest that such views were current in Judaism before that Epistle was ever written? I suggest the answer is yes. In fact, I suggest this view is found in Psalm 110, which we shall look at in chapter four. But first, let's see if there are any hints of the same thing in Genesis itself.

Genesis 14 in Context

In Genesis 12, the Holy One tells Avram to go to another land and he will bless him. But when Avram arrives in the land, the first person who blesses him is not the Holy One but Melchizedek, saying, *Blessed be Avram by El Elyon* (Gen. 14:19).

After meeting Melchizedek, the 'word of YHVH' comes to Avram in a vision (Gen. 15:1). A vision, of course, implies that something is seen, not simply heard. This visible 'word' takes him outside and shows him the stars, which sounds like a bodily thing for 'a word' to do. He promises to be Avram's shield and reward, to make his offspring as many as the stars, and he makes a covenant with him. But the all-important word 'bless' (cf. Gen. 48:15–16; 49:25–26), is not spoken.

Next, in Genesis eighteen, three men appear to Avraham at the trees

[22] So Jerome, Epistle 73.2. See Appendix 2.
[23] Epiphanius, Panarion 55; Marcus Eremita, Against the Melchizedekites.
[24] *Faith* 3:11 (before 380); *Abraham* 1:3 (380) ; *Six Days of Creation* 1:3 (386-90).

of Mamre. Two of them are later identified as *mal'akhim*, that is, 'messengers' or 'emissaries' or 'angels' (Gen. 19:1). But the one who speaks to Avraham is YHVH himself in human form (18:1, 13, 22). His feet are washed. He eats Avraham's food, promises him a son within a year, and seeks his advice on Sodom. But he does not bless him.

Finally, decades later, God tells Avraham to take Isaac *and go to the land of Moriah and offer him there as a burnt offering on one of the mountains of which I will tell you* (Gen. 22:22). Years later, in Solomon's time, Mount Moriah became the Temple Mount (2 Chr. 3:1). One might ask exactly which mountain *in the land of Moriah* was meant. But *the land of Moriah* was the territory of Jerusalem or, as it was then, Shalem, Melchizedek's city. So Avraham goes to sacrifice his son not in some uninhabited rural area where none could see, but in the city of Melchizedek, the one who first blessed him.

Did Melchizedek not know that Avraham, his friend, the great prince (Gen. 23:6), the commander of armies, had come to town? One imagines he did, and that this sacrifice did not proceed without his knowledge. Then we learn that although *God* commanded Avraham to sacrifice Isaac, the one who tells him to desist is the 'Angel of YHVH' (Gen. 22:11). This 'Angel' countermands the command of God! And then the Angel, speaking as YHVH himself, finally bestows the promised blessing upon obedient Avraham.

> [15]The Angel of YHVH called to Avraham from heaven a second time [16]and said: I swear by myself, declares YHVH, that because you have done this and have not withheld your son, your only son, [17]I will surely bless you and make your descendants as numerous as the stars in the sky and the sand on the seashore. Your descendants will take possession of the cities of their enemies. [18]And through your offspring all nations on earth will be blessed, because you have obeyed me.

So, in all this, the first to fulfil YHVH's promise to bless Avraham is Melchizedek, while the last is the Angel of YHVH.

The Visible God

But who is this 'Angel of YHVH'? In Hebrew, he is called *mal'akh yhvh*, which means both 'angel' and 'messenger' of YHVH. And he appears in visible, human form. Grammatically, the Hebrew is unclear whether he is *the* angel or just *an* angel. But, in context, it is clear that he is a single, unique being, who speaks as if he is YHVH himself, who accepts the worship due to YHVH, and who seems to be YHVH himself.

He first appears to runaway Hagar and foretells her son's future. She calls him 'the *elohim* who sees me'. Later, when she is driven out, the 'Angel of *elohim*' saves her and her son (Gen. 16:7–14; 21:17–19).

Then, as said above, the 'Angel of YHVH' calls to Avraham from heaven. He countermands the divine command to sacrifice Isaac (Gen. 22:11). Speaking like YHVH himself, he says, 'You have not withheld *from me* your son' (Gen. 22:12–17). And Avraham's last recorded words are about the Angel (Gen. 24:7). As Michael Heiser says, 'Abraham's spiritual journey includes a divine figure that is integral to Israelite Godhead thinking: the Angel of Yahweh [YHVH].'[25]

The 'Angel of God' appeared to Jacob in a dream, saying that he was the same one who appeared to him at Bethel, where he called himself, 'YHVH the God of your father Avraham and the God of Isaac' (Gen. 31:11–13; 28:13). Later, at the fords of the Jabbok, Jacob struggles with a mysterious man to obtain his blessing, a man whom Hosea tells us is both *elohim* and the 'Angel of YHVH' (Gen. 32:24–30; cf. Hos. 12:3–4). Later still, at the end of Jacob's life, he says that the God of Luz or Bethel (whom we now know to be the Angel of YHVH) was El Shaddai, the almighty God; and he calls the God of his fathers the 'Angel' who has delivered him from all harm, and blesses his grandsons in the name of the Angel (48:3–4, 15–16).[26]

The one who appears to Moses in the burning bush is called the Angel of YHVH, then YHVH, then *elohim*; he is the God of Avraham, Isaac and Jacob (Exod. 3:2–6). This Angel of *elohim* and of YHVH moved in the pillar of cloud and fire that accompanied the Israelites on their way out of Egypt (Exod. 13:21; 14:19, 24). God appointed him to lead the Israelites up from Egypt, saying, 'my name is within him'; he has the divine prerogative to forgive transgressions, although he may not always do so (Exod. 23:20–21; Num. 20:16). It was this Angel who drove out the Canaanites before Israel (Exod. 33:2).

[25] Heiser, *The Unseen Realm*, 135. Heiser's writing reflects much on the Angel and the two powers in heaven.

[26] There is also the mysterious man who finds Joseph wandering and sends him for his fateful meeting with his brothers (Gen. 37:15). Unnamed figures are rare in biblical narrative, yet this man, inessential to the plot, dominates the narrative for three verses. Tg Neof. says he is 'an angel in the form of a man'. Tg Y. says he was the angel Gavriel.

Balaam, going west at the behest of the King of Moab, encountered the Angel of YHVH—first invisible, then visible, with drawn sword—who eventually let him pass with a warning (Num. 22:22–38).

Joshua, at Gilgal by Jericho, met a mysterious warrior with drawn sword who called himself the 'commander of the army of YHVH' (Josh. 5:13–14). Once again, this looks like the Angel. For it was he who was charged with driving out the Canaanites (Exod. 33:2), his sword recalls how Balaam saw him (Num. 22:23; 1 Chron. 21:16), and his command that Joshua remove his sandals are the Angel's words in Exodus 3:5.

In the Judges period, the Angel of YHVH goes from Gilgal to Bokim and speaks to the Israelites (Judg. 2:1). The Angel of YHVH, who is also YHVH and the Angel of *elohim*, appears to Gideon and accepts his offering (Judg. 6:11–24). Later still, he appears to Samson's parents, making Manoah exclaim, 'We have seen God' (Judg. 13:3–22).

David saw the Angel of YHVH encamp around him and pursue his foes (Ps. 34:7; 35:5–6). Later in David's time, the Angel of YHVH, with drawn sword, sends plague on Israel (2 Sam. 24:16; 1 Chr. 21:15–16). It is the Angel of YHVH who tells Elijah not to call fire from heaven a third time, but to go with Ahaziah's soldiers and not be afraid (2 Kgs 1:15). It is the Angel of YHVH who destroys the invading Assyrian army (Isa. 37:36). Later, Zechariah sees the Angel of YHVH, imploring mercy for Jerusalem and purging the sins of the *kohen gadol* Joshua (Zech. 1:12; 3:4).

Finally, as the era of prophecy draws to a close, YHVH tells Malachi, *Behold I am sending my angel* [mal'akhi] *and he will prepare the way before me. And suddenly YHVH, whom you seek, will come to his temple; the messenger-angel of the covenant, whom you desire, behold, he shall come, says YHVH of hosts* (3:1).

All these reports of the visible divine Angel of YHVH tie in with other biblical reports of visible manifestations of YHVH. Moses and the elders ascended Mount Sinai and saw the God of Israel and ate with him (Exod. 24:9). *YHVH spoke to Moses face to face, as a man speaks to his friend*, and later revealed some part of his 'glory' visibly to Moses (33:11, 17). In Samuel's time, *YHVH continued to appear at Shiloh* (1 Sam. 3:21). David said, *I have beheld you in the sanctuary, seeing your power and glory* (Ps. 62:2).

All in all, then, the oldest histories of Israel speak of continual visible manifestations of a divine Lord. He is usually called the Angel of YHVH, or sometimes the Angel of God (*elohim*). Yet he is closely identified with YHVH himself.

The Angel, the Logos

None of this was lost on ancient readers of the scriptures. Philo of Alexandria (c. 20 BC–AD 50), a Greek-speaking Jewish philosopher, sought to harmonize Platonic philosophy with Moses and the prophets. He is particularly known for his theology of the divine Word, in Greek, the Logos. Philo took the term from the 'Word'—in Hebrew ***davar***—who appeared to Avraham and Samuel (Gen. 15:1; 1 Sam. 3:21). And Philo says this Word-Logos-Davar is the Angel of YHVH, the Angel of God. They are one and the same.

He says, 'There is a lesser God, God's eldest Word or Logos, God assuming the place and likeness of an angel-messenger, the image (*eikona*) of God, the outshining halo of God's radiance; he is to God as sunlight to the sun' (*On Dreams* I:239). He is the one through whom all things were created and who sustains all things (*Planting* 10). He is 'God's man, the Logos of the Eternal, who must be immortal' (*Tongues* 41). He is 'the high priest, his firstborn, the divine Logos' (*On Dreams* I:215) and 'the high priest and king' (*On Flight* 118). It was the Logos whom Moses saw on Sinai (*Confusion of Tongues* 97). He was the Angel of YHVH who appeared to Hagar and Balaam (*Cherubim* 3, 35).

Soon after Philo's time, Christians began to speak of the Logos. John says he is the eternally pre-existent Son, the co-agent of creation, present with God in the beginning, becoming flesh in Jesus (John 1:1). And while John doesn't exactly call the Logos a 'lesser' God, as Philo does, his incarnate Logos does speak of the 'greater' God (John 14:28).

Paul, echoing Philo, says the Messiah is the visible image (*eikôn*) of the invisible God (Col. 1:15). He believes that Jesus was the Angel of YHVH who accompanied the Israelites in the desert. For he says the Corinthians must not test 'the Lord', that is Jesus, lest he punish them as he—the divine Angel—did to the Israelites in the desert (1 Cor. 10:9). And he alludes, in 1 Cor. 10:4, to the Israelite tradition that the Rock Moses struck followed them through the desert.

> The well, which was with Israel in the wilderness, was like a rock of the size of a *k'bara*, and was flowing out and rising as from the mouth

> of this flask, travelling with them up the mountains and going down with them to the valleys. Wherever Israel encamped, it encamped opposite them before the door of the Tabernacle. (T. Suk. 3:11)

And, says Paul, this Rock, the Angel of the Exodus, was the Messiah.[27]

The early Fathers take up the same theme. In the second century, Justin Martyr says:

> There is, and there is said to be [in scripture], another God and Lord subject to the Maker of all things, who is also called an Angel, because he announces to men whatsoever the Maker of all things—above whom there is no other God—wishes to announce to them. (Dial. 56) Therefore neither Abraham, nor Isaac, nor Jacob, nor any other man, saw the Father and ineffable Lord of all (and also of Christ), but [they saw] him who was, according to his will, his Son, being God, and the Angel, because he ministered to his will; whom also it pleased him to be born man by the Virgin; who also was fire when he conversed with Moses from the bush. (Dial. 127)

And Tertullian says,

> Now, then, he must be a different Being who was seen, because of one who was seen it could not be predicated that he is invisible. It will therefore follow, that by him who is invisible we must understand the Father in the fullness of his majesty, while we recognise the Son as visible by reason of the dispensation of his derived existence, even as it is not permitted us to contemplate the sun, in the full amount of his substance which is in the heavens, but we can only endure with our eyes a ray, by reason of the tempered condition of this portion which is projected from him to the earth. (Against Praxeas 14)

So the visible God, though taken up by Christians, was no Christian invention. It was deeply rooted in the Hebrew scriptures. And it was taught by Philo who lived a generation before the apostles, and whose teaching was unrelated to the Christian movement.

Yet, when Christians began to make these claims about Jesus, the Jerusalem hierarchy and the Pharisaic community became uncomfortable with it. Soon they forbade any talk of divine plurality and the oneness of God became a required belief in the rabbinic community. In the third century, R. Yoḥanan bar Nappaḥa advised how to counter any claims about divine plurality.

[27] 1 Cor. 10:4. Other texts do not clearly identify the mobile Rock with the Angel. But it is implied in LXX and Mekhilta Exod. 17:6; cf. Hanson, *Jesus Christ*, 17–23.

> Rabbi Yoḥanan says: Any place where the heretics prove their heresy, the response to it is right alongside. [It says] *Let us* [plural] *make man in our image* (Gen. 1:26) but it says: *And God created man in his* [singular] *image* (Gen. 1:27). [It says] *Come, let us* [plural] *go down and there confound their language* (Gen. 11:7), [but also] *And the Lord came down* [sing.] *to see the city and the tower* (Gen. 11:5). [It says] *There God was revealed* [plural] *to him* (Gen. 35:7), [but also] *To God who answers* [sing.] *me in the day of my distress* (Gen. 35:3).

Yet, even among the rabbis, belief in divine plurality never quite disappeared.[28] In rabbinic texts, the exalted Angel is called the Prince of the Presence or Metatron.[29] He appears in the ancient liturgy for the *shofar*-blowing of Rosh ha-Shanah, where he is named Yeshua.[30]

> May it be pleasing in your sight that the blowing of *tekia-shebarim-tekia* that we blow before you be embroidered in the curtain by the hands of the overseer just as you received it by the hands of Elijah, peace be upon him, and Yeshua, Prince of the Presence and Prince Metatron, and fill us with mercy. Blessed are you, the Merciful One.

He appears in the Talmud. There it is clear that the Nazarenes, the early Hebrew Christians, wanted to engage the rabbis in debating this figure. In one such encounter, Rabbi Idith agrees that Metatron was the Angel of the Exodus, but denies that he should be worshipped as divine.

> A certain *min* [a Nazarene] said to R. Idith: 'It is written, *And to Moses He* [God] *said, Come up to Ha-Shem* [YHVH]. (Exod. 24:1). But surely it should have said, "Come up to me."'
>
> [R. Idith replied] 'It was Metatron [who spoke], whose name is like that of his Master; as it is written, [*Behold I send my Angel before you...Do not defy him...*] *For my name is in him.* (Exod. 23:21).
>
> [The *min* replied] 'If so, we should worship him!'
>
> [R. Idith replied] 'It is written: *Do not defy* [tammer] *him* (Exod. 23:21) means "Do not replace Me [temireni] with him."'
>
> [The *min* replied] 'If so [*i.e.,* if the Angel is not the divine Lord himself], why is it said: *He will not pardon your transgression?*
>
> [R. Idith replied] In truth, we did not accept him [the Angel] even

[28] Segal, *Two Powers*, thinks Judaism condemned such ideas as heresy in the first century. Others say it was later and unofficial (McGrath and Truex, 'Two Powers').

[29] Metatron is the defender of Israel (cf. Hag. 15a). The name may be an augmentative of Heb. *metator* (guide); or from Greek *meta thronos* (beside the throne); or Aramaic *sar matarta* (Chief of the Service) (Jastrow 1950: 767).

[30] Professor Leibes of the Hebrew University thinks the name Yeshua here is of early Nazarene, rather than later Christian, origin (מלאכי קול השופר). My view is that it is older still and reflects ancient belief in a Joshua Messiah. More of that in chapters 3 and 13.

> as a guide, as it is written: *And he said to him: If your Presence* [*i.e.*, the personal presence of God, rather than the Angel] *does not go* [*do not bring us up from here*] (Exod. 33:15).

In the seventh-century, Metatron appears in the Book of Zerubbabel.

> And Metatron spoke again and he told me, 'I am the angel who led Abraham in all the land of Canaan, and I am he who preserved Isaac, and wrestled with Jacob at the fords of the Jabbok. I am he who led Israel in the wilderness for forty years in the name of the Lord. I am he who appeared to Joshua at Gilgal. And I am he whose name is like the name of my Master, and his name is in my inmost being.'[31]

Later still, Rashi, commenting on *my name is in him* (Exod. 23:21), says that the name of Metatron is numerologically equal to Shaddai.

So belief in the second God was endorsed by Christians, but banned in rabbinic circles, yet persisted there as a clandestine teaching.

Is the Angel YHVH?

As we saw, the Angel of YHVH is often identified with YHVH himself. He speaks for, and in the person of YHVH. He accepts the worship due to YHVH. The two morph into one another during a single narrative (e.g. Gen. 22:15–16; Exod. 3:2–4; 14:19, 24). All this might lead us to ask whether the Angel of YHVH is entirely the same as YHVH. In other words, is YHVH the lesser God—to borrow Philo's phrase—while other terms, like El Elyon, that is, 'God Most High', should be reserved for the greater God?

Theroretically, it's a plausible idea. After all, if the Logos is God speaking-forth, then it seems reasonable that he is the deity who spoke to Israel.

Some Bible passages seem to support this idea. Moses says Elyon divided the oversight of the nations among the sons of God—one nation to each tutelary deity—but Israel was apportioned to YHVH.

> When Elyon divided the inheritance of the nations, when he separated the sons of Adam, he set the boundaries of the peoples according to the number of the sons of God. But the portion of YHVH is his people—Jacob the portion of his inheritance. (Deut. 32:8–9)

[31] For the text of *Sefer Zerubbabel*, see my *Messiah ben Joseph,* chapter 11§5.

Daniel 7:13 looks similar.

> [13] In my vision at night I looked, and, behold, with the clouds of heaven, came one like a son of man. He came to the Ancient of Days and was brought into his presence.

The one coming with the clouds looks like YHVH. It is he who rides the clouds throughout the Bible. As Emerton says, 'The act of coming with the clouds suggests a theophany of Yahve [YHVH] himself.'[32] And so the Cloud-Rider would be YHVH and Daniel's 'Ancient of Days' would be the greater God. One could see something similar in Psalm 87, where YHVH loves Zion and so Elyon will establish her.

New Testament writers, who saw Jesus as the Logos, often identify him with YHVH. John says that when Isaiah saw YHVH in the temple, he saw Jesus (12:41). He says no-one has ever seen God, but the Son, who is the Logos, alone has revealed him (1:18). So, for John, every divine appearance is the Logos. That includes his appearing to Moses—to which John alludes (cf. 1:17 and Exod. 34:6)—and the prophets. In John 5:37, Jesus speaks to the Jews about the Father, saying, *You have never heard his voice nor seen his form* (5:37). If this is addressed to Israel in general, then all divine speech, including every word to the prophets, is from the Logos.

In the same vein, Paul consistently uses the word 'God' (*theos*) for the greater God, that is, in Christian terms, the Father, and he reserves 'Lord' (*kurios*) for the Messiah, the incarnate Logos.

> For even if there are so-called gods, whether in heaven or on earth (as there are many so-called gods and lords), yet for us there is but one God, the Father, from whom all things came and for whom we exist. And there is but one Lord, Jesus Christ, through whom all things came and through whom we exist. (1 Cor. 8:5–6)

Indeed, since 'Lord' (*kurios*) was, by Paul's time, the widely-accepted Greek substitute for the name of YHVH, it suggests that he too was equating the Logos with YHVH.

James too uses 'Lord' to refer interchangeably to Jesus and YHVH. The Lord, whose coming the church awaits, is the same Lord of the prophets and of Job, who told Moses of his compassion and mercy.

> [7]Be patient, then, brothers, until the coming of the Lord. Behold, the

[32] Emerton, 'Son of Man Imagery', 231; cf. Ps. 18:9–12; 68:4; Isa. 19:1.

> farmer waits for the land to yield its precious crop, patiently awaiting the early and latter rains. [8]You too be patient and stand firm, because the Lord's coming is near. [9]Do not grumble against one another, brothers, or you will be judged. Behold, the Judge is standing at the door. [10]Brothers, as an example of patience in the face of suffering, take the prophets who spoke in the name of the Lord. [11]Behold, we count blessed those who have persevered. You have heard of Job's perseverance and the outcome the Lord brought about. The Lord is full of compassion and mercy. (James 5:7–15; Exod. 34:6)

The same theme is taken up robustly by some of the Fathers. Justin Martyr cites Psalm 99:7 to Trypho as applying to Jesus: *He spoke to them in a pillar of cloud.* Trypho is astounded: 'You think you can persuade us that this crucified man was with Moses and Aaron and spoke to them in the pillar of cloud!'

Melito of Sardis, in his Homily on the Passion, rhetorically addresses the Jews, saying of Jesus:

> He it was who led you down into Egypt and guarded and nourished you there. He it was who gave you a guiding light in the pillar and sheltered you in the cloud, who cut the Red Sea in two and led you through and destroyed your enemy. He it was who gave you manna from heaven, who gave you drink out of the rock, who gave you the law on Horeb, who gave you the land for your inheritance, who sent forth prophets to you, who raised up kings for you. He it was who came to visit you.

Irenaeus speaks the same way in his Proof of the Apostolic Preaching:

> 45. Jacob, when he went into Mesopotamia, saw him in a dream, standing upon the ladder, that is, the tree, which was set up from earth to heaven; for thereby they that believe in him go up to the heavens… For it was not the Father of all, who is not seen by the world, the Maker of all, who said: *Heaven is my throne, and earth is my footstool: what house will ye build me, or what is the place of my rest?* and *Who holds the earth with his hand, and with his span the heaven*—it was not He that came and stood in a very small space and spake with Abraham; but it was the Logos of God, who was ever with mankind, and made known beforehand what should come to pass in the future, and taught men the things of God.
>
> 46. He it is who spoke with Moses in the bush, and said: *I have surely seen the affliction of thy people that is in Egypt; and I am come down to deliver them.* He brought us out from the cruel service of the nations, and made a stream of water in the desert to flow forth in abundance from a rock; and that rock is himself.

So early Christians often identify the Angel-Logos-Messiah with YHVH. Yet they do not conclude that YHVH is always the Angel. And their reticence is surely correct. For, if some Hebrew Bible texts distinguish between Elyon and YHVH, there are others which say that Elyon is YHVH (2 Sam. 22:14; Ps. 9:2; 97:9). And, as we shall see, it would be difficult to insist that YHVH is the Logos in Psalm 110:1.

So we must conclude that, in the revelation to the patriarchs and the prophets, the name YHVH could mean either the greater or the lesser God, or both. Just as the Son is God but God is not the Son, so the Logos is YHVH but YHVH is not always the Logos. Not every reference in the Hebrew Bible to YHVH indicates the Logos-Angel. But many do.

Summary

Melchizedek appears only briefly in Genesis 14. But themes of the surrounding chapters shed light on this enigmatic figure.

First, there is the unfolding promise to bless Avram. The first to speak the promised blessing on him is Melchizedek. The last to speak it, in Melchizedek's city, is the divine Angel. Both are special envoys of the One who called Avram forth. They have much in common.

Second, there is the backdrop of Melchizedek's city, Shalem. There Melchizedek blesses Avram. There Avraham offers up Isaac. There he is finally blessed by the Angel of YHVH. His dealings with Melchizedek are less isolated than a casual reading of Genesis might suggest.

Third, a divine being repeatedly appears in Genesis in visible, human form—to Avram as a Word and as YHVH and his Angel, to Hagar, and later to Jacob. This same divine Lord could certainly have appeared visibly to Avram in the persona of Melchizedek.

And so, only within Genesis, Melchizedek looks suspiciously like the visible Angel of YHVH. Later, we shall find firm evidence in Psalm 110 to confirm this hunch. But, first, a little history.

2

Tribes...

ABRAHAM begat Isaac. Isaac begat Jacob. And Jacob begat Joseph and his brothers in the Plain of Aram. By his first wife, Leah, Jacob had six sons: Reuben, Simeon, Levi, Judah, Issachar, and Zebulun. By his concubine Bilhah, he had two: Dan and Naphtali. By his concubine Zilpah, two more: Gad and Asher. Finally, his beloved second wife, Rachel, bore him Joseph, the cream of all, and his brother Benjamin.

The order of priority was clear enough. The foremost honour would go to firstborn Reuben. He could expect a double portion: twice as much land, livestock, wealth, and honour as his brothers, along with headship over the whole family. The other sons of Jacob's wives would be ranked in line with their birth position. The concubines' sons would come last in the queue for honour and inheritance.

That was how it normally worked. But Leah's sons had issues.

Reuben got into a sexual adventure with an older woman. She happened to be his stepmother and his father's concubine, Bilhah. Reuben's escapade brought upon him his father's curse (Gen. 49:3–4).

Next in line were Simeon and Levi. They slew their sister Dinah's betrothed, Shechem, a local prince, with all his clan and people, looted the town, and seized its lands (Gen. 34:1–31; 37:12). True, Shechem had violated Dinah. But he intended marriage, and his family wanted trade relations with Jacob's clan. Simeon and Levi, in their pride and violence, did their sister no good and endangered the family. Jacob feared that the Amorites would rise against them. (According to some later texts—*The Book of Jubilees* and *The Testaments of the Twelve Patriarchs*—that is just what happened.[1] They tell how Jacob, with 6,000 men, slew the Amorite uprising.) Simeon and Levi protested that their motive for the slaughter was family honour (34:31). But Jacob saw that their true motive was plunder; they too received his curse (Gen. 49:5–7).

Next in line for honour was Judah. But, riding his chariot one day, he came upon his daughter-in-law, Tamar, disguised as a Canaanite shrine prostitute (Gen. 38), and impregnated her. Now Judah was no novice with prostitutes, as his easy approach to the wayside woman showed. And Tamar knew well enough how to catch him when she baited her trap. Finally, when her pregnancy became known and she was led out to die at Judah's command, she revealed him as the author of her condition. Judah's deed, his consorting with Canaanite prostitutes, probably did not impress Jacob very much either.

JOSEPH

Leah's brightest and best having each besmirched his escutcheon, Jacob cast around for another firstborn. Rachel had given birth to a fine boy, her firstborn, Joseph, implored through years of barrenness. In the Bible, long-awaited children are always special. And Joseph was no exception. From his early years he showed wisdom and aptitude in all he did. As he grew, he became perfect, handsome and presentable, unflawed by his brothers' unruly passions. Jacob loved Joseph more than all his other sons. He entrusted to him, young as he was, the management of all his property. He made him an expensive robe with long sleeves, a robe fit for one who did no manual work. He bid him oversee not only his flocks and herds, but also his ten older brothers. Rachel's firstborn took the place of Leah's.

How his older brothers, big men well into their twenties, felt about a teenager being their boss can be imagined. They hated him because he was perfect and they had messed up. They hated him because their

[1] Jub. 34:1–9; T. Jud. 3–7; *Midrash Vayyisa'u* and *Sefer Ha-Yashar* record the same tale. Dinah's rape is rewritten in Jubilees, where the act of Simeon and Levi is counted as righteousness, but Jacob fears its consequences (30:3, 23, 25). T. Lev. 5–7 records Jacob's wrath but says Simeon and Levi were guided by an angel.

father loved him most. They hated him because he reported their misdeeds to their father. They hated him most because he foretold that they would one day bow to him. So they planned to kill him. When the chance came, they seized him and threw him in a pit, like a man buried in a grave.

But Judah figured that gaining a profit from selling his brother to passing slave-traders beat bloodying his hands for nothing. Reuben was away. Twenty pieces of silver divided neatly among ten brothers. So Judah and his brothers sold Joseph into virtual death and told their father he had been eaten by wild beasts.

Joseph descended into Egypt, the land of the cult of the dead. He was sold as a slave to Potiphar, a powerful official, captain of Pharaoh's guard. Potiphar saw Joseph's abilities and entrusted to him the running of all his estate. Joseph hoped that things might go well for him if he pleased his master. But his master's wife wanted Joseph to please her too. When Joseph, fearing God, refused, she accused him of attempted rape. Such an accusation would normally mean death. But Potiphar knew his wife's ways and valued Joseph. Potiphar oversaw Pharaoh's prisons. So he sent Joseph to work there, away from the house, but still in his service and still under his eye. So innocent Joseph was back again in a pit, in an underground dungeon. But Potiphar appointed him manager of the prison. And there Joseph remained eleven long years, all the days of his youth.

Finally, Joseph's abilities as a dream-interpreter came to Pharaoh's notice. He interpreted Pharaoh's dreams about a coming famine in Egypt. He proposed a solution to survive the famine, and was appointed vizier of all Egypt. Pharaoh gave him his signet ring and authority over all Egypt. Just as on his father's farm, in Potiphar's house, and in prison, Joseph was a blameless manager. He stored up surplus grain in the time of plenty so there would be food in the famine.

When the famine came, it struck the land of Canaan where his family lived. Joseph's brothers, hearing of grain in Egypt, came to buy. Joseph dealt with them personally, tricking, troubling and testing them, until finally Judah, the author of his sorrows, offered himself as a slave to spare the lives of his brother Benjamin and his father. Then Joseph revealed himself to his amazed brothers—*I am your brother Joseph, whom you sold into Egypt!*—and sent them to bring their father Jacob to Egypt. And Israel sojourned in Egypt.

JACOB BLESSES EPHRAIM AND MANASSEH

As his death approached, Jacob blessed his sons. But he began with his grandsons, Joseph's sons, Manasseh and Ephraim. He did three things.

First, he announced that Joseph's two sons would be reckoned as Jacob's own. Each would receive an inheritance in place of Joseph's one portion. In this way, Joseph received the firstborn's double portion and became two tribes instead of one. As the Chronicler said:

> The sons of Reuben, the firstborn of Israel. (For he was the firstborn, but when he defiled his father's bed, his birthright was given to the sons of Joseph, the son of Israel, so that he is not reckoned as the firstborn. And although Judah was mightiest among his brothers, and rulers came from him, the birthright was Joseph's.) (1 Chr. 5:1).

Second, to go with his sons' double portion, Jacob gave Joseph a choice property in the green hill country of the Promised Land.

> And to you I give a ridge [Shechem] of land more than to your brothers, the ridge [Shechem] I took from the Amorites with my sword and my bow.

We learn a little more about this piece of land and its conquest in the above-mentioned passages from *The Book of Jubilees* and *The Testaments of the Twelve Patriarchs.* They tell how, after Simeon and Levi destroyed the town of Shechem, the Amorite kings gathered to slay Jacob's family, but Jacob defeated them and took their land.

Third, Jacob blessed Ephraim, Joseph's second-born, above Manasseh, the firstborn. Joseph protested. But Jacob insisted, saying Ephraim would be greater than Manasseh. So, all in a row, Jacob, Joseph, and Ephraim, became *de facto* firstborn, although none was actually his father's firstborn. The 'firstborn' title was becoming important to Joseph's clan.

THE FORGOTTEN JOSEPHITES

Looking back from the vantage point of four millennia later, we tend to see the history of Israel as a Judahite or 'Jewish' history. People speak erroneously of 'Abraham the Jew' or 'the Jewish general Joshua', or inaccurately of 'the Jews in slavery in Egypt' or 'the exodus of the Jews' or 'the Jews conquering the Promised Land'. But the Judahites—later called in English 'the Jews'—were only one of the twelve tribes. And while they were prominent among the tribes, they were not always the chief. For there were also the tribes of Joseph.

Joseph was Israel's first ruler. He was head of his brothers in Egypt, governing and protecting them. It was Joseph who got Jacob's best blessings and the rights of the firstborn. It was Joseph who, on his father's death, took the firstborn's role of leading the funeral rites.

Toward the end of the captivity, Moses, from the tribe of Levi, became Israel's ruler in his lifetime. Yet, as we shall see, even Moses's best blessings were given to Joseph's tribes.

After Moses's death, the headship returned to Joseph's sons. Joshua, from the Josephite tribe of Ephraim, led Israel into the Land, with Judahite Caleb as his assistant. It was Joshua who allotted the land, setting the tabernacle and the ark in his own chosen home territory of Shiloh, giving Ephraim and Manasseh swathes of fruitful terrain in the midlands and northern Transjordan, and giving Judah the dry land leading down to the Negev desert. Of course, the land was apportioned by divine lot. It seems even the Almighty loved Joseph's sons best.

The allotment of the land led to the geographic division of the tribes. For Joshua's conquest did not dislodge from Jerusalem the Jebusites and their Egyptian backers, whose power extended east and west across the land.[2] Nor did it break the chain of Canaanite forts that divided the land further north, through the Plain of Jezreel. And so Israel held the land in three separate layers, like a cake, from south to north.

At the bottom, in the Judean hills and desert, confined by the might of Egypto-Jebusite Jerusalem, lived the Judahites and Simeonites under Judahite judges—Caleb, Othniel, Ibzan.

In the middle of the cake lay the rich midland valleys, populated by Ephraim, Manasseh, and Benjamin. Further north, in the top layer, above the line of Canaanite forts, was the fertile region of the Galil. But all the tribes in the top two-thirds of the land looked to Rachel's children—the tribes of Ephraim, Manasseh, and Benjamin—for leadership. From them sprang Ehud, Deborah, Gideon, Jair, and Jephtah. They survived fine without any help from the Judahites to the south (Judg. 5:13–18). In fact, the only time in the Judges period when

[2] At this time, Jerusalem was an Egyptian vassal city-state, as the Amarna letters show (Na'aman, 'David's sojourn').

the southern and northern Israelites co-operated was in the nigh-extermination of Benjamin by the other eleven tribes (Judg. 20–21).[3]

The head of the northern confederation were the Ephraimites, quick to quarrel with anyone who showed military independence, even their brothers from Manasseh (Judg. 8:1; 12:1–4). It was in Ephraim, at Shiloh, that the all-important ark of the covenant rested for over three hundred years; it was there the Israelites gathered and offered their sacrifices (Josh. 18:1; 21:2). Even after Shiloh was destroyed—probably by the Philistines after the battle at Aphek (1 Sam. 4)—the ark still rested within the Josephite confederation, at Gibeon in the territory of Benjamin.[4]

Figure 2. The tribal territores of Israel

[3] The book of Judges, redacted in Judah to legitimize David's kingdom, propounds Israel's need of a Judahite king (Brettler, 'Judges'). It therefore points to the ongoing political threat posed by the Josephites all through the time of David and Solomon.

[4] Jer. 7:12–15; 26:5–9. Rashi (1 Sam. 9:13) says Shiloh was razed before Saul's time.

Then Samuel, a Korahite Levite from the hill country of Ephraim, united the tribes against their common foes. Under his rule, the Canaanite power across the Jezreel valley was broken.

At the people's insistence, Samuel anointed a king, Saul ben Kish from the tribe of Benjamin, from the children of Rachel. Then, while Saul was still alive, Samuel also anointed the Judahite David as the new king over Israel.

Upon Saul's death, David became king of Judah and ruled in Hebron for seven years, while the northern tribes, under Saul's son Ishbosheth, grew weaker. Finally, even the Ephraimites accepted David as king.

JUDAH GAINS THE CROWN

So it was that, for the first time in their 900-year existence, Israel was led by a Judahite. It was a sharp break with tradition, which succeeded only due to David's military and political *élan*. With his characteristic strategic genius, he conquered Jerusalem on the border of the territory of Benjamin. Thus, in one stroke, he removed the main obstacle to Israel's geopolitical unity and established a capital in the geographic centre of the land, right on the border of the territories of Judah and Rachel's children. Since Israel had never conquered the city, it was free of tribal associations. It was militarily important. And it was the sacred city, the city of Melchizedek, where Abraham placed Isaac on the altar. So, when David brought to Jerusalem the Tabernacle of Meeting and the Ark of the Covenant, he concentrated the military, political, and cultic authority of Israel in one place, and the city's psalmists sang the praises of the 'city of God'.[5]

David ruled a united Israel for thirty years, leading it from oppression under foreign nations to mastery of the whole land, from the Wadi of Egypt to the Euphrates. God told him, through the prophet Nathan, that a line of kings would come from him and his son would rule for ever. David received by divine revelation the plans for a great temple in Jerusalem. He gathered the materials and procured the land for the building project. Then he died and the kingship passed to his son Solomon.

[5] Cf. Pss. 46:4; 48:1, 8; 76:1–2; 122.

Solomon's forty-year reign was famed for its wealth and splendour. He built the temple according to David's plans. But he turned to idolatry. Meanwhile, the Ephraimites had never acquiesced in Judahite rule. Even in David's time, Benjamite clan leaders related to Saul—Shimei ben Gera and Sheva ben Bikhri—took advantage of Absalom's revolt to rise up. They were dealt with. But Solomon's idolatry emboldened his enemies. The prophet Ahijah of Shiloh—in the last hurrah of the rejected house of Eli—instigated a revolt against the house of David.[6] He prophesied to Jeroboam ben Nevat, an Ephraimite prince of Joshua's line, that Solomon's kingdom would be torn apart, giving ten tribes to Jeroboam and leaving only one tribe to Judah and his assimilated Simeonites (1 Kgs 11:29–37).

After Solomon's death, Jeroboam did not fail. He led the entire Ephraimite coalition away from Judah, leaving the house of David as masters only of Judah and Simeon. Judahite leadership of united Israel had lasted all of seventy years.

The Kingdoms of Ephraim and Judah

Control of greater Israel reverted once again to the house of Joseph. They had the largest share of the land. They took the name 'Kingdom of Israel'. They set up their capital in Shechem, the extra portion Jacob had given Joseph. And for two hundred years (930–724 BC), they mostly dominated the small Kingdom of Judah to the south, coercing them into uneasy alliances, seizing their land, plundering Jerusalem, and killing their kings and nobles.

Yet the Ephraimite kingdom was idolatrous, for Jeroboam had instigated the worship of golden bull calves at Dan and Bethel. It was, one imagines, an easy mistake for Joseph's children to make. Moses himself had called them the conquering bull (Deut. 33:17). Initially, they saw their golden bull-calves as representing the God of Israel. This in itself was a breach of the second commandment. But the bull-calf was not only Joseph's sign. It was also Baal's. And the Ephraimites

[6] It is open to question whether Aḥijah ben Aḥitub ben Pinḥas ben Eli of 1 Sam. 14:3 is the same as the prophet Aḥijah the Shilonite. But since the latter lived and ministered at Shiloh, he was of the descendants of Eli, the *kohen gadol* at Shiloh, rejected by God (1 Sam. 2:27–36) and deposed by Solomon, in the person of the *kohen (gadol)* Abiathar ben Aḥimelech ben Aḥitub ben Pinḥas ben Eli (1 Kgs 1:7, 19, 25; cf. 1 Sam. 22:20).

sank ever deeper into Canaanite Baal worship. Ahab married the Tyrian princess Jezebel, who brought with her priests of Baal. In this way, worship of the Canaanite deity became established in Ephraim. The prophets—Elijah, Elisha, Hosea, Amos—denounced the apostasy. They had victories, as Elijah did at Carmel. Yet the Baal cult continued, with all its consequent moral anarchy.

The Ephraimite kingdom was politically anarchic too. They had six dynasties in two centuries, most of which lasted only two generations, and a succession of solo usurpers, some of whom lasted as little as seven days. Yet they also prospered under strong kings like Omri.

Occasionally, they joined forces with Judah against a common foe. But relations were mostly hostile. And just as the Ephraimites, in league with Aram, were gearing up for a total assault on little Judah, the words of the prophets were fulfilled. Assyria invaded the land, conquered the Ephraimites, and swept Joseph's children into exile.

Yet some of them remained in the land, under Assyrian overseers, as did also their ancient priesthood, which traced descent from Aaron. These remnants of the house of Joseph gathered around their ancient capital Shomron, or Samaria, and came to be called Samaritans.

Then the Kingdom of Judah had over a hundred years' rest from Ephraimite aggression. During this time, they sought to extend their power into northern Israel, and to gather the remnant of the Ephraimites into the Kingdom of Judah.

THE BABYLONIAN CAPTIVITY AND RETURN OF JUDAH

But then the Babylonians invaded Judah. Eventually, they destroyed the glorious temple and took the Judahite nobles captive to Babylon.

Yet the Judahite captivity was brought to an end after seventy years—as Isaiah and Jeremiah foretold—by Cyrus's decree. Some of the Babylonian Judahites returned to re-establish Jerusalem and rebuild the temple. Others remained in Babylon where they established a Judahite kingdom—a state within the Mesopotamian state—on the Euphrates. This kingdom later gave birth to the Babylonian Talmud and the great Jewish *yeshivot* of Sura and Pumbedita. The Jewish community in Babylon remained strong right into Ottoman times until only declined in the twentieth century with emigration to Israel.

The Judahite captivity began to weld the disparate southern Israelite groups together for the first time. For instance, Mordecai, a Benjamite, is called 'a Judahite of the tribe of Benjamin', something that would have been unthinkable in the land of Israel (Est. 2:5).

The captives who returned from Babylon to Judah included a mix of people from the tribes of Judah, Levi, Simeon, and Benjamin, with a few others from the old northern kingdom. They spoke Hebrew. Their province was dominated by the city of Jerusalem. Power was vested in the ruling council, the Great Assembly (*Knesset Ha-Gedolah*), led by the *nasi*, the prince of the house of David, or by the Zadokite *kohen gadol.* Later, it was called the Sanhedrin—from Greek *sunedrion*, 'assembly'—and the Pharisees, especially those who could claim royal descent, rose to prominence. Within the Sanhedrin all these groups strove and plotted for influence over the life of the nation.

The Zadokites, known in the New Testament as Sadducees, from the Greek form of their name, were the priestly caste. They traced their descent from Aaron through Zadok, the *kohen gadol* of David's kingdom. They concerned themselves with running the vast and wealthy temple establishment and its multitudinous sacrifices. They held only the five books of Moses to be Scripture, and, as a result, were little concerned with eschatology and angels, as the New Testament points out. Nonetheless, the master copies of all the books that were to become the Jewish Bible were preserved in the temple under their eye, as they had been since ancient times (2 Macc. 2:13). Any Torah scroll newly-written for synagogue use had to be verified against the master copy by a team of Levite proof-readers, who were paid from temple funds lest financial dependence on the scroll's owner should sway their judgement.[7]

The Pharisees, on the other hand, strove for perfect knowledge and observance of Torah. Their environment was not the temple, but the synagogues, where they taught and debated in Hebrew. They were mostly Judahites, although other Israelites were numbered among them. Nor did they all live in Judah. Some lived in Galilee, but had a Jerusalem-centric worldview. They held not only the five books of Moses to be sacred, but also the prophets, the psalms, and the other books. In time, their synagogues set the pattern for Christian churches

[7] B. *Ket.* 106a; Y. *Shek.* 4:2; Y. *Sanh.* 2:6; Rashi on B. *Ket.* 106a.

and their collection of scriptures became the Jewish Bible and the Christian Old Testament. Their other teachings ultimately became the Mishnah, the Talmud, and the other texts of what was to become Rabbinic Judaism.

As for the Ephraimites taken captive in Assyria, some grew to become large eastern nations. To this day, the Kurds and the royal house of Afghan claim descent from Ephraim. Others spread out into the furthest reaches of the world, in fulfilment of Jacob's prophecy that the seed of Ephraim would fill the nations (Gen. 48:19). Yet others stayed in Assyria, practising Torah faith, until some of their descendants were repatriated to the Galilee by Judah Maccabee.

So it was that, by the first century BC, the Holy Land had two communities tracing descent from the house of Joseph; namely, the Samaritans, who had their own temple on Mount Gerizim, and the Galileans, who travelled south to worship in Jerusalem.

Both these groups had their own distinctive beliefs, often closer to one another than to the Judahites down south. As regards the Messiah, the Samaritans said he would be a son of Joshua and of Joseph.[8] It is likely that some Galileans thought the same way. Both groups kept their own ancient calendar, quite independent of the Judahites, which led them to celebrate Passover a day before the Judahites. (It is the divergence between the Galilean and Judean calendars that gives John and the other gospels different days for the crucifixion of Jesus.[9]) The Galileans did not celebrate Judahite feasts like Hanukkah or Purim, which John calls 'a feast of the Judahites' (John 5:1).[10] Further, the Samaritans and the Galileans, like the Zadokites, held only the books of Moses to be scripture. Meanwhile, the Samaritans spoke a later form of Ephraimite Hebrew, whereas the Galileans spoke Aramaic, the

[8] See Appendix 2 to my *Messiah ben Joseph*.

[9] The Galileans, or some of them, along with the Essenes, Samaritans, and Zealots, kept Israel's pre-exilic calendar as opposed to the Judean calendar of the Sanhedrin which was altered, probably during the Exile in Babylon. The existence of different calendars and customs is implied in M. Pes. 1:1–3, where we learn that Galileans did not work all day on the 14th; and T. Pes. 4:8, which rejects Passover sacrifices offered on the morning of the 14th. Josephus also tells of Galilean Zealots and Jews attacking one another on Passover days considered holy to one party but not the other (Roth, 'The Zealots'). For the variant calendars as the solution to the date of the crucifixion, see Humphreys, *Mystery*.

[10] This takes place after winter (4:35), but before Passover (6:4), and can therefore only be Purim.

ancient tongue of Abraham, which they brought back with them from the lands of their northern captivity. Both groups were quite at ease speaking Greek too.

But the Aaronite Zadokites and Judahite Pharisees, with classic capital-city mindset, despised both the Galileans and the Samaritans.

They mocked the Galileans, but tolerated their presence, mostly since they worshipped in Jerusalem and contributed to temple funds.

But if they mocked the Galileans, they despised the Samaritans. It began when Ezra forbade the Samaritans any part in rebuilding Jerusalem. The ground for the Judahites' hatred was the Samaritans' alleged racial impurity, for their land had been settled by Assyrians. So the Samaritans worshipped on Mount Gerizim until, around 128 BC, the Zadokite-Hasmonean king John Hyrcanus destroyed their temple there with much slaughter.[11] Relations became more bitter still in the following century. But the Samaritans knew when they were licked and kept their heads down when the Judahites were around.[12]

Although the Judahites saw the Samaritans as mongrels, the Samaritans still regarded themselves as Israelites. Their priestly caste, in particular, claimed to be of pure Israelite stock. (Samaritan *kohanim* maintain their Aaronite genealogies to this day.) Other Samaritans may have been no more impure than many Judahites. For all the Israelite groups in the land were to some extent genetically mixed. If the Samaritans and returned Ephraimite exiles had interbred with non-Israelites, not a few of the Judahites had too. Yet the prominent families in each community maintained their own Israelite patrilineal genealogies. Patrilineal descent from the twelve tribes still made one an Israelite.

Of all these groups, the most influential by far in Roman-period Judah was the Zadokites. But among the Zadokites themselves, the biggest hitters were the Hasmoneans. They were descendants of the *kohen* Mattathias of Modiin who instigated a revolt against Greek rule in 167 BC. His son, Judah Maccabee, 'The Hammer', led a successful military campaign that gave the Judahites a brief autonomy for the first

[11] Schwartz, 'Destruction', says this event was not seen unfavourably by Samaritan conservatives. It was rather events in the first century that aggravated the schism.

[12] The Talmud is more gracious to Samaritans than might be expected. Shimon b. Gamliel II said, "Every command the Samaritans keep, they are more scrupulous in observing than Israel" (Kid. 76a); the maxim was widely quoted (Ber. 47b; Git. 10a).

time in 400 years. On Judah Maccabee's death, his brother Simon founded a dynasty that was to result in the Hasmoneans eventually taking upon themselves both the high priesthood and the kingship, even though they were not of an established high-priestly family, much less of the royal blood. The Hasmoneans ruled Israel until the ascendancy of Herod, a converted Edomite, in 37 BC.

Judahites and Non-Judahites

The house of Joseph held sway over the twelve tribes of Israel for most of their shared history from 1900 to 722 BC. Even after the division of Rehoboam's kingdom in 925 BC, the Josephites still held the whip. It was not until after the Babylonian exile, in the fifth century BC, that the Judahites emerged as the foremost tribe.

Yet many people are quite unaware of the ancient prominence of Joseph. They see the history of Israel simply as a history of the Jews, that is, the Judahites. There are several reasons why.

First, the Ephraimites preserved no scriptures other than the five books of Moses. Although some Bible books arose in Ephraimite territory—Hosea, Amos, Jonah—as well as the sagas of Elijah and Elisha, they were ultimately preserved by Zadokite scribes in the temple in Jerusalem. And the greater part of non-Moses books which make up the Hebrew Bible—that is, the prophets, the histories, the Psalms and writings—were written and preserved entirely in Judah. Since these books are written from a Judahite perspective, they have given us a Bible in which Judah is central and Joseph is peripheral.

The second reason is that the most prominent Israelites for the last two thousand years have been the Judahites. After the Roman destruction of Jerusalem in AD 70, and the split between Pharisaic and Nazarene forms of the Israelite faith, most Israelites who were not Nazarenes ultimately flowed into the group which came to be called 'Judaism'. Into Judaism, for instance, flowed the survivors of the Zadokite *kohanim.* And so, to this day, people who claim descent from Israel's *kohanim* self-identify as 'Jews'—that is, Judahites—something they would not have done 2,000 years ago when Judah and Levi were distinct tribes. Of course, small Israelite groups still survive who do not trace their descent from Judah: like Samaritans and

Karaites. But the prominence of Jews in today's world has led to all Israelite history being seen as Jewish history.

All this has added up to a Judeocentric view of first-century Israel. But in Jesus's time, many—like Galileans and Zadokites—saw things differently. This non-Judah-centric view of Israel will become important in the chapters which lie before us.

3

...and Messiahs

JACOB, on his deathbed, blessed his sons. He began, as said above, with Joseph's sons, Ephraim and Manasseh. But then he turned his attention to his own twelve sons, foretelling the future of their tribes. 'Gather round,' he says, 'so I can tell you what will happen to you in the last days' (Gen. 49:1).

JACOB'S BLESSING ON JUDAH

This passage is often called 'Jacob's blessing', but, to be honest, some were more blessed than others. Reuben, in case he still harboured any hopes, was written out of the firstborn's honour: *You will not excel* 49.3–4). The cruel anger of Simeon and Levi against the Shechemites is cursed: they will be scattered in Israel (49.5–7). Most of Jacob's other sons obtain run-of-the-mill sort of blessings. Zebulun will live by the coast; Naphtali like a doe among the game-fields of the foothills of Mount Hermon; Benjamin will be a ravening wolf (49:13–27).

But two special prophecies are reserved for Judah and Joseph. Judah's is well known.

> The sceptre will not depart from Judah,
> and the staff from between his legs,
> until Shiloh come (*'ad ki yavo shiloh*)
> and the obedience of the nations [shall be] his. (Gen 49:10)

The reference to the 'the staff...between his legs' suggests that the prophecy points to Judah's offspring, as the Septuagint makes clear, with its translation, 'a prince from his loins'.

But what this 'Shiloh' has to do with Judah's offspring has always been a puzzle. Views fall into two camps: first, those who see it as short-term prophecy pointing to the town of Shiloh; second, those who see it as long-term prophecy pointing to the Messiah. The latter view is older. But let us begin with the former, moving from lesser to greater.

We spoke of Shiloh in the previous chapter. It was Joshua's hometown. He set up the ark there and it became Israel's cultic and political centre from the time of the settlement of the land till just before the time of David's kingdom. Medieval rabbis try to make sense of this reference to Shiloh in Jacob's prophecy.

Ibn Ezra (c. 1089-1167) is first. He speaks of those who say it means that Judah's rule will begin after *it* [destruction] *comes to Shiloh.* But the prophecy clearly says Shiloh is the end, not the beginning, of Judah's rule. So this view is not convincing.

Rashbam (1085-1158) says it means *until he comes to Shiloh.* Taken this way, it refers to Rehoboam's arrival at Shechem—which Rashbam says is near Shiloh—to be crowned as the third Judahite monarch, only to flee for his life from Jeroboam and the Ephraimite rebels. Thus Judah ruled until *he* [the Judahite king] *comes to Shiloh*, meaning Shechem. But we now know that Shechem was over thirty kilometres—a good seven hours walk—from Shiloh. So that is not convinving either.

Hizquni (c. 1250-1310) says it points to the time when Ahijah the priest of Shiloh prophesied the end of Solomon's kingdom (1 Kgs 11:26–39), instigating Jeroboam's rebellion and the division of the kingdom in 925 BC. Thus Judah ruled *until* [*Ahijah of*] *Shiloh comes.*

The problem for Hizquni (and Rashbam) is that they make Jacob's prophecy and David's kingdom a very short-term business indeed. If it concerns only the reign of David and Solomon until the division of the kingdom, then it was a reign of only seventy years. Such a kingdom was hardly worth prophesying.

The better view by far is the one based on the alternative reading in the Hebrew Masoretic text which reads Shiloh as *she-lo*, 'that which is his'. So the phrase reads, 'until he comes whose it [the kingdom] is'.

It seems very likely that this was how the passage was understood by Ezekiel, when he says that the royal line of Judah shall be overturned *until he comes whose it is* (Ezek. 21:27). Ezekiel's phrase is very close to Jacob's prophecy. The main difference is that the early relative particle *she-* is replaced by the later Judean form *asher.*[1]

The Septuagint too seems to follow this interpretation. It translates the phrase as 'until there come the things stored up for him'.

The Targums too all take the passage in the same way, saying that the one who is to come is the Messiah to receive the kingdom prepared for him. Targum Yerushalmi says:

> Kings shall not cease from the house of Judah, nor scribes teaching the law from his children's children, until the time that the King Messiah shall come, whose is the kingdom, and to whom all the kingdoms of the earth shall be obedient. How beauteous is the King Messiah, who is to arise from the house of Judah.

Targum Onkelos says:

> He who exercises dominion shall not pass away from the house of Judah, nor the *saphra* from his children's children for ever, until the Messiah come, whose is the kingdom, and unto whom shall be the obedience of the nations.

And Targum Neofiti:

> Kings shall not cease from the house of Judah, nor scribes teaching Torah from his children's children, until the time of the King Messiah comes, and the kingdom shall be his, and to him shall all the kingdoms of the nations be subject.

The Talmud merges the messianic interpretation with the name Shiloh:

> What is his [the Messiah's] name? The school of R. Shilah said: His name is Shiloh, for it is written, *until Shiloh come.* (B. Sanh. 98)

So does Midrash Rabbah on Genesis.

> *Until Shiloh come:* This is the King Messiah. (Gen. R. 98:8)
>
> *Until Shiloh come:* the one to whom the kingdom is his (*shelo*: which is his)...the shoot of Jesse. (Gen. R. 99:8)

And Midrash Rabbah on Lamentations 1:52 says:

> Those of R. Shilah say: Shiloh is the name of the Messiah.

[1] Gen. 49:10: *'ad ki yabo shelo.* Ezek. 21:27 [Heb. text 21:32]: *'ad bo asher lo.*

So the evidence is that *she-lo* is a much older reading than *shiloh.* The *she-lo* reading seems to have been current even in Ezekiel's time, while *Shiloh* is unattested before the amoraic period. We can only guess how this later reading became the principal reading in the Hebrew text.

Through the ages, the Judahites clasped this part of Jacob's prophecy to their heart as a promise of a Messiah to arise from their tribe. Yet there is one detail they overlooked. The prophecy does not actually say that Shiloh will come from Judah. It only says Judah will rule until this figure called Shiloh comes.

Jacob's Blessing on Joseph

Jacob's prophecy to his darling Joseph, on the other hand, is much greater yet much less famous. It goes like this.

> [22] A fruitful shoot [*or* son] is Joseph,
> a fruitful shoot upon a spring,
> whose branches run over the wall.
> [23] They attacked him and shot at him;
> they hated him, the bowmen.
> [24] But his bow abode steady
> and the arms of his hands became supple,
> from the hands of the Might of Jacob;
> from thence [will come] a Shepherd, Rock of Israel;
> [25] from the God of your father, who shall help you,
> and from Shaddai, who shall bless you.
> with blessings of heaven above,
> blessings of the deep that crouches below,
> blessings of the breasts and the womb.
> [26] The blessings of your father are mightier
> than the blessings of my progenitors
> to the limits of the eternal hills;
> let them be upon the head of Joseph
> and on the crown of the head
> of the *nazir* of his brothers (Gen. 49).

Jacob, as if enraptured at the vision seen, pronounces upon Joseph the biggest and best blessing of all. As the *Zohar* says, 'Jacob inherited the cream of all, beyond the other patriarchs, and being perfect in all, he gave all to Joseph' (Vayeḥi: I:247b).

Jacob makes Joseph the *nazir*—that is, the prince set-apart—among his brothers. He speaks the word 'bless' or 'blessing' over Joseph six times. (Judah got it only once.) Joseph is to get the blessings of heaven and earth and sea, the utmost fecundity, the bounty of the eternal hills. Joseph's blessing is longer and more lavish than Judah's. It is longer and more lavish than anyone's. And we can note three things about it.

First, Jacob gives Joseph exceeding fruitfulness. His branches—that is, his offspring—will climb over the wall. Jacob had already said as much to Joseph's son, Ephraim: *His seed shall fill the nations* (Gen. 48:19). But the promise is repeated to Joseph.

Second, Jacob recalls the bitter arrows of Joseph's fate—his brothers' treachery, the slavers' whips, Potiphar's wife's lies. And he says that Joseph overcame these things by the hand of the Might of Jacob, that is, by Shaddai, the Almighty, who is Jacob's God.

Third, he foretells that from thence—that is, from the Might of Jacob, from Shaddai—there will arise to Joseph a great hero and leader, a 'Shepherd Rock of Israel'. He is called a Shepherd, because he will be a good and just ruler, caring for his flock. And he is called a Rock or Stone, because he will be an unshakeable foundation and defense.

Yet it is not actually said that the Shepherd-Rock will be Joseph's son, just as it is not actually said that Shiloh will be Judah's son. They are heroes promised to each tribe.

Yet the patriarchs foreshadow their offspring. As the Hebrew saying goes *Ma'aseh avot siman la-banim*, 'The deeds of the fathers are a sign for the sons.' Or, as Ramban says:

> Everything that occurred to the Patriarchs is a portent for their descendants. (On Gen. 12:6; cf. Midr. Tan. Lekh lekha §9)

Just as Judah led his brothers in the land of Canaan, so the Messiah promised to Judah will be a ruler. Likewise, Joseph will prefigure his Shepherd-Rock. As Joseph was beloved, blameless, betrayed, buried in the underworld, and exalted, so will it be with the Shepherd-Rock. He too, beloved by his father and innocent, will be betrayed by his brothers and buried, but will rise to splendour and authority over them all.

We will have more to say on this soon, when we look at how Moses, in Deuteronomy 33, develops Jacob's prophecy to Joseph. But, for now, lest anyone think that no-one ever saw what I see in this Shepherd-Rock of Genesis 49:22, I refer again to Ramban. Living in 13th-century Palestine, he commented on Deuteronomy 32:4:

> [*The Rock, his work is perfect*, etc. (Deut. 32:4)]. And all Israel will say also the Rock is Joshua, a sign about this land, for, *From thence a Shepherd-Rock of Israel* (Gen. 49:24). And it was interpreted long ago: *The rock rejected by the builders has become the capstone; this is from HaShem*, etc. (Ps. 118:22–23). And that is why Joshua said, *This rock will be a witness between us* (Josh. 24:27). Also, *For behold the rock which I have set before Joshua: upon one rock are seven eyes* (Zech. 3:9). Let the wise understand.

Ramban's comments are intentionally opaque. Let the wise understand. But he is saying that the Shepherd-Rock promised to Joseph is none other than the Rock of Deuteronomy 32:4, who is the God of Israel himself, the Angel who followed the Israelites through the desert as a thirst-quenching Rock. And he is also the Rock-rejected-by-the-builders of Psalm 118. Further, just as Jacob's promise to Joseph was first fulfilled in Joshua ben Nun, so the Shepherd-Rock, the Angel, will be a second Joshua. And Ramban, in 13th-century Palestine, is hoping for this greater Joshua to come and restore the Holy Land to Israel.

All in all, Joseph is the star of Jacob's blessing. And Joseph's stellar blessing is the climax of Genesis. After this prophecy of his glorious future, one chapter ties up his last acts. He buries his father, pardons his brothers, foretells the Exodus, and directs the Israelites to take his bones to the Promised Land. Then Joseph dies, is mummified, and laid in a sarcophagus. And the book comes to an abrupt close without any further details of Joseph's brothers or their seemingly irrelevant fate.

So ends Genesis. Israel's first great leader, Joseph, has saved them all. He is the prince-set-apart among his brothers. He is the father's chosen firstborn, inheriting the double portion, as two tribes with an extra bequest of land. He is the chosen heir to the blessings promised to Abraham. He will be fruitful beyond his brothers. From him will come a hero who will suffer and rise to rule. Meanwhile Judah, rather in second position, is briefly promised a line of kings.

Moses's Blessing

In time, Israel left Egypt and journeyed through the Sinai, each tribe marching under its banner and encamping around the ark at night. Finally, in the Plains of Moab, just before the conquest of the Promised Land, Moses, like Jacob before him, blesses the twelve tribes.

Moses's Blessing in Deuteronomy 33 is the direct offspring of Jacob's Blessing in Genesis 49. Each forms the last great discourse in its scroll. Each foretells the future of Israel's tribes. Each bestows symbols upon the tribes. Each favours some tribes above the others. And Moses's language frequently echoes Jacob's.

Moses serves his own tribe, Levi, generously. Jacob's sentence that Levi would be 'scattered in Israel' is now redeemed to Levi's benefit. They are to dwell in cities throughout the Israelite confederation; scattered, yes, but living off the tithes of the other tribes. Most of the other tribes get perfunctory blessings, even Judah, although, echoing Jacob, Moses gives him triumph in battle.

But Joseph's blessing, once again, is the cream of the cream. It is worth quoting in full.

> [13] And of Joseph he said,
> Blessed of YHVH be his land,
> from the treasures of heaven, from the dew,
> and from the deep that crouches below.
> [14] And from the treasures brought forth by the sun
> and from the treasures put forth by the moons.
> [15] And from the chief things of the ancient mountains
> and from the treasures of the eternal hills.
> [16] And from the treasures of earth and its fullness,
> and the favour of the one who dwelt in the bush;
> let it come upon the head of Joseph
> and on the crown of the head of the *nazir* of his brothers.
> [17] The firstborn of his *shor* is his [Joseph's] splendour;[2]
> and the horns of a *rem* are his horns;
> with them he shall gore the peoples, all as one,
> even to the ends of the earth.
> And these are the ten thousands of Ephraim;
> and these are the thousands of Manasseh (Deut. 33:13–17).

Moses reserves the word *bless* for Joseph alone. In the first four verses, he bestows, like Jacob, the fullest prosperity on Joseph—the blessings of heaven and the deep, the fertility of the hills. To these he adds the blessings of the sun and moon, the best of all that earth contains, and the favour of the one who appeared in the burning bush. He confirms Joseph's headship over the twelve tribes. And he directly quotes the last words of Jacob's blessing: *Let all these [blessings] rest on the head*

[2] *Or* The firstborn of his shor—splendour is his!

of Joseph, on the crown of the head of the nazir among his brothers.

Then he goes on to add to Joseph's head a crown or corona of fearsome horns. For he foretells a champion to arise from Joseph, whom he compares to two beasts, a *shor* and a *rem.* The *shor* and the *rem* are both oxen. But they are different kinds of oxen. And it is the difference between them that takes us to the heart of what Moses is saying.

FIRSTBORN *SHOR* AND *REM*

The Hebrew word *shor* means the domestic ox. The *rem* (or more precisely, *r'em*), on the other hand, is the Hebrew word for the aurochs.

The domestic ox, *bos taurus*, needs little introduction. It is the barnyard bull, the holy cow of India, the Texan cowboy's longhorn, the dewlapped beast of the Masai herder, the shaggy Highland strain. The best of the breed can, of course, be fierce when provoked, as a slow matador may find to his regret. But in general it is a servile animal, fulfilling the needs of mankind—bearing burdens, pulling loads, yielding milk, and surrendering its flesh and hide for beef and leather.

But more, the *shor* or domestic ox of Moses's blessing is the *firstborn of a shor*, that is, the male firstborn, since the Hebrew word for *firstborn* specifies its gender. It's a phrase which appears elsewhere in the Torah in the law of the firstborn. And it amounts quite simply to this: in ancient Israel every firstborn male ox was destined to die as a sacrifice. As Moses himself wrote:

> The firstborn of a shor or the firstborn of a sheep or the firstborn of a goat you shall not redeem. They are holy. Sprinkle their blood upon the altar and burn their fat in the fire, an aroma pleasing to YHVH. (Num. 18:17)

There was no negotiation about this. The law touched every Israelite herder. Every time a cow gave birth to a firstborn male calf, that calf was destined to a bloody end at the altar.

On the other hand, Moses's other ox, the *rem* or aurochs, is the ancient Eurasian wild ox, *bos primigenius.* Nowadays, the aurochs is much less familiar than *bos taurus*, but it very much merits our attention.

The aurochs is now extinct. It died out in Europe as late as 1627, in

Poland's Jaktorów Forest. But its near-eastern cousins died out 2,000 years before, before 500 BC.[3] Yet, for those who knew it, in the days of Jacob, Moses, Job, and David, when it roamed freely throughout north Africa and Eurasia, the aurochs was a dreaded beast. A large bull stood two metres high to the withers, with its head and great black horns rising another metre into the air.

All were in awe of this monstrous creature. From Neolithic Lascaux to Babylon's Ishtar gate, it barged and bellowed its way through the imagery of the ancient world. It was worshipped in one form or another by most of the Mediterranean peoples—the Egyptians, Canaanites, Minoans, Hittites, and Greeks.

Figure 3. Aurochsen from Lascaux.

Balaam ben Beor, in his curse-turned-to-blessing, compares the strength of Israel to the aurochs.

> God brings him out of Egypt; he has strength like an aurochs. (Num. 23:22)

The aurochs appears in 'Job's zoo', among the superbeasts, Behemoth and Leviathan. There, the Holy One himself admiringly contrasts its unyielding belligerence with the sweet docility of the poor *shor*.

[3] Tsahar *et al.*, 'Distribution and Extinction of Ungulates', places its extinction in the Levantine Iron Age (1,200–586 BC).

> Will the aurochs agree to serve you?
> Will he bed down by your manger?
> Can you bind an aurochs to the furrow with a harness?
> Will he plough the valleys behind you?
> Will you rely on him for his great strength?
> Or will you consign to him your hard work?
> Will you trust him to bring home your grain
> And gather it to your threshing-floor? (Job 39:9–11)

Julius Caesar saw the aurochs during his campaign in the Black Forest. He wrote,

> They are only a little smaller than elephants, but have the appearance, colour, and shape of a bull. Their strength is very great, and also their speed. They spare neither man nor beast that they see. The Germans trap them with much pains in pits and kill them. The young men harden themselves with this exercise, and practice themselves in this sort of hunting, and those who have slain the greatest number of them, having produced the horns in public, to serve as evidence, receive great praise. But not even when taken very young can they [the aurochsen] endure the sight of men, nor can they ever be tamed. (*Gallic War* VI:28)

Rabbinic tales of the auroch's immense size and ferocity abound. They say it did not enter the ark, but only its calves, for it was too large; or how King David found an aurochs asleep in the desert and, thinking it a hill, climbed upon it, and being borne away, vowed to build a temple a hundred cubits high—like its horns—in return for his safety; or how its horns are larger than those of all beasts, and it is called *rem* because its horns are *ram*, or 'high'; or how even the lion fears the aurochs.[4]

So there is a total contrast between the firstborn of a *shor* and a *rem*. What the one is, the other is not. While the *shor* is a slave, the *rem* is a conqueror. While the *shor* passed unheeded, the *rem* inspired fear and awe. While the *shor* pulled burdens amidst human habitations, the *rem* roamed unyoked in virgin forest and field. While the firstborn of a *shor* was destined to a victim's death, the *rem* had no place in Israel's sacrifical system (Lev. 1:2). One was lowly, enslaved, and bound to slaughter. The other was sovereign, free, and bound to life.

[4] Gen. R. s. 31; Midr. Pss. on 22:22; Yalkut Shimoni on Ps. 22 (§ 688); Midr. Pss. on 92:11; Rashi on Ps. 22:22.

Joseph's Conquering Ox

So these are the two oxen that Moses promises Joseph. But, of course, he is not speaking about oxen at all. For the horns of this beast are the tribes of Ephraim and Manasseh. Moses is actually speaking of a hero who will lead the tribes of Joseph. And he describes him as a firstborn *shor* and *rem*. As a firstborn *shor*, he is glorious even in his humility; as it is said, he is Joseph's *majesty* (v. 17). And so he is finally crowned with the majestic horns of the *rem*. Being so crowned, the *shor* becomes the *rem*. Our hero undergoes a striking transformation.

But how exactly does the firstborn-*shor* hero become the *rem*? By what process does this transformation take place? Or how does one destined to sacrifice become triumphant? Clearly, it is not by evading his fate. Dereliction of duty is not the hero's way. No. The path to glory must be through the destiny of sacrifice and death.

Lest anyone think this is just my own idea, here is the 'Animal Apocalypse' of 1 Enoch, dating from before the mid-second century BC. (It is an ancient Hebrew text. But, although Hebrew fragments still exist, it is preserved complete only in the Ethiopic text.) Here is its interpretation of Moses's prophecy.

> And I saw that a white bull was born, with large horns, and all the beasts of the field and all the birds of the air feared him and petitioned him all the time. And I saw till all their generations were transformed, and they all became white bulls; and the first [white bull] became an aurochs. (The aurochs was a great beast and had great black horns on its head.) And the Lord of the Sheep rejoiced over them and over all the oxen. (1 Enoch 90:37–38)[5]

This ancient writer sees a white bull born. This bull represents the Messiah, as all the commentators agree.[6] His whiteness shows his spotless purity; his large horns show his mighty power; the fact that he is an ox shows that he is the one promised to Joseph. All the nations of the earth—the beasts and birds—adore him. But this unblemished creature is destined to die. Why? Because he is born a 'first' white bull,

[5] For more on the passage, including the translation of Ethiopic *nagar* as aurochs, see my *Messiah ben Joseph*, chapter 5.

[6] Dillmann, *Henoch*, 286; Buttenwieser, 'Messiah', 509; Charles, *Enoch*, 258n.; Martin, *Livre d'Hénoch*, 235n; Isaac, '1 Enoch', 5; Torrey, *Apocryphal Literature*, 112; 'The Messiah Son of Ephraim', 266; Lindars, 'A Bull, a Lamb and a Word', 485; Milik, *Enoch*, 45, Tiller, *Animal Apocalypse*, 388.

and such is the lot of the firstborn bull.

Although his death is not described, its results are. All mankind is transformed into his likeness, into white bulls. Meanwhile, the Messiah himself, the first white bull, is transformed into something greater, into an aurochs. Then follows an explanation—either by the author or the Ethiopic translator—of what an aurochs actually is, for his readers had never seen one. And finally, the Messiah and all redeemed mankind live in the favour of the Lord of the Sheep, the God of Israel. This ancient writer perfectly grasped what Moses meant about Joseph's firstborn *shor* and *rem.*

Does this mean then that Joseph's promised hero must die and then reappear in glory? Could Moses ever have imagined such a scenario? Well, perhaps. Even in Moses's time, the people of the Nile Delta already worshipped some form of the bull-deity, Apis. To Apis they sacrificed bulls and buried them, believing that they would rise again as gods. Likewise, in Ugarit, just north of the land of Canaan, the bull-calf Baal was dying, rising, and ruling in the mid-second millennium BC. So the idea of a dying and rising bull was quite familiar to Moses. It is not impossible that he would speak like this of the death and post-mortem resurgence of the ox-hero promised to Joseph.

WHO IS THIS HERO?

But who is this hero Moses speaks about? Some rabbinic sages thought he was speaking about Joseph himself? Joseph was the one who held himself in check, restrained his passions, bent his neck to the divine law, and yet was cast into servitude and buried in pits and dungeons. But, at length, his subjugation complete, he was set free and became a ruler at whose feet all bowed. Yes, the two oxen mirror the life of Joseph quite nicely. But there's a snag. Moses's words are prophecy, not history. He speaks of a future figure, not of Joseph who was already long dead. Joseph's firstborn *shor* cannot be Joseph himself.

Others, more reasonably, think Moses was speaking of Joshua. For in Moses's time, Joshua's destiny still lay in the future. Joshua, of course, was the chief prince of the house of Joseph in his own day. 1 Chronicles 7:20–27 traces the single stirps from Ephraim to Joshua. Joshua, like Joseph, knew a path of lowliness and exaltation. Although he was a prince and a mighty commander in battle, he did not join Korah's rebellion, but waited upon Moses as a servant, and sought God late into the night. Finally, Moses appointed him prince and commander over all Israel to lead them to victorious conquest of Canaan. Like Joseph, and like a firstborn *shor*, his sacrificial humiliation gave life to Israel. Yet again there's a hitch: Joshua did not *gore the peoples, all as one, to the ends of the earth* (Deut. 33:17). He merely fulfilled his own remit, the conquest of the seven nations of Canaan (Josh. 3:10).

There is, therefore, a third interpretation, the most popular by far among the rabbis: the firstborn *shor* is a Messiah like Joshua who is to arise in the latter days. In fact, such a figure is implied in the text itself. It arises naturally from the discrepancy between Moses's prophecy and the limited nature of Joshua's conquest. For while Joshua's conquest was modest in extent, Moses's hero was promised the whole earth. And so the idea inevitably arose of a greater son of Joseph, a second Joshua, who would fulfil the prophecy entirely, a hero from Joseph's line, a Messiah ben Joseph.

And so we leave the books of Moses with two pillars in place. Moses gave Joseph an animal symbol just as Jacob did to his brothers. If Jacob made Judah the lion, Moses made Joseph the aurochs, whom even the lion fears. If Jacob promised Judah a hero who would rule 'until Shiloh comes', he promised Joseph a Shepherd-Rock from Shaddai. But Joseph's symbol is unique. It is the only sacrificial animal. More, his firstborn *shor* is destined to sacrifice. Moses points to one who must suffer as a sacrifice and then rise to rule the world.

The Priest-Prophet Messiah

So the Israelites entered the Promised Land with promises of two champions, one from Judah, one from Joseph. We see eager hope for both these heroes early in Israelite history. The Judahites hoped for a Messiah from their tribe. This hope found its focus in David and his offspring, who ruled the Judahites for almost a thousand years.

Meanwhile, the Ephraimites looked to their succession of sorry kings for their messiah. We see their hope in the story of Zedekiah ben Kenaanah prancing before King Ahab with iron horns on his head. His words, *With these horns, you will gore the nations altogether* (2 Chr.

18:10) refer directly to Moses's words in Deuteronomy 33. Zedekiah is saying Ahab is the hero that Moses foretold.

Two tribes, then, waiting for two messiahs. But, just to make things more interesting still, Moses also spoke about yet another saviour.

> YHVH said to me, 'What they say is good. I will raise up for them a prophet like you from among their brothers. I will put my words in his mouth, and he will tell them everything I command him. If anyone does not listen to my words that the prophet speaks in my name, I myself will call him to account.' (Deut. 18:18–19)

Since Moses was from the tribe of Levi, this was taken as pointing to a prophet to arise from that tribe. A similar hope rises again in the fateful oracle brought to Eli by the unnamed man of God. He foresees a future priest who will minister before the Messiah.

> And I will raise up for myself a faithful *kohen*, who shall do according to what is in my heart and in my mind. And I will build for him a sure house, and he shall walk before my *mashiaḥ* forever. (1 Sam. 2:35)

Finally, to make things more interesting still, Malachi told how Elijah the prophet would come to prepare the people for the day of YHVH.

> Behold, I will send you the prophet Elijah before that great and terrible day of YHVH comes. He will turn the hearts of the fathers to the children and the hearts of the children to the fathers, or else I will come and strike the land with a curse. (Mal. 4:5–6)

From these prophecies arose the idea of a priest and prophet Messiah. Since it was thought that Elijah was a *kohen*, that made the priest and the prophet Elijah the same.[7] So it was understood there would be another hero—a latterday prophet and priest to stand at the Messiah's side as counsellor and *kohen*. Of course, this *kohen* figure was treasured by the Levites. After all, Moses, Elijah, and most of the prophets were *kohanim*. And Israel's *kohanim* felt they also deserved a role in the coming salvation. That is why the Zadokite *kohanim* who wrote the Community Rule (a text found among the Dead Sea Scrolls) even gave the priestly messiah precedence over the King Messiah.

> The Priest shall enter at the head of all the congregation of Israel, then all the chiefs of the sons of Aaron, the priests, called to the assembly,

[7] For Elijah's priestly descent, see Tg Y. on Exod. 40 overleaf, and *Messiah ben Joseph*, chapter 7.

> men of renown. And they shall sit before him, each according to his rank. Afterwards, the Messiah of Israel shall enter. (1Q28a 2.11–14).

Three tribes, then, waiting for three heroes. Or should that be four? For the blurred border between the latterday priest and prophet came and went, depending on the writer's viewpoint and the fortunes of the temple *kohanim.* Sometimes it was one figure, sometimes two. After the temple was destroyed, the priest messiah faded out, but the prophet remained. Sometimes the latterday *kohen* was even said to be Melchizedek, who of course was not a Levite at all. There was no one view.

Hope in these three or four figures developed throughout the Greek and Roman period. We see them, for instance, in a one-page Dead Sea Scrolls document called 4QTestimonia, dating from around 100 BC. It offers four messianic proof-texts. The first is Deuteronomy 18:18–19 foretelling the Prophet like Moses. The second is Numbers 24:15–17, the 'Star from Jacob' which is the Messiah from David. The third is Deuteronomy 33:8–11, Moses's blessing on the Levites, which points to the priestly messiah. And the fourth is Joshua's curse on Jericho (Joshua 6:26), pointing to the Joshua Messiah from Joseph.

We find something similar in the 'Four Craftsmen' adage which recurs throughout rabbinic literature. The oldest version dates from the late first or early second century AD. It features the prophet Elijah, the King Messiah from Judah, the priest Melchizedek, and the War Messiah from Joseph.

> *The flowers appear on the earth* (Song 2:12). R. Isaac said, 'It is written: *And the Lord showed me four craftsmen* (Zech 2:3). These are they: Elijah, the King Messiah, Melchizedek and the War Messiah.'[8]

A later version of the same tradition replaces Melchizedek with the Righteous Priest:

> *And the Lord showed me four craftsmen* (Zech. 2:3). Who are these [four craftsmen]? Rav Ḥana bar Bizna said in the name of Rav Shimon Ḥasida: 'Messiah ben David, Messiah ben Joseph, Elijah, and the Righteous Priest.' (B. Sukkah 52b).

[8] Pes. R. 15:14-15 (cf. PdRK 5:9, and Song R. 2:13:4). The eds. of Buber and of Braude and Kapstein attribute it to the fourth-generation *tanna* R. Isaac (*fl.* 140-165); Wünsche, *Bibl. Rab.* 3:61, gives the second-generation *tanna* R. Eleazar (*fl.* 80-120). For more on the Four Craftsmen, see my *Messiah ben Joseph*, pp. 140–143. For the identity of the War Messiah as Messiah ben Joseph, see chapter 10 of the same book.

We find the same figures in the Targum Yerushalmi, except that now the Priest Messiah and Elijah the prophet have melded into one.

> [9] You shall take the anointing oil and anoint the tabernacle and all that is in it; you shall consecrate it for the sake of the crown of the kingdom of the house of Judah, and of the King Messiah who is destined to redeem Israel at the end of days.
> [10] You shall anoint the altar of burnt offerings and all its utensils, and consecrate the altar, and the altar will be most holy for the sake of the crown of the *k'hunah* of Aaron and his sons, and of Elijah the *kohen gadol* who is to be sent at the end of the exiles.
> [11] You shall anoint the laver and its base, and consecrate it for the sake of Joshua, your attendant, the head of the Sanhedrin of his people, by whose hand the land of Israel is to be divided, and of Messiah bar Ephraim, who will proceed from him, and by whose hand the house of Israel will conquer Gog and his horde at the end of days. (Tg Y. to Exod. 40:9–11)

So whether three or four, these were the messiahs the tribes of Israel awaited. Each great tribe—Ephraim, Judah, and Levi—had its own promised champion, borne as an ensign upon the heart. This was their hope as they earnestly served God night and day.

4

O Melchizedek

IT IS TIME to revisit our friend Melchizedek. Apart from Genesis 14, the only other Hebrew Bible text to mention him is Psalm 110. This little psalm, only seven verses long, is one of the deepest texts of the Bible. Long before Jesus's time, it gave rise to a host of other texts—Habbakuk 3, Daniel 7, Zechariah 14. Then it became the most quoted text in the New Testament. It appears there more than two dozen times, from Matthew through to Revelation.[1]

Yet it is riddled with engimas and beset by thorny issues of translation, interpretation, and variant readings. This is not surprising. For what it says is so astonishing that some have sought to bend it to their understanding. Still, with careful reading, we may uncover what it says.

Here's the issue. In this psalm, the Holy One makes two oaths. In verse 1, he promises someone worldwide rule. In verse 4, he promises someone eternal priesthood. But whom? Some say the one receiving these promises is a nameless figure.[2] But I do not think that is true. It seems to me that he does have a name. But to discover it we must first answer two questions: "Who's who in Ps. 110:1 ?" and "Who's who in Ps. 110:4 ?"

[1] Matt. 22:44; 26:64; Mark 12:36; 14:62; 16:19; Luke 20:42, 43; 22:69; Acts 2:34, 35; 1 Cor. 15:25; Eph. 1:20; Col. 3:1; Heb. 1:3; 1:13; 5:6; 6:20; 7:17, 21; 8:1; 10:12, 13; 12:2; 1 Pet. 3:22. The conqueror of Rev. 19:14 is based on Ps. 110:3, 5–7. There are also frequent references to Melchizedek throughout Heb. 7 without direct quotation from the Psalm.

[2] Gerstenberger, *Psalms 2*, 264.

WHO'S WHO IN PSALM 110:1 ?

The opening verse of the psalm runs as follows.

> 1 Of David, a psalm.
> YHVH vows to my lord: Sit at my right hand;
> till I set your enemies [to be] a stool for your feet.

There is a solemn oath—*YHVH vows* to *my lord.* We know who YHVH is. But who is *my lord* to whom he speaks? And who is the narrator of the promise? Let's visit the answers in chronological order.

JESUS'S VIEW: THE OLD INTERPRETATION

The earliest recorded explicit interpretation is from Jesus. It forms the climax of an extended debate with the Pharisees.

> 41 Now while the Pharisees were gathered together, Jesus asked them, 42 saying: "What do you think of the Messiah? Whose son is he?"
> They said to him, "The son of David."
> 43 He said to them, "How is it then that David by the Spirit calls him Lord, saying, 44 *The Lord said to my lord, Sit at my right hand, until I put your enemies under your feet*? 45 If David thus calls him Lord, how can he be his son?"
> 46 No one could answer him a word, nor from that day did anyone dare to ask him any more questions. (Matt. 22:41–46)

Here our English translation follows the Greek of Matthew's gospel in translating both YHVH and *my lord* as 'Lord'. But Jesus, debating with the Pharisees in Hebrew, would certainly have used quite distinct terms. We cannot be certain what these terms were, though the ancient Hebrew texts of Matthew may provide some clues.[3]

[3] Jesus spoke Hebrew in halakhic debate (cf. Joosten, 'Hebrew or Aramaic'), so he would have cited the psalm in Hebrew. For 'my lord', he would have said *adoni*, as in the psalm text. For the Tetragrammaton he may have said *Ha-Shem* ('the Name') or a periphrasis, like *Adonai* ('my Lords', the plural of majesty reserved for the Name). Matthew's gospel was probably written in Hebrew, as Papias, Origen, Eusebius (*Hist.* 3:24, 39), Irenaeus (*Adv. Haer.* 3.1.1), Jerome, and others, relate, adding that it was preserved by the Nazarene-Mandean community in their own day. Three Hebrew Matthew texts exist to this day: Shem Tov, Münster (Quinquarboreus), and Du Tillet, the last being perhaps the Hebrew original of the Greek text (Schonfield, *Old Hebrew Text*; Howard, 'Textual Nature'; Edwards, *Hebrew Gospel*). Shem Tov and Münster have ה' for *HaShem.* But Du Tillet has three *yodhs* in triangle, maybe implying that

So Jesus assumes, from the title of the psalm—*Of David, a psalm*—that the psalm is spoken by David, that *my lord* is the Messiah, and that David is recounting an oath uttered by YHVH to the Messiah. Three people: David the psalmist, YHVH the promiser, Messiah the promisee.

Now, if *my lord* is the Messiah, several things follow. First, David knew or knew about the Messiah, and about an oath made to him by YHVH.

Second, the Messiah is not David's son. We must not reduce this to meaning the Messiah is David's greater son, as some do. The Pharisees would have agreed to that too and so the debate would have been pointless. Jesus is really saying the Messiah is not David's son.

Third, the Messiah is greater than David. And, since it is understood that no mortal can be greater than David, the implication is that the Messiah is more than mortal.

Now Jesus did not invent this interpretation. It was already well established in his own time. You see, the Pharisees share it too. After Jesus speaks they do not say, 'We reject your interpretation because we do not believe David spoke about the Messiah.' On the contrary, they share the same view. That is why they feel the force of his argument and *no one could answer him a word* (Matt. 22:46). Nor should we imagine that Matthew is just giving a one-sided picture of the debate while, in reality, the Pharisees did not share Jesus's view at all. Matthew wrote his gospel for a Hebrew-speaking community. His hearers knew what the Pharisees believed. The credibility of his gospel depended on representing the Pharisees' view squarely.

THE ANTIQUITY OF THE OLD INTERPRETATION

So the Pharisees' reaction shows that this interpretation of Psalm 110, where the vow is made to the Messiah, was ancient and was shared by Jesus and the Pharisees alike. This is confirmed by three texts which are older than the gospels and share the same interpretation; namely, Daniel 7, 11QMelchizedek, and the Similitudes of Enoch.

Daniel 7. In Daniel chapter seven, the prophet sees a grim vision of

Jesus spoke the Name explicitly, as the Talmud and *Toldot Yeshu* claim he did (cf. chap. 10 below). By Jesus's time, speaking the Name was forbidden except to the *kohen gadol* on Yom Kippur. Such a violation of *halakhah* would have given the authorities one more reason to hate him.

the successive empires of history, depicted as savage beasts. Then, in bright contrast, he sees the divine throne-room where the Ancient of Days sits in state.

> [9] I looked until thrones were set in place,
> and the Ancient of Days took his seat.
> His garment was as white as snow;
> and the hair of his head like wool.
> His throne was a pure flame of fire,
> its wheels a burning fire.
> [10] A river of fire was flowing,
> coming forth from before him.
> A thousand thousand attended him;
> ten thousand times ten thousand stood before him.
> The court was seated,
> and the books were opened.

Daniel describes the demise of the beasts. Then he continues:

> [13] In my vision at night I looked, and, behold, with the clouds of heaven, came one like a son of man. He came to the Ancient of Days and was brought into his presence. [14] To him was given dominion and glory and a kingdom; and all nations, peoples, and tongues shall serve him. His dominion is an everlasting dominion that will not pass away, and his kingdom is one that will never be destroyed.

Daniel sees the heavenly throne room, where *thrones are set in place*, and the Ancient of Days presides amidst the myriads of his court (7:9–10). Then another figure appears (7:13). He is certainly a divine being, for he comes riding the clouds of heaven.[4] But he is also a human figure, for he is called *one like a son of man.* This divine man is given a place beside the Ancient of Days. That is implied in the *thrones.* And the Ancient of Days gives him authority to go forth and establish an everlasting kingdom over the whole earth.

Now, while Daniel's vision is a vision, yet, one way or other, heavenly visions relate to biblical texts. And Daniel's vision mirrors Psalm 110. No other passage in scripture speaks of a man enthroned beside God. The whole passage—heavenly man, seated beside the divine throne, conquering the earth—reflects the imagery of the psalm.

The rabbis long saw the Messiah in Daniel 7. A second-century dispute between Rabbis Akiva and Yose suggests there was an older

[4] Emerton, "The Origin of the Son of Man Imagery", 225–242.

tradition—a *baraitha*—that the one seated beside the Ancient of Days was 'David', which probably means the Messiah from David.[5]

> *Till thrones were placed* (Dan. 7:9). One [throne] for Him and one for David, as it is taught [in a *baraitha*]: One for Him and one for David. This is R. Akiva's view. Rabbi Yose said to him: Akiva! How long will you profane the *Shekhinah*. (B. Sanh. 38b)

The early seventh-century midrash, *Pirqei Hekhalot Rabbati*, says:

> And you should learn that Messiah, when he is revealed, like flesh and blood shall he be revealed, or like an angel shall he be revealed, as was explained by Daniel: *And behold, with the clouds of heaven, came one like a son of man* (Dan. 7.13).[6]

A mid-seventh century midrash, *Otot Rav Shimon ben Yoḥai*, says:

> He [the Holy One] will bring Menahem ben Ammiel, Messiah ben David, from the place of imprisonment, as it is said: *For one came out of prison in order to reign* (Eccl. 4.14). And he will carry him on a cloud, as it is said: *And behold with the clouds of heaven* [*one like a son of man*] (Dan. 7.13).[7]

And a late seventh-century midrash, *Pirqei Mashiaḥ*, says:

> Now it is said in praise of King Messiah that he is going to come with the clouds of heaven and two seraphim, [one] at his right hand and [one] at his left, as it is said, *Behold, with the clouds of heaven, one like a son of man is coming* (Dan. 7.13).[8]

An eighth-century midrash, *Nistarot Rav Shimon ben Yoḥai*, says:

> The King Messiah will spring up there, as it is said, *And behold, with the clouds of heaven* (Dan. 7.13). And it is written afterwards, *And he was given dominion* (Dan. 7.14).[9]

And the tenth-century *Midrash Vayosha* says,

> And after that Messiah ben David will come, as it is said: *And behold with the clouds of heaven one like a son of man* (Dan. 7.13), and it is written afterward, *He will have authority and royal dignity* (Dan. 7.14).

[5] As the Soncino Talmud footnote also recognizes.
[6] See Mitchell, *Messiah ben Joseph*, chapter 11 §4, for the text and dating.
[7] See Mitchell, *Messiah ben Joseph*, chapter 11 §6, for the text and dating.
[8] See Mitchell, *Messiah ben Joseph*, chapter 11 §7, for the text and dating.
[9] See Mitchell, *Messiah ben Joseph*, chapter 11 §8, for the text and dating.

So, all in all, Daniel's figure, who comes straight from Psalm 110, was widely recognized as being the Messiah.

11QMelchizedek. A similar interpretation of Psalm 110 is found in the Dead Sea text called the Melchizedek Scroll (11QMelchizedek or 11Q13).[10] The scroll dates from about 100 BC, but its date of composition was obviously earlier. It tells of a heavenly hero called Melchizedek. The text has many gaps—or lacunae—marked here by square brackets.[11] But even so, what emerges is striking. It is worth quoting at length.

> *Column 2*
> 2 [...] And as for what he said: *In this year of jubilee, [you shall return, each one, to his respective property* (Lev. 25:13), as is written: *This is*]
> 3 *the manner of the* [*release: every creditor shall release what he lent* [*to his neighbor. He shall not coerce his neighbour or his brother when*] *the release for God* [*has been proclaimed*] (Deut. 15:2).
> 4 [Its inter]pretation for the last days refers to the captives, of whom he said: *To proclaim liberty to the captives* (Isa. 61:1). And he will make
> 5 their rebels prisoners [...] and of the inheritance of Melchizedek, for [...] and they are the inheri[tance of Melchi]zedek, who
> 6 will make them return. He will proclaim liberty for them, to free them from [the debt] of all their iniquities. And this will [happen]
> 7 in the first week of the jubilee after the ni[ne] jubilees. And the day [of atonem]ents is the end of the tenth jubilee
> 8 in which atonement will be made for all the sons of [light] and for the men of the lot of Melchizedek. [And on the heights] he will decla[re in their] favour according to their lots; for
> 9 it is the time of the *year of favour* of Melchizedek, to exa[lt in the tri]al the holy ones of God through the rule of judgement, as is written
> 10 about him in the songs of David, who said: *God will stand up in the assem*[*bly of El,*] *in the midst of the gods he judges* (Ps. 82:1). And about him he said: *Above it*
> 11 *return to the heights, God will judge the peoples* (Ps. 7:8–9). As for what he sa[id: *How long will yo*]*u judge unjustly and show partiality to the wicked? Selah* (Ps. 82:2).
> 12 Its interpretation concerns Belial and the spirits of his lot, who were rebels [all of them] turning aside from the commandments of God [to commit evil].
> 13 But Melchizedek will carry out the vengeance of God's judgements

[10] So García Martínez 1992a: 176. Its date of composition is, of course, earlier.

[11] Square brackets reconstruct missing text; round brackets and Bible verses are editorial clarification. My translation is indebted to García-Martínez, *Dead Sea Scrolls*, pp. 139–40.

[on this day, and they shall be freed from the hands] of Belial and from the hands of all the sp[irits of his lot].
[14] To his aid (shall come) all *the gods of* [*justice*; he] is the one [who will prevail on this day over] all the sons of God, and he pre[side over] this [assembly].
[15] This is the day of [peace about which God] spoke [of old through the words of Isa]iah the prophet, who said: *How beautiful*
[16] *upon the mountains are the feet of the herald who announces peace, of the her*[*ald of good who announces salvation*], *saying to Zion: Your God* [*has become king*] (Isa. 52:7).
[17] Its interpetation: The mountains are the pro[phets ...]
[18] And the herald is [the one ano]inted of the spirit (*mashiaḥ ha-ruaḥ*) about whom Dan[iel] spoke [...*until the time of an Anointed Prince* (*mashiaḥ nagid*) *there will be seven weeks . . . after sixty-two weeks, an Anointed* (*mashiaḥ*) *shall be cut off* (Dan. 9:25–26). [... and *the herald of*]
[19] *good who announces salv*[*ation* (Isa. 52:7)] is the one about whom it is written that he will send him *to comfo*[*rt the afflicted, to watch over the afflicted ones of Zion*] (Isa. 61:2–3).
[20] *To comfo*[*rt the afflicted*, its interpretation:] to instruct them in all the ages of the worl[d...]
[21] in truth. [...]
[22] [...] it has been turned away from Belial and it [...]
[23] [...] in the judgements of God, as is written about him: *Saying to Zion: 'Your God rules'* (Isa. 52:7). [*Zi*]*on* is
[24] [the assembly of all the sons of justice, those] who establish the covenant, those who avoid walking [on the pa]th of the people. *Your God* is
[25] [Melchizedek, who will fr]ee [them] from the hand of Belial. And as for what he said: *You shall blow the hor[n in every] land* (Lev. 25:9).

As said, the name Melchizedek appears in the Hebrew scriptures only in Genesis 14 and Psalm 110, and this Dead Sea Scrolls figure reflects elements of both these Bible texts. Like Melchizedek of Genesis 14 and Psalm 110:4, he is a priest, coming to make atonement (ii.7–8). But he is also a conquering warrior (ii.11–12), as in Psalm 110:5–7.

He comes to make lasting atonement and to usher in the year of liberty proclaimed by Isaiah (ii.4). He will free his people, the Sons of Light, from their iniquities and atone for their sins (ii.6, 8, 13, 25). He will judge the peoples and their gods (ii.10–11). He will make war on the followers of Belial and destroy them (ii.13, 25). In accord with Daniel's prophecy, he will bring in everlasting righteousness and seal up vision and prophecy (ii.18; Dan. 9:24). Since he is not of the sons of Aaron, his atonement will inaugurate a new *k'hunah* or priesthood, presumably making the *k'hunah* of Aaron obsolete.

But who is this figure? He must be seen, first, as the Messiah. For he is identified, in lines 15 to 20, with Isaiah's herald of peace to Zion (Isa. 52:7) who is also the servant of YHVH, the one anointed (*mashiaḥ*) by the spirit to comfort the afflicted of Zion (61:1–3). He is also identified with Daniel's 'cut off' *mashiaḥ* prince (ii.18).

Yet he is certainly no ordinary human being. Professor Vermes said he was an angel. But he is no ordinary angel either.

It seems that he is the God of Israel. For the author identifies him with YHVH, making *the year of the favour of YHVH*, spoken of in Isaiah 61:2, into 'the year of the favour of Melchizedek' (ii.9). Again, he is the God who judges the gods in Psalm 82:1, which, in context, refers to the God of Israel (ii.10). In the same way, he is the *elohim* of Psalm 7:8 who, in the original psalm, is YHVH (ii.10–11).

So, if this Melchizedek is an angel, then he seems to be that same Angel of YHVH who appeared to the Patriarchs, to Moses, Joshua, and David, as the divine Lord in human form.

Altogether, then, the central figure of the Melchizedek Scroll reflects Psalm 110 in several ways: first, in his name; second, in being a king; third, in being a priest; fourth, in being a divine warrior sent from beside the heavenly throne to establish his kingdom on earth.[12]

The Similitudes of Enoch, dating probably from the first century BC, take a similar line.[13] Here is chapter 48.

> [1] And in that place I saw the fountain of righteousness
> which is inexhaustible,
> and is surrounded by many fountains of wisdom;
> and all the thirsty drank of them, and were filled with wisdom,
> and their dwellings were with the righteous and holy and elect.
> [2.] And at that time that Son of Man was given a name
> in the presence of the Lord of Spirits,
> the Ancient of Days.

[12] Flowers, 'Two Messiahs', sees two *mashiaḥ* figures and the 'angel' Melchizedek. I see no basis to divide the central figure of the text in this way. But, either way, the Melchizedek of the text is still *elohim*, YHVH, and divine saviour.

[13] Estimated dates for the sections of the Enoch compendium vary widely. The Similitudes are usually said to date from the time of Herod the Great. See Walck, *Son of Man*, 15–23.

[3] Yea, before the sun and the signs were created,
before the stars of the heaven were made,
his name was named before the Lord of Spirits.
[4] He shall be a staff to the righteous to lean upon and not fall,
and he shall be the light of the Gentiles,
and the hope of those who are troubled of heart.
[5] All who dwell on earth shall fall down and worship before him,
and will praise and bless and celebrate in song the Lord of Spirits.
[6] And for this reason hath he been chosen and hidden before him,
before the creation of the world and for evermore.
[7] And the wisdom of the Lord of Spirits hath revealed him
to the holy and righteous;
for he hath preserved the lot of the righteous,
because they have hated and despised this world of
unrighteousness,
and have hated all its works and ways
in the name of the Lord of Spirits:
for in his name they are saved,
and according to his good pleasure
hath it been in regard to their life.
[8] In these days the kings of the earth shall be downcast in face,
and the strong who seize the land by the works of their hands;
for on the day of their anguish and trouble
they shall not save themselves.
[9] And I will give them over into the hands of my elect,
as straw in the fire so shall they burn before the holy ones:
As lead in the water shall they sink before the righteous,
and no place shall be found for them.
[10] And on the day of their affliction there shall be rest on the earth,
and they shall fall before them and not rise again:
[11] And no one shall take them by the hand to raise them up;
for they have denied the Lord of Spirits and his Messiah.
Blessed be the name of the Lord of Spirits.

From this, and the surrounding chapters, we learn that the Son of Man is the chosen of the Ancient of Days (46:1–2); he shall be summoned before the throne of the Ancient of Days (47:3; 48:2) and there sit enthroned (45:3); he is eternally pre-existent (48:6), he is the Messiah (48:11), with universal dominion to destroy the wicked and console the righteous (46–48). It is all built on Psalm 110 and Daniel 7.

All the above passages grow out of Psalm 110. And they all interpret the psalm just as Jesus did, with a divine Messiah-figure sent forth from heaven to establish his rule over the earth. And, since they all date from before Jesus's time, they confirm that Jesus did not invent this interpretation of the psalm. It was current long before he was born.

THE PERSISTENCE OF THE OLD INTERPRETATION

But there is another reason to think that this ancient messianic view of Psalm 110 was the main one in Jesus's time; namely, it persists right through the first millennium AD, despite new views which emerge.

We find it, for instance, in Midrash Aleph Beth, from the fifth or sixth century.[14] 'Ephraim' signifies the Messiah from Joseph, while *Gog and Magog* sets him in the great end-time battle of Ezekiel 36–37.

> Ephraim my firstborn, come, sit at my right hand until I bring down the power of the horde of Gog and Magog, your enemies, beneath your footstool. As it is said, *HaShem says to my lord, Sit at my right hand*, etc. [Ps. 110:1] (§11b:1)

The midrash *Otot Ha-Mashiaḥ,* from the early seventh century, also applies the psalm to the Messiah.

> And Messiah ben David will go, and Elijah the prophet, with the righteous ones who returned from the desert of Judah, and with all of gathered Israel, and he will go to Jerusalem. And he will ascend the steps to the remains of the temple and take his seat there. And Armilus will hear that a king has arisen for Israel and he will say, "How long will this contemptible little nation act like this?" Thereupon he will gather all the armies of the nations of the world and go to make war with the Messiah of the Lord. And then the Holy One, blessed be he, needs nothing for the battle, but to say to him [Messiah ben David], *Sit at my right hand* [Ps. 110:1].[15]

The midrash on Psalm 18, from the eighth or ninth century, says,

> R. Yudan said in the name of R. Ḥama: In the time to come, the Holy One, blessed be he, seats the King Messiah at his right hand, as it is said, *HaShem says to my lord, 'Sit at my right hand'* [Ps. 110:1].

Later still, in the Crusades period, *Tefillat Rav Shimon ben Yoḥai* says,

> The Holy One, blessed be he, will fight on behalf of Israel. He will say to the Messiah, *Sit at my right hand* [Ps. 110:1]. And the Messiah will

[14] For the dating, see Sawyer, *Midrash Aleph Beth* 26–27.
[15] See Mitchell, *Messiah ben Joseph*, chapter 11 §2, for the text and dating.

> say to Israel, "Assemble yourselves and *stand and see the deliverance of the Lord!*" [Exod. 14:13].[16]

As late as the 13th century, the *Zohar* makes the same interpretation, once again of Messiah ben Joseph.

> Jacob, *changing his hands* [Gen. 48:14], placed ox [Ephraim] on the right and lion [Judah] on the left, for which reason *HaShem says to my lord: Sit at my right hand* [Ps. 110:1]. This is the *tsadik* Messiah ben Joseph (*Zohar,* Pinhas, §567).

All these texts show that the messianic reading of Psalm 110 remained widespread in Judaism, despite the emergence of new views.[17]

So Jesus's messianic interpretation of the psalm was no novelty. It dated from at least the time of Daniel, it was widely accepted in his own day, even by the Pharisees, and it persisted well into medieval times. And this view saw three people in the psalm, namely, David the psalmist, YHVH, and David's *my lord*, who is the Messiah.

So what was Jesus's point?

But what was Jesus's point in this whole debate? Well, of course, Jesus claimed to be the Messiah (Matt. 16:15–17; Mark 8:29; 14:61–62; John 4:25–26). Everyone understood that (Matt. 12:23; 21:9), despite his occasional reticence on the subject (e.g. Matt. 16:20). But his first-century hearers had differing views on the Messiah. Some thought that, as a second David, he might be only an exceptional mortal. So Jesus's point in citing this psalm is to say that he is the Messiah whom David called *my lord.* He is therefore not David's son but a divine man, sent from heaven, like the Messiah Daniel spoke of.

This agrees with what he says elsewhere. Jesus never calls himself 'son of David' in the canonical gospels. Others do: Matthew (Matt. 1:1), the angel Gabriel (Luke 1:32), blind Bartimaeus (Matt. 20:30–31; Mark 10:47), a Canaanite woman (Matt. 15:22), the Palm Sunday

[16] See Mitchell, *Messiah ben Joseph*, Appendix 3, for the text and dating.

[17] Still other texts might be cited. The 'Four Craftsmen' traditions see Melchizedek of Ps. 110:4 as a messianic figure (Pesikta Rabbati §15:14/15, Pesikta de Rav Kahana 5:9, Song of Songs Rabbah 2:13:4). See too the midrash *Pirqei mashiaḥ* §5, where *uzzkha yisrael,* cited as scripture, is not a biblical expression, but, in context, describes the Messiah's sceptre and is an emendation of *uzzkha yishlakh* '(the sceptre of) your strength will send (YHVH)' (Ps. 110:2).

crowds; the children in the temple (Matt. 21:9, 15; Mark 11:10); the apostles (Rom. 1:3; Heb 7:14). But Jesus says he is not even a son of Abraham (John 8:58). His chosen title for himself is, of course, 'son of man', the same title as the heavenly Messiah of Daniel's vision.

The Pharisees would certainly not have missed the implication of Jesus's words. Nor would they have liked it one little bit. In fact, this debate became something of a *cause célèbre* between the Nazarenes and Pharisees. That is surely why it appears in all three synoptic gospels. But while the Nazarenes continued to uphold the interpretation endorsed by Jesus, the Pharisees soon found alternatives.

THE TARGUM ON PSALM 110

The earliest such alternative is in the targum—the ancient Aramaic translation—of the Psalms. The Targum of Psalms we now possess was compiled in the mid-first millennium.[18] But it sprang from older versions, from before the time of Jesus, which were modified over the years, as desired. The targum preserves two variants for the first verse of Psalm 110. (YY is the targum abbreviation for YHVH.)

> By the hand of David, a psalm. YY said in his decree [*b'memreh*] to make me lord of all Israel. But he said to me, 'Wait yet for Saul of the tribe of Benjamin to die, for one reign must not encroach on another. And afterwards I will make your enemies a stool for your feet.'
>
> [By the hand of David, a psalm.] YY said in his decree [*b'memreh*] to give me the dominion in exchange for sitting in study of Torah. 'Wait at my right hand until I make your enemies a stool for your feet.'

The first variant links the psalm's *my right hand* (*y'mini*) with Saul the Benjamite (*ben-y'mini*). But both variants really enshrine the same idea, namely, that David is both the speaker and *my lord* who receives the promise. The three figures of the original psalm have become two: David the psalmist, YHVH the promiser, David the promisee.

When did this happen? I imagine it happened early. By the early second century, R. Akiva said of Daniel's vision, 'Two thrones: one for himself and one for David' (B. Ḥag 14a). Akiva wants to give the Messiah's seat to David. For this, he was rebuked by Rabbi Yose ha-

[18] Stec, *Targum of Psalms*, dates it from fourth to sixth century.

Galili: 'Akiva, how long will you profane the Shekhinah?' The Shekhinah, the abiding glory of God in the temple was widely seen as the Angel, the visible God. Rabbi Yose holds to the old interpretation and is not impressed by Akiva's idea. This was around the same time when Justin Martyr said the Jews were saying the psalm was not about the Messiah but about King Hezekiah (Dial. 33), a view hinted at in Sanhedrin 99a: *There shall be no Messiah for Israel because they have already enjoyed him in the days of Hezekiah.*

How did this change happen? Well, let's imagine *b'memreh*, 'in his word', was formerly *l'memreh*, 'to his word'. Yes, I know *b'memreh* is standard targum locution for divine speech. Perhaps it shouldn't arouse any suspicions. Still, the change of this single letter would change the sense of the text smoothly and completely. In that case, '*in* his word' would first have been '*to* his Word' or '*to* his Memra', the Aramaic term for the divine Logos. If so, the earlier targum would have read:

> By the hand of David, a psalm. YY said to his Memra [Logos], 'Sit at my right hand', etc.

Now, there is no hard evidence for the existence of such a text.[19] But it would fully reflect the ancient three-person interpretation: David, YHVH, and *my lord* the divine Logos Messiah. And we must surely agree that the earliest Aramaic translations would have followed the original Hebrew, where YHVH speaks to *my lord*, not 'in his word'.

So, one way or another, the fact is that the targum has lost someone from verse one. David the speaker and *my lord* have melded into one; *my lord* has vanished as a third person. And that is quite at odds with the original Hebrew psalm and its whole long history of interpretation.

Talmud Bavli, Nedarim 32b

We already saw, in chapter one, how a Talmud passage, Bavli Nedarim 32b, identifies Melchizedek with Shem ben Noah. The gist of it is that Melchizedek aka Shem was in line for the eternal priesthood or *k'hunah* spoken of in Ps. 110:4. But, when he flouted protocol—blessing Avram before El Elyon—the *k'hunah* went to Avram and his seed.

[19] Pietro Galatino (1460–1540) testified to such a targum (so John Gill on Ps. 110), but Galatino's polemical intent might lead to doubt of his testimony.

> Avraham said to him, 'And does one preface the blessing of the slave to the blessing of his master?'
>
> Immediately he [God] gave it [the *k'hunah*] to Avraham, as it is said, *HaShem said to my Lord, 'Sit at my right hand until I set your enemies as a stool for your feet'* (Ps. 110:1). And after this it is written, *The Lord has sworn and will not repent. You are a priest forever* 'al-dibrati *Malki-zedeq* (Gen. 110:4), that is, on account of that which Melchizedek had said [*l'divoro shel malki-tsedeq*].

Now, David is not even mentioned here. But the point is that, if David could not call his son *lord*, he could call his ancestor Abraham *lord*. In other words, there is an implied rebuff of Jesus's interpretation. And the result is another three-person reading of verse 1: David the psalmist, YHVH, and Abraham, who is *my lord*.

This interpretation became standard in the Talmud and among many later authorities, including Rashi.[20] But, as Ibn Ezra pointed out, in his comments on Psalm 110, it does not really make sense. Avraham did not become an eternal priest, nor did he ever rule from Zion.

The Rishonim

Ibn Ezra (c. 1089–1167) developed a new version of the targum interpretation: the psalm was not written *by* David but *for* David by one of the temple singers. And so David was *my lord*, but the psalmist was one of the temple singers. So again we have three people: Levite psalmist, YHVH the promiser, and David (*my lord*) the promisee. This view is followed by Radak (1160–1235), Yeshayahu Mitrani (d. 1260), and by many modern scholars. But it has two weaknesses. First, David did not become an eternal priest (110:4). Nor did his sons, although they maybe held some kind of priestly role (2 Sam. 8:18).[21] So, if the prophecy concerns David, it is a false prophecy. Second, it assumes

[20] Cf. B. Sanh. 108b: R. Hana b. Liwai said: Shem Rabba [*i.e.*, Melchizedek] said to Eliezer [Abraham's servant]: 'When the kings of the east and the west attacked you, what did you do?' He replied, 'The Holy One, blessed be he, took Abraham and set him at his right hand, and they threw dust which turned to swords, and chaff which turned to arrows, as it is said, *A Psalm of David. HaShem said to my lord, Sit at my right hand, until I make your enemies your footstool.*' Cf. Lev. R. 25:6; Midr. Ps. 76 §3; 110 §4.

[21] The verse has many interpretations, including that David's sons were the managerial staff for palace relations with the *kohanim*.

that the heading *l'david* can be understood as *concerning David.* This assumption was accepted by no-one in ancient times—neither Jesus nor the Pharisees nor the apostles nor the targum nor the talmud.[22] Nor could Ramban accept it.

Ramban (1194–1270), at the Barcelona Disputation, offered an upgrade of Ibn Ezra's theory. He said the psalm was indeed written *by* David, as the title implies. But he wrote it for the singers to sing about himself. Menachem Meiri (1249–1306) agreed, sagely adding that if David had written, 'HaShem says to me', then it would have been untrue when sung by the Levite singers. So again we have three people: Levite singer, YHVH the promiser, and David the psalmist, promisee, and *my lord.* But this view has weaknesses too. As with Ibn Ezra's view, David was not a priest for ever, so the prophecy is false. Further, it paints a lonely picture of David writing praise-songs and prophecies about himself, which isn't how it's supposed to be (Prov. 27:2).

PSALM 110:1 SUMMARIZED

Therefore Jesus's interpretation of Psalm 110:1 was ancient and widespread in his own time. It was followed, naturally, by Patristic writers. Yet the disciples of the Pharisees, apparently in reaction to Christian use of the psalm, produced a series of alternative interpretations.

But, strangely, modern scholarship—even conservative Christian scholarship—routinely ignores Jesus's interpretation and tends toward the later alternatives, especially Ibn Ezra's. Yet these views ignore the authorial sense of the title which Jesus clearly endorsed (Mark 12:36; Luke 20:42) and which the Pharisees also accepted. They reduce the psalm to false prophecy, leaving it as no more than an ancient panegyric on David, legitimizing his inheritance of a supposed line of Jebusite sacral kingship—Melchizedek, Adonizedek (Josh. 10:1–3)—which can perhaps be vaguely understood as pointing to the Messiah.[23]

[22] In fact, the evidence is that the *lamedh* preposition of the Psalms should normally be seen to indicate authorship. See my *Songs of Ascents*, 73–74, or Ross, *Psalms*, 1:43.

[23] From a generation ago, see Ishida, *Royal Dynasties*, 137–40; Allen, *Psalms*, 81; Bruce, *Hebrews*, 159–60. Yet there have been, and still are, those who hold by the old interpretation: Delitzsch, *The Psalms*, 187; Kaiser, *Use of the Old Testament*, 77; Waltke, *Old Testament Theology*, who says, "The New Testament has priority in 'unpacking' the meaning of the Old Testament."

But why has Jesus's interpretation been so shunned? Surely the answer is that, while it is perfectly coherent, it's a lot to take on board. For it means that David is reporting an oath made by YHVH to the Messiah. This implies, in turn, a pre-existent Messiah—alive in David's time. It implies further that David had inside knowledge of the promise made by the Holy One to the pre-existent divine Messiah. That seems like a lot to handle if any other explanation can be found.

Yet, I suggest, there is no other possible explanation. None of the other interpretations bear scrutiny. The old interpretation is still the only cogent one. It is exactly what the psalm is saying. And, by way of confirmation, we must turn now to verse four.

WHO'S WHO IN PSALM 110:4?

Most English translations of Psalm 110:4 run something like the NIV version below.

> The LORD [YHVH] has sworn and will not change his mind:
> 'You are a priest forever, in the order of [*'al-dibrati*] Melchizedek.'

According to this translation, YHVH is appointing someone as an eternal priest in the order of Melchizedek's priesthood. Perhaps this person is *my lord* of verse one, but it is not at all clear.

Yet all such translations have at their core an unbearable conundrum. Let's break it down into three puzzles.

Puzzle #1. If YHVH makes someone a priest forever like Melchizedek, then that implies that Melchizedek is a priest for ever.

Someone might object: 'No, no. This person is made an eternal priest *like* Melchizedek, but the original priesthood of Melchizedek was temporary, not eternal.'

But that would be as if a voice should call to me from heaven and say, 'I hereby make you Archbishop of Canterbury forever and ever, just like Thomas à Becket.'

I would reply, 'Wow! That's really nice. For ever and ever? Wow. What can I say? But hang on! Thomas à Becket wasn't archbishop forever. He's dead!' In the same way, it makes no sense at all to appoint someone to be an eternal priest in the image of a mortal.

Puzzle #2. If this promised priesthood of verse four was not eternal, then who would want it? After all, the promise was made in David's time, when the sons of Aaron had a functioning priesthood. That was worth something. But to bestow on someone the defunct priesthood of a defunct priest was not better but worse. Perhaps Melchizedek's ancient priesthood was originally in some unknown way better than Aaron's. But in what way can it possibly be better now, being extinct? Better a live dog than a dead lion.

So, if Melchizedek is not a priest forever, then verse four is absurd. But if he is a priest forever, then he is most certainly an immortal. In that case, one must ask, 'Where is Melchizedek and what is he doing now?'

Puzzle #3. If Melchizedek is indeed an eternal priest, and YHVH makes someone else an eternal priest in verse four, then there are now two eternal priests. How can this be? Either there are two rival priests eternally offering access to the one God. Or else there is something badly wrong with the translation.

IN THE 'WHAT?' OF MELCHIZEDEK?

The translation 'in the order of Melchizedek' represents the Hebrew '*al-di*b̲*rati malki-tsedeq*. The word *'al* means 'upon' or 'according to'. And *malki-tsedeq* is Melchizedek. The key issue is what does *di*b̲*rati* mean?

*Di*b̲*rati*—the *b̲* is soft, like Spanish *sabio*—is a form of the feminine noun *di*b̲*rah.* It's a rare word. But it comes from a common root—*dbr*—which gives rise to a constellation of related words meaning 'word', 'speak', 'matter', 'thing', 'reason', or 'promise'. The noun *di*b̲*rah* never appears in the Bible in its simple form, but only with its ending modified to *di*b̲*rat* or *di*b̲*rati.* These two forms look similar, but their meanings are different.

*Di*b̲*rat* is a noun in the Hebrew possessive or 'construct' case. The Hebrew possessive differs from its English equivalent. In the English possessive, the possessor noun takes a genitive ending: 'The king's sons' (adding the genitive ending to king). But in Hebrew the possessee noun is modified to the construct state: 'sons-of the king' (*b'nei ha-melekh*).

When feminine nouns ending *–ah* are in the construct case, the ending becomes *–at.* So the Torah-of Moses is *tor**at** mosheh.* The Queen (*malkah*)-of Sheba is *malk**at** sheva.* The fear (*yirah*)-of YHVH is *yir**at** yhvh.* The year (*shanah*)-of Jubilee is *shan**at** yovel.* It's a pattern.

In the same way, *diḇrat* (without the *–i* on the end) means '*diḇrah*-of [something]'. This is how it appears once in Daniel and three times more in Ecclesiastes, where it has the sense 'sake of' or 'matter of'.

> Dan. 2:30. For the sake that (*'al-diḇrat*) the king may know the interpretation and that you may understand the thoughts of your heart.

> Eccl. 3:18. I said in my heart about the matter of (*'al-diḇrat*) the sons of men.

> Eccl. 7:14. Consider that God has appointed this one as well as that, so that/for the sake that (*'al-diḇrat*) man may not find out anything that will be after him.

> Eccl. 8:2. Keep the king's command for the sake of (*'al-diḇrat*) your oath to God.

But *diḇrati*, on the other hand, has quite a different meaning. The final letter *–i* is the first-person singular possessive suffix. So *diḇrati* means '*diḇrah*-of-me' or 'my *diḇrah*'. It occurs only one other time in the Bible, in Job, where it means something like 'my matter' or 'my case' or 'my cause'.

> Job 5:8. But I would seek God and to God would I commit my cause (*diḇrati*).

So, taking *diḇrati* as it stands, the plain reading of Psalm 110:4 is:

> You are a *kohen* forever, according to my order/matter/cause (*'al-diḇrati*).

Since that is so, those who translate '*al diḇrati Malki-tsedeq* as 'in the order' of Melchizedek are ignoring the plain sense of the Hebrew. So we must ask how they justify it and why they do it.

No 'Order of' Melchizedek

They justify it by taking the *i*-vowel on the end of *diḇrat-i* not as a possessive suffix, but as either:

(1) a filler-vowel flourish—called a 'paragogic *yodh*'. We use such

filler vowels in English words like thingamy-jig or tickety-boo.

(2) or as the ancient proto-semitic form of the construct ending. We see this in the name *malki-tsedek* itself, which is indeed an ancient proto-semitic or Canaanite name. There *malki* means 'king-of'.

Either way, they can take *di<u>b</u>rati* to mean just *di<u>b</u>rat*: 'the *dibrat* [of] Melchizedek'.

Why do translators resort to this manoeuvre? Well, it dates from at least the Vulgate translation of Jerome, as we shall see shortly. And it continues to this day because reading the *i*-vowel as a possessive pronoun has really quite enormous implications, as we shall also see.

Yet the phrase *'al di<u>b</u>rati Malki-tsedeq* makes perfect sense as plain classical Hebrew. There is absolutely no reason at all to propose filler vowels or to read it as ancient Canaanite. The rest of the psalm is pure classical Hebrew, and it was written, apparently by David, in the time of the Israelite monarchy. So there is no reason to assume it is anything other than classical Hebrew. And so we should simply take the *–i* of *'al-di<u>b</u>rati* as it stands, as a first-person possessive suffix, just as in Job. In that case, the Holy One is calling someone a *kohen* for 'my sake' or 'my cause'.

But who? Well, if *di<u>b</u>rati* is no longer in the construct case, then it is no longer joined to *Malki-tsedeq.* There is no longer anything 'of Melchizedek'. The name Melchizedek has been cut free, and can now be read only as a vocative, that is, a direct address to a person present.

So the whole phrase, following the example of Job 5:8, must now become,

> You are a *kohen* for ever according to my cause, [O] Melchizedek.

But, since *di<u>b</u>rah* is a rare noun, and since nouns from the root *dbr* often carry the meaning of something said, we might be better to take it as 'promise' or 'saying' or 'decree'. That is how R. Zechariah took it in Nedarim 32b (cited above) when he took *'al-di<u>b</u>rati* to mean 'that which Abraham said' (*l'divoro shel malki-tsedeq*). That would give the following translation:

> You are a *kohen* for ever according to my decree, [O] Melchizedek.

Bam! The veil is lifted. The light comes on. The nameless figure in verse four, who was to be made *like* Melchizedek, is gone. With him is gone the intolerable conundrum of two eternal priests. There are not two priests, but one. And *my lord* of verse one is now not nameless either. His name is Melchizedek. It is Melchizedek alone who is promised both universal dominion (v. 1) and eternal priesthood (v. 4). And therefore the martial and triumphant tone of verses five to seven follows perfectly as Melchizedek goes forth from the throne to impose his rule upon his enemies.

This reading is strongly confirmed by the cantillation of the Hebrew Masoretic text. (These symbols show how the text was chanted or sung in ancient times.) The symbol at *'al-diḇrati* is pausal or 'disjunctive'. It is equivalent to separating *'al-diḇrati* from *Malki-tsedeq* with a comma, as I have given it above: 'for my sake, Melchizedek'. But if *diḇrati* were really a construct form, 'the order *of* Melchizedek', then there would be a conjunctive sign instead.[24]

By way of further confirmation, permit me to call to witness a passage from *Zohar Ḥadash* where the psalm is read in exactly this way, with *'al-diḇrati* being understood as a promise from the Holy One to Melchizedek, that is, to Shem ben Noah. (Remember, in rabbinic tradition Melchizedek is Shem ben Noah.)

> The Holy One, blessed be he, took Shem ben Noah and made him *kohen* of Elyon to serve him, and his *shekhinah* rested upon him. And he called his name Melchizedek, King of Shalem. And his brother, Japheth, learned Torah from him in his school, until Avraham came and taught Torah in the school of Shem. And the Holy One, blessed be he, turned his [Japheth's] attention to Avraham and he forgot all the others. Avraham came and prayed before the Holy One, blessed be he, that his *shekhinah* should always dwell in the House of Shem, and he consented, as it is said: *You are a kohen forever according to my promise, Melchizedek* (al-diḇrati malkhi-tsedeq). (Noah §128).

In fact, the same interpretation even underlies the passage from Bavli Nedarim 32b, cited above, where Melchizedek is ousted in favour of Avraham. For when R. Zechariah deflects the promise of *k'hunah* from Melchizedek-Shem to Abraham, the argument presumes that the promise was originally made to Melchizedek.

Therefore, with this reading, Melchizedek is no longer a faceless

[24] '*al-diḇrati* is marked with *revia mugrash*, a disjunctive sign-pair. In the next psalm, we see how the cantillation would feature on the construct: *yirat* and *yhvh* (the fear of YHVH) are indeed joined with the conjunctive sign *illuy* over *yirat* (Ps. 111:10); so too in Pss. 19:9 and 34:11, the same phrase is joined with conjunctives—*mahpakh* and *merkha* respectively.

Levantine who met Avram a thousand years before David's time. He is no mortal. He is an eternal *kohen.* David knew him in David's own time and called him *my lord.* Our hunch in chapter one was correct: Melchizedek is the Logos, the visible God. David overheard words from the invisible God to Melchizedek. He heard the vow and recorded it. It may be mind-boggling. It may go against all current understanding of the psalm. But there it is. It is the plain sense of *'al-dibrati.*

THE ORIGIN OF THE MISTRANSLATION

If then 'the order of Melchizedek', which we find in our English Bibles, is the mother of all mistranslations, how did it arise?

Let's begin with the Septuagint, the old Greek translation dating from the third century BC. It translates the Hebrew as follows.

> You are a priest for ever *katà tên taxin Melchisedek.*

The noun *taxin* is the accusative of *taxis.* (*Katà* is always followed by the accusative.) The word's range of meanings include a position in the line of battle, an arrangement or order, an orderly kingdom (*katà táxin basileia*). But the closest parallel—the exact words—is from Plato: *katà tên taxin tou nomou*, that is, 'according to the decree of the law'.[25] This agrees well with our translation of *dibrah* above.

But what about the name *Melchisedek*? Is it in the genitive case: *according to the decree* of *Melchizedek*? Or is it vocative: *according to the decree, O Melchizedek*?

Apollonius Dyskolos, the 'Prince of Grammarians', stated that a head noun and an attached genitive noun must either both have the article or both lack it. This rule is called Apollonius's Canon. We find it confirmed throughout Greek literature. We see it, for instance, in the quote from Plato above: 'according to *the* ordinance of *the* law'. Apollonius's rule means, simply, that if *Melchisedek* were in the genitive, it would likely have its own article to agree with the article before *taxin*: that is, *katà tên taxin* ***tou*** *Melchisedek.* But it does not have that. Therefore, all things considered, it appears to be not genitive, but vocative.

Nor should anyone object that the Hebraized Greek of the

[25] Liddell & Scott, *taxis*; the quotation is from Plato, Legg. 925 B.

Septuagint might not follow Apollonius's Canon. Yes, Septuagint Greek shows semitisms, but it is not barbaric. The Septuagint was written in Alexandria, one of the greatest cities of Hellenic civilization. The Library of Alexandria made the city a cultural crossroads of scholarship and learning. An educated Alexandrian was as unlikely to be ignorant of Greek grammar as a Harvard professor to be ignorant of English grammar. More, Apollonius himself was born and lived in Alexandria. His rules of grammar reflect the Greek of that very city.

Further, it is likely that, if Melchizedek were in the genitive, it would have a genitive suffix: *katà tên taxin tou Melchisedek**ou**.* But that too it does not have. Nor can any objection can be mounted on the basis of a missing omega for the 'O' of 'O Melchizedek'. The omega is the exception rather than the rule in the Greek vocative.

Of course, one might finally object that proper nouns follow their own rules. And that can be true. But let us at least agree that there is no evidence at all here that *Melchisedek* is genitive. It looks vocative. And, since that is so, the English translation should be:

> You are a priest for ever, according to the decree, [O] Melchizedek.

But what the Greek translation does omit from the Hebrew original is the 'my' of 'my decree'; that is, the possessive *yodh*-suffix of *dib̲rati.* Why the Greek translator omitted it, I cannot say. Its omission does not justify taking *Melchisedek* as genitive, but it did provide the seed for later confusion.

It is perhaps in the Syriac translation that the seed first sprouts. The Peshitta renders the verse:

> You are a priest for ever *ba-dmutha di-malkhizedek.*

The noun *dmutha* follows Greek *taxin* in the sense that it can mean an 'order' or 'manner'. But it more properly means a 'form' or 'pattern' or 'image'. Meanwhile, the possessive prefix *di–* has been added to Melchizedek. So the verse now reads:

> You are a priest for ever in the image *of* Melchizedek.

Why the Peshitta took this line, who can say? Apart from the rarity of the noun *dib̲rah*, and the enormity of what is implied, perhaps the translator, in reverence at the mystery revealed, wished to veil the striking vision of the psalm by blurring the sharp edges of the sense.

Or perhaps it was influenced by rabbinic views or by the view of Jerome.

Jerome, remember, was far from neutral in this matter. He lived in Bethlehem and studied Hebrew with rabbis there. But his own Hebrew was apparently not solid enough to enable him to make independent interpretations, as we can see from his comments in Epistle 73, where he is unaware of the true etymology of 'Jerusalem', claiming it arises from Hebrew and Greek.[26] And, in that same Epistle 73, he propounds the rabbinic neo-orthodoxy that Melchizedek was Shem ben Noah.[27]

Jerome produced two translations of the Psalms. His Gallican Psalter, that is, the Vulgate Psalter, was translated from the Septuagint, and his Hebrew Psalter, he said, from the Hebrew. But in both he rendered Ps. 110:4 in exactly the same way:

> *Tu es sacerdos in aeternum secundum ordinem Melchisedech.*
>
> You are a priest for ever according to the order of Melchizedek.

The deed was done. Thanks to Jerome, the Pharisaic riposte to Jesus's teaching in Matthew 22:41–46 found its way to the heart of the Christian Psalter. And it is propagated there to this very day by our translators.

But let us be absolutely clear that it is not at all the natural reading of the Hebrew text. The natural reading is,

> You are a *kohen* for ever according to my decree, [O] Melchizedek.

Now, we're not done with Melchizedek. Not by a long chalk. But we need to take a break here, if only to draw breath.

[26] See his comments in §7 of his Epistle 73 in my Appendix 2.
[27] Jerome, Epis. 73.

5

Before Avraham Was

PSALM 110 says, then, that the Holy One has made Melchizedek an eternal priest and ruler of the world. It says too that he was seen and known by David in his day. From this, we may perhaps deduce that Melchizedek is that one who appeared to Avram also as the Word and the Angel of YHVH. He is the Logos. Lest anybody think this is just my idea, permit me to cite a few others who suggest the same thing. Let's begin with those we have already visited.

We spoke in the last chapter about 11QMelch, and how it makes Melchizedek to be the Messiah and *elohim* of Israel. With my proposed reading of Psalm 110:4, the two texts now match up perfectly. For, in Psalm 110:5–7, it is now divine Melchizedek who conquers the world from Zion, while, in 11QMelch, it is divine Melchizedek who does just the same thing.

Philo Judaeus, as we saw in chapter one, was the first theologian of the Logos, the 'second God', the Angel of YHVH. When he talks of Avram's meeting with Melchizedek, he says plainly that Melchizedek, priest of God Most High, is the Logos, who, in time to come, shall refresh his devotees with heavenly wine, just as he refreshed Avram.

> Melchizedek shall bring forth wine instead of water, and shall give your souls to drink, and shall cheer them with unmixed wine, in order that they may be wholly possessed by divine intoxication, more sober than sobriety itself. For the Logos is a priest, having, as his inheritance the true God, and entertaining lofty and sublime and magnificent ideas about him, *For he is the priest of the most high God* (Gen. 14:18). (*Allegorical Interpretation* 3:82)

Melchizedek as Logos in the Epistle to the Hebrews

Melchizedek is a matter of great interest to the author of the Epistle to the Hebrews, who wrote some years before the destruction of the temple in AD 70 (Heb. 10:11). He says:

> [1]This Melchizedek was king of Salem and priest of God Most High. He met Abraham returning from the defeat of the kings and blessed him. [2]And Abraham gave him a tenth of everything. First, the name Melchizedek means 'king of righteousness', then also, 'king of Salem' means 'king of peace'. [3]Without father or mother, without genealogy, without beginning of days or end of life, but having been made like the Son of God, he remains a priest forever. (Heb. 7:1–3)

From this, we may conclude the author of Hebrews believed that:

(a) *Melchizedek was not begotten of human parents.* Anyone who has no father or mother or genealogy is not a human being. He is a deity. The very same words are used in Greek literature to describe the gods. Pollux says Athene is 'without mother' and Hephaistos is 'without father' (*Onomastikon* 3:26). Yet even they were not uncreated deities. Hephaistos was the virgin-born son of Hera—fatherless, not motherless. And Athene was born from the head of Zeus—motherless, not fatherless. As Neyrey writes,

> The three terms in Hebrews beginning with the alpha privative (ἀπαάτωρ, ἀμήτωρ, ἀγενεαλόγητος) [without father, without mother, without genealogy] are typical of the negative descriptions used in Hellenistic god-language.[1]

But this is not just a Greek usage. We find it in Israelite writers too.[2] Josephus, in *Contra Apion* 2.167, says,

> Our lawgiver [Moses]...represented him [God] as One, unbegotten and immutable to all eternity, in beauty surpassing all mortal thought.

And in the Apocalypse of Abraham 17:8–10 the angels sing to God:

> Eternal One, Mighty One, Holy El...
> Without father, without mother, ungenerated.

[1] See Neyrey, 'Without Beginning', 440–41.

[2] Bauckham, 'Divinity of Jesus', 30, cites to the same effect Philo, the Sybilline Oracles, and Pseudo-Orpheus in addition to Josephus, *Apion*, and the Apocalypse of Abraham; for Philo cf. Neyrey, 'Without Beginning', 442–44, 446.

In other words, both in Hellenistic and Hebraic parlance, someone without father, mother, or genealogy is an uncreated deity.

But some object. Epiphanius, bishop of Salamis in Cyprus in the fourth century, said: '*Without father, without mother* is not said because he had no father or mother, but because his father and mother are not explicitly named in the scripture.'[3] Then he proceeds to tell us the name of Melchizedek's father and mother which he got from an unnamed source.

> Still, some have said that his father was a man named Heracles, and his mother was Astarth, the same as Astoriane. He was one of the inhabitants of the country at that time, and he lived in the plain of Save.

He adds that the parentage of Daniel and Elijah is not given in the scriptures, yet they had parents. But nothing could be more irrelevant. The issue is not that Melchizedek's parents are not named. It is that the author to Hebrews tell us plainly that they did not exist.

More recently, F.F. Bruce took a similar line, claiming that the author to the Hebrews, if asked, would no doubt have agreed with him at once, for he did not really mean what he said.

> When Melchizedek is described as "having neither father nor mother, without a genealogy," and having "neither beginning of days nor end of life," it is not suggested that he was a biological anomaly, or an angel in human guise. Historically, Melchizedek appears to have belonged to a dynasty of priest-kings in which he had both predecessors and successors. If this point had been put to our author, he would have agreed at once, no doubt; but this consideration was foreign to his purpose.[4]

But Bruce, like Epiphanius, utterly misses the point. The words of the author of Hebrews are not just some rhetorical cadenza. They mean that Melchizedek is an unbegotten deity. And, to avoid any ambiguity, he follows with another statement saying virtually the same thing.

(b) *Melchizedek is without beginning of days or end of life* (v. 3). Anyone described in such terms is certainly not a mortal, but an immortal. And, once again, he follows it up by another statement saying the same thing.

(c) *Melchizedek remains a priest for ever* (v. 3). Only an immortal

[3] Epiphanius, *Panarion* 55.
[4] Bruce, *Hebrews*, 159–160.

remains anything for ever. Mortals die and leave their places and titles to others. But, lest there be any doubt, he repeats the same thing a few verses later: Melchizedek is greater than Abraham or Levi, because they die, but he *is declared to be living* (7:8). And again, Melchizedek became *a priest not on the basis of a legal requirement of ancestry, but on the basis of the power of an indestructible life* (7:16).

For the author of Hebrews, then, Melchizedek is no dead historical figure, but an ever-living one, alive in his own time, alive to all ages. But he says much more about Melchizedek.

(d) *Melchizedek is greater than Abraham* (7:4–7). Now, we must ask, who might our author regard as greater than Abraham? We can exclude all gentile rulers. They meant nothing to him. We can also exclude all Israelites, like Moses, Aaron, Joseph, or David. For, as he says in 7:9–10, they were present in the body of Abraham and so are less than he. Nor can Melchizedek be an ordinary angel, for, according to this author, angels are servants of God's elect (1:14), of Abraham and the fathers. Who then can Melchizedek be, if not the Messiah?

He then proceeds to make direct comparisons between Jesus and Melchizedek.

(e) *Melchizedek is Jesus.* Jesus is a priest for ever; so is Melchizedek (6:20; 7:3). Both became priests *on the basis not of ancestry but of an indestructible life*, that is, by virtue of their immortality (7:16). Now, just as in Psalm 110, there cannot be two eternal high priests. So, if Jesus and Melchizedek are both high priests for ever, then Jesus and Melchizedek are one and the same person.

We see this again when he speaks of Jesus becoming priest with a divine oath (7:21). He brings forth Psalm 110:4 as his proof-text, but drops the phrase *like Melchizedek* and applies the psalm direct to Jesus.

> He [Jesus] became priest with an oath when God said to him, 'The Lord has sworn and will not change his mind, You are a priest for ever.'

Yet Jesus is not named in Psalm 110. The one there who has an eternal priesthood is Melchizedek. And so the promise of eternal priesthood to Melchizedek in Psalm 110:4 is also a promise to Jesus. Therefore the author of Hebrews believes Melchizedek is Jesus.

(f) *Melchizedek-Jesus was designated priest in David's time.* In Heb. 5:5–10 we learn that Christ—that is the Messiah Jesus—was designated high priest at a specific point in the past. (Such is the implication of the aorist passive participle *prosagoreutheis* in v. 10.) Then we read that Aaron's priesthood is inferior to Melchizedek's. The question is posed, 'What further need would there have been for another priest to arise?' (7:11). This implies that the institution of the Messiah's priesthood took place after the institution of Aaron's priesthood in the time of Moses. This is further confirmed by the statements that the former regulation concerning Aaron's priesthood was set aside in favour of the new priesthood (7:18), and that the oath of the new priesthood came later than the regulations of the first (7:28). Thus Messiah was designated priest after Aaron. When did this take place? It could only have been in the events spoken of in Psalm 110:4, which is specifically cited in this regard (5:6, 10). Thus the Messiah was designated priest in the time of David, as recorded in Psalm 110:4.

(g) Some, like Bruce again, object to this conclusion. They say that *like the Son of God* (Heb. 7:3) means Melchizedek is not the Son of God, but only resembles the Son of God.

Let's start where they start. Even if the meaning is simply that Melchizedek resembles the Son of God, one must ask 'Who resembles the Son of God?' And the answer must surely be, 'No-one but the Son of God.' If Melchizedek resembles him, then the resemblance must be so unique that the Son of God could have it only to himself.

But there is more. They, and the translations on which they lean—like RSV, NIV—oversimplify the Greek when they render it 'like the son of God'. The phrase should really read, *having been made like the Son of God.* Two things are said here. First, Melchizedek was made in the likeness of the Son of God, not the other way round: the Son of God was the pattern for Melchizedek. Second, when Melchizedek appeared to Avram, he was made manifest in the likeness of the Son of God.

Now that elicits at least two other questions. 'First, who made him in the likeness?' And second, 'In what way was he made in the likeness of the Son of God?'

The implied answer to the first question is, I suspect, that the greater God, with the agreement of the Logos, made the latter to be Melchizedek in the likeness of the Son of God.

The second question is harder. It depends on what is meant by 'the son of God'. Scholars see in this phrase a range of meanings, from the historical king of Israel to the third Person of the Trinity. But the author to the Hebrews provides his own answer. He repeatedly describes the man Jesus as the 'Son of God' (1:2, 5, 8; 3:6; 4:14; 6:6). So Melchizedek, when he appeared to Avram, was made in the likeness of the Son of God as he was to be incarnated in Jesus.

This 'likeness' surely refers to Melchizedek's manifestation rather than to his being. After all, Melchizedek, being the Son of God, could not be made to resemble himself in essence any more than he already did. But his manifestation to Avram was made to foreshow his future, incarnate ministry as Jesus. How then did Melchizedek foreshadow the work of Jesus? First, he brought salvation to his friend—to Avram in the battle with the kings. Then he offered bread and wine to refresh the soul of his friend. And, carrying through to Genesis 22, he provided a sacrifice to redeem those under divine sentence of death (Gen. 22:12–14).

(f) *But if the author of Hebrews thought Jesus is Melchizedek, why does he keep translating Psalm 110:4 as* 'in the order of Melchizedek'? Why does he not render it as I said above, making Melchizedek a vocative?

Let's recall the linguistic foundations. Any natural reading of the Hebrew of Psalm 110:4, must read as follows:

> You are a priest forever according to my decree, Melchizedek.

But the Septuagint Greek translation is rather more ambiguous. It literally reads:

> You are a priest forever according to the decree Melchizedek.

Someone who knows the Hebrew would understand the Greek to mean the same thing. But someone who does not might just take it to mean,

> You are a priest forever according to the order [of] Melchizedek.

Now the text of the Epistle to the Hebrews was written in Hebrew. Eusebius says so.[5] And it makes sense too, doesn't it? The author was a Hebrew (1:1), writing to Hebrews. If you were a Bosnian writing to Bosnians, you would write in Bosnian, not English. So this letter was written in Hebrew and translated into Greek. This is not crucial to our argument. The crucial thing is that the ambiguity of the Greek distorts Psalm 110:4. But let's bear the Hebrew in mind.

[5] Eusebius, *History*, 6.14, says it was written in Hebrew by the apostle Paul.

So, when the author of Hebrews cited Ps. 110:4, the meaning, for a Hebrew speaker who knew the psalm—and Hebrew speakers did know the psalm—was quite clear. Either in a reconstructed Hebrew text or in our New Testament Greek text, it makes perfect sense.

> He [God] says [to Christ] in another place...*You are a priest forever according to my/the decree, [O] Melchizedek.* (5:6)

> For it is declared [of Christ]...*You are a priest forever according to my/the decree, [O] Melchizedek.* (7:17)

No problem there. Such citations of Psalm 110:4 are not at all at odds with the view of the author of Hebrews that Melchizedek is Jesus. The problem is only in our English translations. But two other texts are harder to explain.[6]

> Where the forerunner has entered for us, Jesus, according to the order of Melchizedek, become a high priest for ever. (6:20)

But, once again, this verse makes good enough sense if we allow that the author is giving a direct quote from the Hebrew scripture. His style of argument is rabbinic. And rabbinic writing abounds in such direct quotes—even if a little awkward in context—for the rabbis always quoted scripture directly without modification.[7] In that case, it should be taken as follows:

> Where the forerunner has entered for us, Jesus, *according to my/the decree, [O] Melchizedek*, become a high priest for ever. (6:20)

But Hebrews 7:11 is rather harder. Translated literally into English, it reads as follows:

> What further need, according to my/the decree Melchizedek [*katà tên taxin Melchisedek*], [for] another to arise priest, and not to be said according to the decree Aaron [*katà tên taxin Aaron*]?

In this verse, the author deliberately contrasts the priests 'according to the order of Aaron' and the new priest like Melchizedek. And, since that is so, one may imagine that, in both cases, the phrase *kata tên taxin*

[6] I see no difficulty in 7:15: *What we have said becomes even more clear if another priest like* (katà tên homoiotêta) *Melchizedek appears.* The Greek is not a direct citation from Ps. 110:4. And Jesus is a priest like Melchizedek.

[7] In fact, Rosenberg ('Allusion', 704–7) defines 'textual awkwardness' as one of fifteen criteria for intentional allusion or citation.

should be taken as 'according to the order of'. Thus our English texts render it something like:

> What further need was there for another priest to arise according to the order of Melchizedek, and not called according to the order of Aaron.

But, let's be clear, it still makes good sense if we allow that the author is quoting the psalm-verse in rabbinic fashion.

> What further need was there for another priest to arise, *according to my decree, [O] Melchizedek*, and not to be named according to the decree of Aaron?

Yes, the phrase *kata tên taxin* is repeated twice. But that does not mean the author meant the same thing each time. It is part of the contrastive force of his rhetoric.

So I suggest the author of Hebrews understood Psalm 110:4 as we interpreted it in the previous chapter. His argument makes good sense read that way. Nor does this depend on a Hebrew original to the epistle, likely though that is. But we must bear in mind the ambiguity of the Greek text of the psalm and the author's rabbinic style of citation.

But, one way or another, we must interpret his citations of Psalm 110:4 in the context of what he says about Melchizedek generally, namely, that he is an uncreated deity, greater than Abraham (as only the Messiah can be), equal to Jesus, and that, like Jesus, he is an eternal high priest (7:3, 8, 16). For, if he did not believe Jesus is Melchizedek, then he is enmired in the unbearable conundrum of two concurrent, uncreated, eternal high priests—Melchizedek and the son of God—forever offering two ways to the one God. That makes no more sense in Hebrews than it did in Psalm 110. It makes no sense in any book in any language. And I think the author to the Hebrews understood that.

English Bibles must rethink their translation, both of Psalm 110:4 and of the Epistle to the Hebrews. The Hebrew text of Psalm 110:4 is perfectly clear. The ambiguity first appears in the Septuagint. Then Jerome, in utter confusion on Psalm 110:4, led astray by the rabbinic notion that Melchizedek was Shem, botched the Latin translation, both in the psalm and in the epistle. Both were then translated into English by translators working in the dismal shadow of Jerome's error. That is why our English text of Psalm 110:4 and of the Epistle to the Hebrews preserves the Pharisaic distortion of Psalm 110:4 to this day.

WHO ELSE THINKS MELCHIZEDEK IS THE LOGOS?

The *Apocalypse of Abraham* is a text dating from the late first or early second century AD.[8] It features a heavenly messenger who appears to Abraham, called Yaoel. His name is a compound of *Yah* or *Yaho* or *Yahu*—short for YHVH—and *el* or 'god'. It means 'Yah-God'. Indeed, this name seems to be a substitute for the Tetragrammaton, for we read that he possesses the power of the Ineffable Name. More, he is the ruler of all angelic beings, the leader of song of the heavenly hosts. He is sent to supervise the sacrifice of Abraham (§10), and calls himself 'the priest of my glorious name' (§25). Attired in turban and glorious raiment, like a *kohen*, he enacts with Abraham the events of the sacrifice of Genesis 15 (§11–13). Since, in Genesis, this event takes place straight after Abraham's meeting with Melchizedek, it seems like this heavenly *kohen* Yaoel is none other than the *kohen* Melchizedek.

In chapter one, we met the Four Craftsmen *baraitha*, with its line-up of messianic heros. The oldest versions of the *baraitha*, from before AD 200, present Melchizedek as a *kohen* who will appear, in the last days, with Messiah ben David, War Messiah ben Joseph, and Elijah.

> *The flowers appear on the earth* (Song 2:12). R. Isaac said, 'It is written: *And the Lord showed me four craftsmen* (Zech 2:3). These are they: Elijah, the King Messiah, Melchizedek and the War Messiah.' (Pesikta Rabbati §15:14-15).

Therefore, according to this text, Melchizedek will appear in the days of the Messiah. That is a view the author of Hebrews would have agreed with. But later versions of this *baraitha* remove the name of Melchizedek and replace it with the *kohen tsedeq*, or Righteous Priest. This was perhaps a later emendment, designed to undercut any identification of Jesus with Melchizedek.[9]

Early Christian writers reached similar conclusions. Origen, as said, thought Melchizedek was an angel. But Ambrose of Milan went further still. He initially believed, like the other Fathers, that Melchizedek was only a type of the Messiah.[10] But over a decade, his view changed. First,

[8] It was originally written in Hebrew or Aramaic, but is now preserved only in Slavonic (Box, *Apocalypse of Abraham,* x).

[9] For more on the variants of the 'Four Craftsmen' *baraitha* and why Melchizedek disappears after tannaitic times, see Mitchell, *Messiah ben Joseph*, chapter 9.

[10] Cf. On Faith 3:11 (before AD 380); On Abraham 1:3 (AD 380).

he said that Melchizedek was the one who initiated the sacrament of communion. Perhaps he was reflecting on Philo's comment about Melchizedek cheering the souls of the faithful with pure wine.

> Can a man be king of righteousness when he himself can hardly be righteous? Or a king of peace when he can hardly be peaceable? The sacrament you received is the gift not of man but of God, brought forth by him who blessed Abraham. (On the Mysteries 8:46; AD 387)

Then, a few years later, he said:

> God is Melchisedech, that is, he is king of peace and justice, having neither the beginning of days nor end of life.' (The Six Days of Creation 1:3; AD 389)

Ambrose had gone over to the Melchizedekites, despite their condemnation by his brother bishops. Yet, for all this, the idea that Melchizedek is the Logos is widely rejected to this day by Christian commentators of all stripes. But there are brave exceptions. The Anglican theologian Anthony Hanson wrote at length on the subject; and Michael Green, another Anglican, spoke of Melchizedek as a 'Christophany'.[11] I, of course, agree with them, and rejoice to be found in such distinguished company.

PSALM 110:3. WHAT IS GOING ON?

Now that we have finally worked out who is who in Psalm 110, we can turn back to verse three of that psalm. It's another knotty verse, but our fresh grasp of the characters speaking within the psalm allows us to proceed with more confidence. Here are two possible readings, from the Hebrew Masoretic text and from the Greek Septuagint.

Hebrew	Your people [are] willingness on the day of your strength. In holy splendours (*or* mountains), from the womb of dawn, to you [comes] dew of your youth.
Greek	With you is dominion on the day of your strength. Amidst the shining lights of your holy ones, I have begotten you from the womb, before the morning star.

There are three sets of alternate readings: *in splendours* versus *on*

[11] Hanson, *Jesus Christ* 67–70; Green, *Empty Cross of Jesus*, 48.

mountains; *your people are willingness* versus *with you is dominion*; and *your youth* versus *I have begotten you.* Then there is also *the womb [of dawn] before the morning star.* None of these readings changes what we saw in verses 1 and 4, but some may confirm it.

(a) We'll start with the little knots. Should it be *holy splendours* or *holy mountains*? The Hebrew text says *b'hadrei* (in/on splendours). But an old variant reading changes one letter to say *b'har'rei* (in/on mountains). It's an easy change. Hebrew R (ר) and D (ד) look very alike. Taken with the next word—*qodesh* or 'holy'—the main text says *in holy splendours* and the variant reading says *on holy mountains.*

Which is correct? Well, the main Hebrew reading is confirmed by the Septuagint and Peshitta. They both say 'splendours'.[12] So that's the best reading overall. But both readings make sense. 'Holy splendours' refers to the general setting or ambience, and perhaps to holy garments. 'Holy mountains' means Jerusalem's Temple Mount and Mount Zion, which also have a holy ambience and holy garments. Perhaps 'holy splendours' might mean a heavenly place and 'holy mountains' might mean an earthly place. But it's a slim distinction. After all, the hill-tops of Jerusalem were seen as the throne of heaven itself.

(b) Next, is it *your people are willingness*, as in the Hebrew text, or *with you is dominion*, as in the Greek? The variant arises from the Hebrew word *'mk̲* (עמך). When written without vowels, as it was in ancient times, it can be read either as '*immkha*, 'with you', or '*ammkha*, 'your people'. Then the following word, *n'dab̲ot* comes from the Hebrew root *ndb*, meaning 'impel', from which is derived 'willing' or 'excellent' or 'noble'. So this word can certainly be read in the sense of *willingness*, or more literally, *willingnesses*, since it is a feminine plural. But it can also be read as *nobilities* or *excellencies* in the sense of royal power. The meanings are different. But both make sense. The Messiah's army will be willing. And dominion will be his.

(c) Next again, is it *your youth* or *I have begotten you*? The Hebrew text, written without vowels, has the consonants *yldtyk.* This can be read two ways. The Hebrew text with vowel marks—the Masoretic text—reads it as *yalduteykha*, 'your youth'. But the Septuagint Greek translator, reading the Hebrew as *y'lid'tikha*, translates it as 'I have begotten thee' (*exegénnêsá se*). There is also an extra word in the

[12] LXX: en tais lamprotêsi tôn hagiôn sou. Peshitta: b'hadrei qodsha.

Hebrew text, 'dew', which is missing from the Greek, while the Greek text speaks of the morning star rather than the dawn.

To choose between them is not at all easy. The Hebrew version can be justified on the basis of Isaiah 26:19: *For dew of the light is your dew; the earth to the shades of the dead will give birth.* Isaiah's text, which speaks of the resurrection of the dead, has the same concurrence of 'youth' and 'dew' and birth as implied in the 'womb of dawn'. So the sense of the psalm might be that the 'dew of youth', which comes to the Messiah, is his army of risen dead, glorious in endless youth, reborn from the womb-red dawn of the glorious new age.

On the other hand, the Septuagint reading seems likely from the fact that the word *y'lid'tikha* appears at the beginning of the Book of Psalms. There YHVH first promises universal dominion to the Messiah.

> [7]I will proclaim the decree of YHVH. He said to me,
> 'You are my son. Today I have begotten you (*y'lid'tikha*).'
> [8]Ask of me and I will give the nations for your inheritance;
> and for your possession, the ends of the earth.' (Ps. 2)

Since Psalm 110 is the fulfilment of the promise of Psalm 2, it seems very natural that the declaration of the Messiah's divine conception would be repeated in this later climactic psalm as well. Read this way, the Septuagint text speaks of the Messiah's heavenly nature rather than of his army. We may well scratch our heads over what is implied in the phrase *from the womb before the morning star*, the more so since most ancient peoples associated that star with goddesses of fertility. But the Greek text is certainly speaking about the pre-existence of the Messiah. And that is how the Greek-speaking Church Fathers understood it.[13]

Now the Masoretic text is usually preferable to the Greek. But the early Christians, especially Justin Martyr, claimed that the Sanhedrin—in the years between the death of Jesus and the Roman destruction of AD 70—changed parts of the Bible text to refute apostolic teaching. Sometimes these claims seem far-fetched. But sometimes it looks like they might have been right. And this verse might just be one of these cases. So, once again, both texts make sense. But in this case the Septuagint perhaps represents the older reading.

We have discussed this psalm at length for it is important. Now,

[13] Justin, *Dial.* 63:3; 76:7; Clement of Alexandria, *Protrepticus.* I; IX; Hippolytus, *Haer.* X:29; Tertullian, *Adv. Marc.* V:9; *Adv. Prax.* VI; cf. XI; Augustine on Ps. 110.

taking into account the Septuagint reading of verse three, here is a more accurate translation of the psalm than the ones we commonly meet.

[1] Of David, a psalm.
YHVH vows to my lord: Sit at my right hand;
till I set your enemies [to be] a stool for your feet.
[2] YHVH will send forth your mighty sceptre from Zion.
Rule amidst your enemies.
[3] With you is dominion on the day of your strength.
Amidst the shining lights of the holy ones I have begotten you
from the womb before the morning star.
[4] YHVH has sworn and will not revoke:
You are a *kohen* for ever, according to my decree, O Melchizedek.
[5] The Lord at your right hand
crushes kings in the day of his wrath.
[6] He executes judgement among the nations—fullness of corpses!
he crushes the head [*or* ruler] of the wide earth.
[7] From a brook by the road will he drink;
so will he lift up [his] head.

Back to Jesus

So, with the plain reading of the Hebrew of Psalm 110:4, we must see three people in the psalm: David, YHVH, and David's lord, who is Melchizedek. And Jesus, following ancient interpretation, also sees three people in the psalm: David, YHVH, and David's lord, the Messiah.

Yet the Messiah is not mentioned in the psalm. And so we must ask a question with a rather obvious answer: 'In which of the three figures of the psalm does Jesus see the Messiah?' The Messiah cannot be YHVH. Nor can he be David, nor David's son, according to Jesus. Only one option remains: Melchizedek is the Messiah. There is no other possible anwer. After all, Jesus, and everyone else who read this text the same way, was savvy enough to realize there could not be two eternal priests in Psalm 110. They took *'al-dibrati* according to its plain sense, which makes Melchizedek inevitably a vocative, and made the link between Melchizedek and the Messiah. In fact, according to any other interpretation, it is difficult to find the Messiah in the psalm at all. But with this reading, the Messiah is crystal clear.

And so it follows that Jesus thought David knew this Melchizedek-Messiah in his own day and called him 'my lord'. And, since Jesus had no doubts about who the Messiah was, we must conclude that Jesus is saying that he himself is Melchizedek, and that David knew him and called him lord. This is surely what is implied in the debate in Matthew 22. I see no other possible conclusion. And that explains why the Jerusalem élite were so unhappy with this claim, and why they later sought to belittle Melchizedek, to cover up the whole idea of the second God, and to assign the promise of Ps. 110:4 to Abraham or David or Solomon or anyone except the Messiah.[14]

JESUS SAID HE WAS MELCHIZEDEK

But if, in Matthew 22, Jesus is claiming to be Melchizedek, why did he not make it a little more plain? Well, perhaps he did. In John's gospel, there's a debate between Jesus and *the Judeans* or *Jews*, which is how styles the Jerusalem elite, especially the Pharisees. The underlying theme of the debate is paternity: whose son are the disputants?

Jesus speaks of his Father. The Judeans ask, 'Where is your father?' Jesus promises them freedom if they believe in him. They, forgetful of history, reply that, as Abraham's children, they have never been slaves, so he cannot set them free (8:33). Jesus replies, yes, Abraham is their father, but they plan to kill him and, in fact, he and they have different fathers (8:37–38). They insist they are Abraham's children (8:39). But Jesus says they seek to kill him, a man who has spoken to them the truth from God; Abraham did no such thing (8:40). The implication is that Abraham knew such a man, one who spoke to him the truth from God. Jesus can only be referring to Melchizedek, for Abraham had no other teacher or priest. He then says that this shows they have, in fact, another father (8:41). They reply in kind, casting against Jesus the rumours of his illegitimate birth. The *we* is emphatic in Greek, as if to say, 'We, unlike you, were not begotten of fornication.' (They forgot about Judah and Tamar.) But they get the gist of what Jesus is saying:

[14] Thus is explained the change to Genesis 14:22 spoken of in chapter one. It initially said, *I have raised my hand to El Elyon*, but was changed to *I have raised my hand to YHVH El Elyon*. Someone wanted to make YHVH and El Elyon into one God, presumably because others were claiming that Melchizedek-Messiah was YHVH in human form. It explains too why Melchizedek is recast as Shem and ritually defrocked in B. Nedarim 32b. And it explains why Melchizedek has been removed from the later versions of the Four Craftsmen *baraitha*.

there is a spiritual paternity. So they claim God is their father (8:41). Jesus says their rejection of him shows that their father is the devil, and they do their father's works (8:44). They reply that he is a demon-possessed Samaritan (8:48). Jesus doesn't object to the Samaritan label, but replies that he does not have a demon. Rather, he honours his father and has the power to bestow eternal life (8:49–51). They find this claim preposterous. Is he greater than Abraham? Abraham and the prophets died. Who does he think he is? Jesus replies:

> Your father Abraham rejoiced to see my day. He saw and was glad.

Now, in this verse, some translations resort to paraphrase, as if to say that Jesus meant that Abraham foresaw the time of the Messiah, but did not actually see him. But the text is just as I have given it.[15] Jesus is claiming that Abraham, in his lifetime, saw him. His hearers grasp his meaning perfectly well: 'You are not yet fifty and you have seen Abraham!' (8:57) He was claiming to have seen Abraham in the flesh.

So when did Jesus see Abraham? Was it when YHVH appeared to Abraham in human form at Mamre in Genesis 18? Or when the divine angel spoke to him in Genesis 22? Perhaps. But these seem like brief encounters, whereas *Abraham rejoiced to see my day* implies a period of residence. Is Jesus not rather speaking of the time when Melchizedek ruled in Shalem and brought Abraham bread and wine at the defeat of the kings of the east?

Whether his opponents grasped this claim is unclear. I imagine they were struck by his words *your father Abraham*, implying that he, Jesus, was not a son of Abraham. And so he is neither Jew nor Samaritan. That surely pleased his hearers, who were insisting on his illegitimacy.

But his next comment pleased them less: *Before Abraham was, I am.* At this they prepared to stone him, but he, 'concealing' himself, passed through the midst of them and left. (8:58–59)

Explosive words

Now, it's clear enough that Jesus's words are making a big claim about himself. But to grasp why they merited stoning, we must remember that

[15] Ἀβραὰμ ὁ πατὴρ ὑμῶν ἠγαλλιάσατο ἵνα ἴδῃ τὴν ἡμέραν τὴν ἐμήν, καὶ εἶδεν καὶ ἐχάρη.

I am was how God revealed himself to Moses in Exodus 3:13–14.

> And Moses said to God, 'Behold, when I come to the children of Israel, and say to them, "The God of your fathers has sent me to you," and they say to me, "What is his name?", then what shall I say to them?'
> God said to Moses, 'I Am Who I Am'. And he said, 'So shall you say to the children of Israel, "I Am has sent me to you."'

Jesus's allusion to this text is pretty clear. It's clear even in English (and in the Greek version of his words in the New Testament).

But let's remember that this was spoken in Hebrew, for that was the language of Jerusalem and its officials. (Remember, Jesus spoke Aramaic with his disciples and in Galilee, but Hebrew in Jerusalem.[16]) And Jesus's Hebrew words were much more weighty than they were in Greek or English.

In the Greek of the gospels, the verb 'to be' does not have any more impact than it has in English. Just as in English we say 'It is me' or 'It is I' (if we are keen on grammar), so Greek says 'I am' (*ego eimi*) to mean 'It's me'. It's the phrase used by the man born blind in John 9:9.

Now Jesus says *ego eimi* over and over again in John's gospel.[17] But with Jesus the phrase is loaded. First, even in Greek, we sense allusions to the divine name of Exodus 3. But the Hebrew words that lie behind Greek *ego eimi* are much less ambiguous.

In Hebrew, the verb 'to be' is not used when speaking of one's own existence in this way. To say, for instance, 'I am he', one says only, 'I he' (*ani hu*). 'I am she' would be 'I she' (*ani hi*). Or again, 'Here I am,' is 'Behold me' (*hinneni*). No verb is required or used.

But once add the verb 'to be' (*hayah*) and the meaning changes totally. If one were to say, with the Hebrew verb, *ani eh'yeh*, it doesn't mean 'I am he' but 'I am being.' Now in Hebrew there are basically only two tenses—perfect and imperfect. Using the perfect tense would simply mean 'I was.' But using the imperfect suggests continual ongoing being: 'I am being what I shall be being.'

And here Jesus is using the imperfect form of the verb. That is pretty clear both from the Greek and the Aramaic Peshitta text.[18] So we can

[16] Joosten, 'Hebrew or Aramaic'.

[17] It appears seventeen times in all. Seven with a predicate: 6:35; 8:12; 10:7; 10:11; 11:25; 14:6; 15:1; and ten without (including the man born blind): 4:26; 6:20; 8:24; 8:28; 8:58; 9:9; 13:19; 18:5; 18:6; 18:8.

[18] The pronoun and verb in Gk points to the same in the Heb. dialogue. The Aramaic

be fairly sure that Jesus's words in Hebrew meant: 'Before Avraham was, I am being what I shall be being.' That was a claim to eternal self-existence by appropriating the divine name of Exodus 3:14. As God said to Moses:

> 'I am being who I am being' [*eh'**yeh** **asher** eh'**yeh***]. And he said, 'So shall you say to the sons of Israel, "I Am [*eh'**yeh***] has sent me to you."'

For any man to apply such words to himself was taboo. It did indeed make him equal with God (John 10:33). It's not surprising they wanted to stone him.

THE TAKE-HOME MESSAGE

His enemies finally got the take-home message. He was claiming to be the visible God who was seen in the flesh by Abraham.

It might not have been a matter for stoning if they had believed he was the Messiah. There would surely have been some there who, like Philo or the author of 11QMelch, believed that Melchizedek was the divine Messiah. In theory, the idea was acceptable enough.

But the claimant was intolerable. The one they called *mamzer*, demon-possessed Samaritan, who presumed to purge their temple and call them vipers, was claiming to be the divine Messiah, to be Melchizedek who blessed Avraham at the defeat of the kings, to be the Angel-Messenger of YHVH who led Israel out of Egypt and through the desert in the pillar of cloud and fire, who travelled with them as the thirst-quenching Rock, who appeared to Joshua at Gilgal, to Moses, Samuel, and David in the sanctuary, to be the Logos, the emanation of the divine glory, sent from the right hand of the Ancient of Days to the earth, to illumine, atone, judge, conquer, and inherit.

He was claiming to be Israel's guide since the beginning, he who was born in shame at Bethlehem.

pronoun (*ena*) and predicator of existence (*ithai*) gives 'I exist', which is dynamically equivalent to Hebrew *ani eh'yeh*. Finally, Jesus must have used the Heb. imperfect, for the Heb. perfect form (I was) would make no sense in context.

6

A Good Genealogy

PRIDE of birth. That's what impressed the Israelites. Pride of birth and purity of lineage. Of course, pedigree was important everywhere in ancient times. But in Israel, who traced descent from God's chosen, it was everything. Forget the trappings of status—urban villas, Egyptian stallions, Roman chariots, silks, linen robes in Tyrian purple, education by eminent rabbis, bejewelled goblets. These were all fine. But what really counted, what they really dug, what they flaunted if they had and envied if they hadn't, what pushed all their buttons, was just this—a good genealogy.

A Good Genealogy

When it came to honour, genealogy was the first weapon in the armoury. Every Israelite family of any worth kept a record of its own genealogy. But there was no chance of vaunting oneself on an imagined family tree. The master copies of the genealogical records of Israel were kept in the temple in Jerusalem, under the watchful eye of God. There the proud father and mother took their newborn son to be presented to God. The father had to acknowledge the boy as his own. That way there could be no faking. He knew best if he had any suspicions about the child's conception. If he believed the child was his own, he made the testimony: *Zeh b'ni*—This is my son.[1] With these

[1] 'A man who says, "This is my son" is believed' (Mishnah Baba Bathra 8.6).

words, the matter was established beyond appeal. The child was recorded in the genealogies of Israel, as Z the son of Y, son of X, of the clan of W, the whole way back to Abraham, the father of the nation. The records were available for scrutiny by all Israel.

Happy the man who scored high in lineage. Eminence and status were his from birth. As he grew, he carried self-worth like a seal on his brow. None could remove it. It was recorded before the face of God.

Any Israelite who could claim descent from the patriarchs of Israel was respected. He could boast, like Paul, 'I am of the people of Israel... a Hebrew of Hebrews.' (Phil. 3:5) But the cream of all—the highest caste—were those descended from the royal line of David or the priestly line of Zadok. They could say, like Josephus,

> The family from which I am descended is no ignoble one, but is descended all along from the priests. And as nobility among different races is of different origin, so with us to be of the sacerdotal dignity is an indication of the splendour of a family. Now I am not only sprung from a sacerdotal family in general, but from the first of the twenty-four courses. And as among us there is not only a considerable difference between one family of each house and another, I am of the chief family of that first course also. Nay, further, by my mother I am of the royal blood. For the children of Hasmoneus, from whom her family was derived, had both the office of the high priesthood and the dignity of a king for a long time together. I will accordingly set down my progenitors in order. (Life of Josephus 1)

And this he accordingly does, in detail, from his Hasmonean great-great-grandfather down to his sons. Then he concludes,

> Thus have I set down the genealogy of my family as I have found it described in the public records, and so I bid adieu to my calumniators.

Normally, the high-born were wealthy. But even if fortunes fell, their status remained untarnished as diamond. Good birth covered a multitude of failings. Neither poverty nor peccadillo could sully the lustre of pedigree.

There was no substitute for lineage. Nothing could compensate for the lack of it. Horror if one had a male progenitor who was not a pure-blooded Israelite. Such was the case of King Herod the Great. He was one of the richest men in the world. As a friend of Mark Antony, the Roman Senate appointed him king of Israel. But the crown lay uneasy on him for, as everyone knew, he was a mongrel. His father, Antipater, was an Edomite convert to Judaism. His mother was a Nabatean Arab. Though many toadied for his favours, the Israelites despised him.

To advance his dynasty, he procured a wife, Mariamme, from the royal and priestly Hasmonean dynasty, of which Josephus spoke. Mariamme, royal and beautiful, was the cream. But she despised Herod like a dog. He crawled on the floor for her attention. But she preferred death to his embrace. Soon, by Herod's jealous passion, she obtained her happy preference, leaving him howling in remorse. Bad luck to the mongrel. For all his wealth, power, or royal office, he was forever banished from the honour that came with lineage.

To produce such mixed offspring was every Israelite family's nightmare. And so marriage was no casual matter. The choosing of a wife was not done for love or attraction, *à la style Hollywood.* It was serious business. The rabbis taught their disciples, 'Young man, lift up your eyes and see whom you will choose. Pay no regard to beauty but to lineage.' (Proem 33 to Lam. R.) Marriage had one purpose—to provide honourable pedigrees for honourable offspring. As Ben Sira taught:

> Seek a fertile field within the plain, and sow it with your own seed, trusting in your fine stock. Then your offspring will prosper, and, having confidence in their good descent, will grow great. (Ben Sira 26:20–21)

The decisions about who should marry whom were initiated by the boy's father as a sacred obligation.

> Our Rabbis taught: The father is obliged concerning his son: to circumcise him, redeem him, teach him Torah, get him a wife, and teach him a trade. Some say, to teach him to swim too. (B. Kid. 29a)

He would approach the family of the prospective bride, chosen for her ancestry. Josephus tells of marriage among the *kohanim*:

> Our forefathers...made provision that the stock of the priests should continue unmixed and pure. For he who is partaker of the priesthood must propagate of a wife of the same clan, without any regard to money, or any other dignities. But he must investigate and take his wife's genealogy from the ancient tables, and procure many witnesses to it. This is our practice, not only in Judea. But wherever any body of men of our nation live, even there an exact catalogue of our priests' marriages is kept: I mean at Egypt and at Babylon or in any other place

> of the rest of the habitable earth, wherever our priests are scattered. For they send to Jerusalem the ancient names of their parents in writing, as well as those of their remoter ancestors: and signify who are the witnesses also. (*Contra Apion* 1:7)

He then tells of the rigour with which the young woman's innocence was investigated.

> But if any war falls out, such as have fallen out a great many of them already, when Antiochus Epiphanes made an invasion upon our country, as also when Pompey the great, and Quintilius Varus did so also, and principally in the wars that have happened in our own times, those priests that survive compose new tables of genealogy, out of the old records, and examine the circumstances of the women that remain. For they do not allow [marriage with] those that have been captives, suspecting they may have had intercourse with foreigners. (1:7)

He concludes:

> But the strongest argument of our exact management in this matter is this: that we have the names of our high priests from father to son set down in our records, for a period of two thousand years. And if any have been transgressors of these rules, they are prohibited to present themselves at the altar, or be partakers of our purifications. (1:7)

Woe to the youth who, in passion or haste, married below his rank. For him there was the *k'tsatsah* or 'cutting-off' ceremony. The Talmud describes how it was enacted:

> How is the *k'tsatsah* performed? If one of the brothers has married an unsuitable woman, members of the family come and bring a barrel filled with fruit and break it in the town square, saying, 'O brethren of the House of Israel, give ear! Our brother so-and-so has married an unsuitable woman and we are afraid lest his seed mingle with our seed. Come and take yourselves a sign for the generations [to come], that his seed mingle not with our seed.' (B. Ket. 28b)

The spilling of the fruit, to be picked or kicked by all and sundry, signified the squandering of the unhappy young man's seed. Any young Israelite was admonished on all hands against such a marriage.

In such a society, the severest attack on a man was to reproach his pedigree. That was what the Pharisees did to John Hyrcanus, in anger at his taking the dual office of *kohen gadol* and king. To force his resignation from the high priesthood, they flung in his face the charge,

'Your mother was a captive,' implying his illegitimate conception and ineligibility for priestly office. Hyrcanus turned on them, abolished their decrees, and punished those who kept them (Josephus, *Ant.* 13:10:6). A generation later, for the same reason, they threw the same accusation at Hyrcanus's son, Alexander Jannai. He drowned their objections in blood (B. Kid. 66a.).

So everything was done to secure an honourable match. When the families of both young people had reached an agreement, the consent of the young maiden was sought. She could, of course, decline. But, in a world where honour scored much higher than sentiment, few did. The couple were then betrothed for a period of one year, to give the husband time to win his wife's affection. The girl was kept under a watchful eye, admonished against all contact with men. Then she was married, often in her fourteenth year.

Betrothal was no casual matter, it was a binding marriage contract. Gifts were exchanged, documents signed. So any girl found to be with child before going to live with her husband was guilty of adultery. Indeed, the rabbis held it to be a greater sin to seduce a betrothed virgin than a married woman. And, since girls were normally betrothed just after puberty, there was no such thing as an illegitimate child in the modern sense, that is, a child born to an unmarried man and woman. There was only a legitimate child or a *mamzer*, that is, a child of adultery or incest.

Woe to the *mamzer*. Woe to his mother. For such there was no presentation in the temple by a proud father, no coveted entry in the genealogies of Israel. Woman and child were outcast. If they survived. Frequently they did not. For, according to the law, the mother could be stoned for her offence, and the child would perish within her.

But if her husband were good enough to commute the death-sentence and divorce her quietly, what then? Disgraced beyond any hope of honourable marriage, rejected by her home on whom she had brought lasting stigma, she might feed herself and her child by begging or drudgery or prostitution. Her child, without genealogy or status, bore the indelible stain of illegitimacy throughout his cursed days, cast out of well-born society to live among the *mamzeri* caste, side-by-side with prostitutes, thieves, and beggars. By divine command, he could not enter the temple of God, neither he nor his offspring to ten generations (Deut. 23:2). They were under an enduring curse.

A Bunch of Peasants

Joseph had no such fears. He had obtained a bride of high pedigree from an honourable family, a bride well-suited to his own royal lineage. Her name was Mariam, a later form of Miriam, the name of Moses's sister. Joseph was glad of the match. Mariam's family were glad too. Her father Joakim smiled to himself, 'She's marrying a prince of the house of David. Who knows? Maybe my little Mariam will bear the Messiah.' But none of it worked out as simply as Joakim envisaged, and Mariam's child was born amidst an uproar of scandal. But we should be clear about this: both Joseph and Mariam came from the highest ranks of Israelite society.

Yet academics stand in line to call Jesus and his family peasants. Crossan says Jesus is 'a mediterranean Jewish peasant' and 'a Jewish peasant with an attitude' and 'a peasant Jewish Cynic'.[2] Ehrman calls him 'a lower-class Jewish preacher…a crucified peasant'.[3] Aslan says he is, 'a marginal Jewish peasant from the backwoods of Galilee'.[4] Chilton thinks he is 'a peasant prophet, a threadbare king', and adds 'Jewish peasants…For the most part, like Jesus, they were illiterate.'[5] Meier says Jesus is, 'a Galilean peasant layman', but magnanimously allows, 'he is not an ordinary peasant.'[6]

But Jesus's family were not peasants. The sources—Christian, Jewish, and pagan—all agree that Joseph and Jesus were *tektōnes*, that is, builders. Of course, it is often said that Jesus was a carpenter. The confusion comes from old English, when a carpenter—as opposed to a mason—was one who built in wood. The same construction methods prevailed in first century Galilee. So Joseph and Jesus were carpenter-builders. They put up houses and roofs as well as making doors and ploughs and yokes.

Now a carpenter-builder is not a peasant. A peasant is a landless agricultural worker who labours in another man's field. A carpenter-builder is a skilled artisan who has mastered his own trade, who owns his own business, workshop, home, and tools. He is skilled in many areas. He takes pride in his work and his customers trust him. Tell a

[2] Crossan, *Historical Jesus*, subtitle; *Birth of Christianity*, xxx; Jesus, 198.
[3] Ehrman, *How Jesus Became God*, 1.
[4] Aslan, *Zealot*, 235.
[5] Chilton, *Rabbi Jesus,* 227, xx.
[6] Meier, *Marginal Jew*, 347, 278.

modern builder—expert in brick-laying, plastering, wiring, plumbing, roofing, and more—that he is a peasant and you will find that he will not agree with you.

But Joseph and Jesus were not only builders, they were landowners. The Emperor Domitian (*r.* 81–96), near the end of his reign, summoned before him the grandsons of Jude, the brother of Jesus, with their uncle, Simeon, the son of Joseph's brother Clopas. He wanted to know if their royal status was a threat to Roman rule. Eusebius relates the story, as recorded by Hegesippus, a second-century Hebrew Christian.

> But when this same Domitian had commanded that the descendants of David should be slain, an ancient tradition says that some of the heretics brought accusation against the descendants of Jude (said to have been a brother of the Saviour according to the flesh), on the ground that they were of the lineage of David and were related to Christ himself. Hegesippus relates these facts in the following words.
>
> Of the family of the Lord there were still living the grandchildren of Jude, who is said to have been the Lord's brother according to the flesh.
>
> Information was given that they belonged to the family of David, and they were brought to the Emperor Domitian by the Evocatus. For Domitian feared the coming of the Messiah as Herod had also feared it. And he asked them if they were descendants of David, and they confessed that they were. Then he asked them how much property they had, or how much money they owned. And both of them answered that they had only nine thousand denarii, half of which belonged to each of them. And this property did not consist of silver, but of a piece of land which contained only thirty-nine *plethra*, and from which they raised their taxes and supported themselves by their own labor. Then they showed their hands, exhibiting the hardness of their bodies and the callouses produced upon their hands by continuous toil as evidence of their own labor.
>
> And when they were asked concerning the Messiah and his kingdom, of what sort it was and where and when it was to appear, they answered that it was not a temporal nor an earthly kingdom, but a heavenly and angelic one, which would appear at the end of the world, when he should come in glory to judge the quick and the dead, and to give unto every one according to his works.
>
> Upon hearing this, Domitian did not pass judgement against them, but, despising them as of no account, he let them go, and by a decree put a stop to the persecution of the Church.
>
> But when they were released they ruled the churches because they were witnesses and were also relatives of the Lord. And peace being

> established, they lived until the time of Trajan. These things are related by Hegesippus. (Eusebius, *History*, 4.19–20; cf. 22, 32)

Jude's grandsons owned a farm of thirty-nine *plethora.* Estimates vary as to how big this was. Bauckham thinks the *plethron* here is equivalent to the Roman *iugerum*, an area ploughable by two oxen in one day, equal to a quarter of a hectare or two-thirds of an acre.[7] If so, their farm was just under ten hectares or about twenty-four acres; that is, fourteen soccer fields. So it was not a huge farm. Yet it would be enough to feed one's family and a few workers, and to have some produce left over to sell. But, if this holding had already been divided between the sons of Joseph and his brother Clopas, and further subdivided between their sons, then it might have been rather larger in Jesus's time.

So Jesus's family were not peasants. They ran a construction business and were landowners who probably employed others on their own farm. Yet, despite this, many writers are determined to see Jesus as a peasant. And there are several reasons why.

First, western academics are rooted in the Greek philosophical tradition which holds manual labour to be demeaning. Plato, Aristotle, and their disciples were united in their contempt for *banausia*, that is, labouring for a daily living.[8] The Greek philosopher had to be a landowner who lived by the sweat of others. Likewise, modern academics tend to lump manual workers together as horny-handed oafs. Anyone who works with hands, they assume, is inferior to the all-wise boffin: a builder is no different from a peasant. Thus Crossan confidently asserts, 'a *tekton* or peasant artisan is but a euphemism for a dispossessed peasant, for a landless laborer.'[9] They imagine that no manual worker is of much value.

The Israelites held quite a different view of things. A manual trade was deemed essential in all stations of life. Said Rabbi Judah bar Ilay, 'Great is labour, for it betters one's lot' (Ned. 49b) and 'Who teaches his son no trade leads him to be a robber' (B. Kid. 29a). And so every boy, high-born or low, had to learn a trade, even if he were to be a rabbi, a *kohen*, or a *nasi*.

[7] Bauckham, *Jude and the Relatives of Jesus*, 104. But Carrington, *Early Christian Church*, 334, says it was equal to four hectares or ten acres; that is, six soccer fields.

[8] See, e.g., Plato, *Republic,* VI:495d-e; Aristotle, *Politics,* I:1260a-b.

[9] Crossan, *Birth of Christianity*, 350.

Shimon ben Shetaḥ, *nasi* of the Sanhedrin, was a weaver of linen.[10] The great Shemaiah, his successor as *nasi*, used to say: 'Love manual work. Despise high position!' (Avot 1). Hillel, Shemaiah's successor, earned in his youth a *tarpeik*—a half-denarius—a day as a lumberman (Yoma 35b). Hillel's successor, Shammai, was a builder (Shab. 31a). Rabbi Joshua the *nasi* was a blacksmith (Ber. 28a). Rabbi Joshua ben Ḥananiah and Abba ben Zemina were both tailors (Y. Sanh. 3:6; Y. Ber. 7d). Rabbi Jose ben Ḥalafta was a tanner (Shab. 49b). Abba Hoshaiah of Ṭurya was a laundryman (Y. B.K. 10:10). Ḥanina and Oshaya were shoemakers (Pes. 113b). Ḳarna was a wine-taster and Huna a water-carrier (Ket. 105a). Ravs Ḥisda and Pappa were brewers (Pes. 113a). Other rabbis bore names that reflected their trade: Yitzhak Nappaḥa (the smith), Yoḥanan ha-Sandalar (the sandal-maker); and Abin Naggara (the carpenter). And of course Shaul-Paul, the Nazarene rabbi, was a tent-maker or, in other words, a leather-worker (Acts 18:3). He said, 'These hands of mine have provided for my own needs and for those of my companions' (Acts 20:34) and 'With toil and labour we worked night and day that we might not be a burden to any of you' (2 Thess. 3:7–8) and 'If anyone will not work, let him not eat!' (2 Thess. 3:10).

So deep was this Jewish commitment to manual labour that the rabbi was expected not to live on payment from his students. 'Make not of your learning an axe to hew out a living' (M. Abot 4). Yes, they might bring gifts, but the ideal rabbi was to be a giver not a taker. He laboured in Torah—studying and teaching—from sunrise till noon, then laboured with his hands from noon till sundown. This was also Paul's practice among his disciples. Gifts were appreciated as tokens of thanks, or in time of need (Gal. 6:6; Phil. 4:15–18). But the noble course was to serve without payment.

The first-century *nasi* and sage, Rabban Gamliel II, descended from David and of great honour and wealth, taught:

> Anyone who has a trade, to what is he similar? To a vineyard that is surrounded by its fence, to a furrow that is surrounded by a hedge. (T. Kid. 1:11)

His great-grandson, the *nasi* Rabban Gamliel beRabbi, taught his disciples:

[10] Y. Bava Metzia 2:5 [8c]; Deut. R. 3:5.

> Lovely is Torah study with daily labour, for persistence in both makes one forget sin. But Torah without daily labour leads to nought and becomes a cause of sin. (Avot 2:2)

In fact, this high view of manual labour was widely held among the peoples of the east. Benjamin of Tudela tells how, in the twelfth century, the Caliph of Baghdad, Emir al-Muminin al-Abbasi, lived entirely by the labour of his own hands.

> He will not partake of anything unless he has earned it by the work of his own hands. He makes coverlets to which he attaches his seal; his courtiers sell them in the market, and the great ones of the land purchase them, and the proceeds thereof provide his sustenance. He is truthful and trusty, speaking peace to all men.[11]

Yet there is another reason why people see Jesus as a peasant, namely, because Mariam and Joseph brought two doves to the temple as an offering at his birth (Luke 2:24). Since this was the poorest offering the law allowed at the birth of a child, then it looks like Mariam and Joseph really were poor. But still, that does not mean they were peasants. They could have been, as we shall see, of noble birth, but thrust into poverty.

PRINCE JOSEPH

In fact, both Joseph and Mariam, rather than being peasants, were of royal descent. We learn this in several ways.

1. The gospel genealogies. Matthew and Luke make a point of tracing Joseph's descent from King David. More importantly, Matthew traces the line of succession from Solomon through the kings of Judah to Joseph. The two evangelists are certainly saying that Joseph was the heir to David's throne in his generation. Even though Herod reigned, the *nasi* of David's line, the rightful king of Israel, was Joseph. We will speak more of this in the next chapter.

2. The royal status of Jude's grandchildren. As we saw, Jude's grandchildren were of sufficiently royal lineage to be on trial for their lives as a live political threat in the late first century. This suggests that they were the apparent heirs to David's throne in their own day. This

[11] Adler (ed.), *Benjamin of Tudela*, 35–36.

suggests in turn that their grandfather, Joseph of Nazareth, was heir to David's throne in his own day.

3. Rabbinic testimony to Jesus's royal connections. A memory of this royal descent is preserved by a passage in tractate Sanhedrin of the Babylonian Talmud which tells of the execution of Jesus. It first relates the regulations for the execution of a criminal. A herald had to go before the condemned man, announcing his crime and the names of its witnesses. Any who had evidence in his favour could then come forward. Here is the text. The Mishnah is in capitals. The Talmudic commentary on it—the *gemara*—follows.

> AND A HERALD PRECEDES HIM etc. This implies, only immediately before [the execution], but not previous thereto.
>
> Has it not been taught? On the eve of the Passover they hanged Yeshu the Nazarene.[12] For forty days before the execution, a herald went before him [crying], 'Yeshu will be brought out to be stoned for he has practised sorcery and enticed Israel to apostasy. Anyone who can say anything in his favour, let him come forward and plead on his behalf.' But since nothing was brought forward in his favour he was hanged on the eve of the Passover.
>
> Ulla retorted: 'Do you suppose that he was one for whom a defence could be made? Was he not a *mesith* [enticer], of whom the Merciful says, *Neither shalt thou spare, neither shalt thou conceal him.* [Deut. 13:8]?' With Yeshu however it was different, for he was near to the kingdom.
>
> Our Rabbis taught: Yeshu the Nazarene had five disciples, Mattai, Nakai, Nezer, Buni and Todah. When Mattai was brought [before the court] he said to them [the judges], Shall Mattai be executed? Is it not written, *Mattai* [when] *shall I come and appear before God?* [Ps. 42:3] Thereupon they replied: Yes, Mattai shall be executed, since it is written, *Mattai* [when] *shall he die and his name perish?* [Ps. 41:6] When Nakai was brought in he said to them; Shall Nakai be executed? It is not written, *Naki* [the innocent] *and the righteous slay thou not*? [Exod. 23:7] Yes, they said, Nakai shall be executed, since it is written, *In secret places does Naki* [the innocent] *slay.* [Ps. 10:8] When Nezer was brought in, he said; Shall Nezer be executed? Is it not written, *And Nezer* [a twig] *shall grow forth out of his roots* [Isa. 11:1]. Yes, they said, Nezer shall be executed, since it is written, *But thou art cast forth away from thy grave like Nezer* [an offshoot] [Isa. 14:19]. When Buni was brought in, he said: Shall Buni be executed? Is it not written, *Beni* [my son], *my firstborn*? [Exod. 4:22] Yes, they said, Buni shall be

[12] The Florentine ms. has On Shabbat, on the eve of Passover.

> executed, since it is written, *Behold I will slay Bine-kha* [thy son] *thy firstborn.* [Exod. 4:23] And when Todah was brought in, he said to them: Shall Todah be executed? Is it not written, *A psalm for Todah* [thanksgiving]? [Ps. 100:1]. Yes, they answered, Todah shall be executed, since it is written, *Whoso offers the sacrifice of Todah* [thanksgiving] *honours me.* [Ps. 50:23] (Bavli Sanh. 43a)

Such is the text. Some say that it is not about Yeshu-Jesus of Nazareth, but about some other Yeshu. But the Yeshu of this narrative was hanged on the eve of Passover, like Yeshu the Nazarene. He was one who led Israel astray—a customary description of Yeshu the Nazarene.[13] He had a band of disciples whom the authorities sought to kill, just like Yeshu the Nazarene. And all the uncensored manuscripts name him fully: 'Yeshu the Nazarene'.[14] So attempts to make him another Yeshu look like wishful thinking.

The first part of the passage—describing Jesus's execution—begins with the introductory rubric, 'Has it not been taught?' This rubric introduces a *baraitha*, that is, a tannaitic oral tradition, dating from before AD 200, preserved in the later Talmud text. Such a date is confirmed by the fact that the passage is in Hebrew, for rabbinic discourse changes from Hebrew to Aramaic in the late second century.

The next short paragraph, about Rav Ulla, is later. Ulla was a late third-century teacher, and the comments, before and after the Bible passage, are in Hebraized Aramaic.

The final paragraph, about the disciples, is again tannaitic, for it is in Hebrew and is introduced with another *baraitha* rubric 'Our rabbis taught' (*tannu rabbanan*). So the linguistic evidence is that, except for the Ulla paragraph, the text dates from no later than 150 years after Jesus's death. Yet, of course, the first and third paragraphs recall events of the 30s AD, so it is quite likely that these passages are earlier.

The gist of the passage is that the Jewish authorities gave Yeshu every chance. It tells how the charges against a condemned man were usually read only as he went to execution, not before. But Jesus got special treatment. In his case, the charges were announced every day for forty days. Yet still no one had anything good to say in his behalf, and so he was hanged.

[13] See the reference to Yeshu at Sot. 47a.

[14] The Firenze, Herzog, and Karlsruhe mss. have *Yeshu the Nazarene* in both the first and third paragrpahs. In all other mss the name has been erased.

Rav Ulla asked why Yeshu deserved such favour. For Moses taught that no mercy should be shown to one who led Israel astray. But, it is explained, this happened because Jesus was 'near to the kingship' (*di-qarov la-malkut hawah*).

Now the obvious sense of this phrase, 'near to the kingship', is that Jesus had royal connections, that is, he was of royal descent. There have been attempts to explain this away. Rashi took the passage to mean that it was Jesus's disciples whom the Sanhedrin tried carefully, because they had connections with the Roman or Herodian *malkut* or kingship. But the 'royal connections' clearly refer to Yeshu, not his disciples. And it was Yeshu who is said to have got the special treatment. Not his disciples. They got rough justice.

Further, any idea that the *malkut* refers to the Roman or Herodian kingdom is unlikely.[15] These authorities offered no protection to Jesus or his disciples. Everyone knew that. Even Tacitus says that Jesus was executed at the behest of Pontius Pilate.[16] Nor were Roman or Herodian rule ever a lawful *malkut* in Jewish eyes. The only lawful Jewish *malkut* was the house of David. That must be the *malkut* the passage refers to. So I suggest the phrase means that Jesus was of royal lineage.

So the passage is a rabbinic defence of the Sanhedrin's execution of Jesus: they gave him every chance, but he had it coming. Of course, its account of Jesus's execution is, as Klausner agrees, less credible than the gospel narratives.[17] But it preserves at its heart the rabbis' awareness that the one the Sanhedrin condemned was heir of the royal house of David.

4. A royal tomb. A final piece of evidence for Jesus's royal lineage can be deduced from the stone which sealed the tomb where Jesus was laid.

More than 900 burial caves from Israel's second-temple period—the centuries before the destruction of the temple in AD 70—are known around Jerusalem. Some are sealed with a square stone plug, others

[15] The Soncino Talmud says 'he was connected with the government [or royalty, i.e., influential].' The William Davidson online Talmud gives the passage as, 'Rather Jesus was different, as he had close ties with the government, and the gentile authorities were interested in his acquittal.' Herford notes that Gamliel II was also said to be 'near to the kingdom' (B. B.K. 83a), which he takes to mean that as Patriarch he dealt with the Roman power (Herford 1903: 89). But Gamliel did indeed claim descent from David.

[16] Tacitus, *Annals*, 15:44.

[17] Klausner, *Jesus of Nazareth*, p. 27.

with a rolling stone disk. The former far outnumber the latter. In fact, only four rolling-disk tombs are known in total, and they all belonged to people of the highest status. One of them belonged to the Assyrian Queen Helena of Adiabene, a convert to Judaism who was buried in Jerusalem. Another belonged to Herod's family.[18]

Now the three synoptic gospels state that the stone was 'rolled against' (*proskulisas*) the door of the tomb and then 'rolled away' (*apokulisen*).[19] Such language suggests that the stone was a rolling disk rather than a stone plug. (John speaks only of the stone being 'taken away' from the tomb, which neither confirms nor denies the synoptics' testimony.) If that is so, Jesus was buried in a tomb befitting royalty.

Of course, the tomb did not belong to Jesus. Matthew says it belonged to Joseph of Arimathea, a wealthy man, of whom Mark adds that he was a prominent member of the Sanhedrin (Matt. 27:57–60; Mark 15:43). It is quite likely that such a wealthy man would have a rolling-disk tomb made for himself. But it is very unlikely that he would give it to a 'crucified peasant'. Rather, in giving his tomb to Jesus, Joseph of Arimathea thought that Jesus was of a status befitting such a tomb, a status as of the apparent heir of the house of David.

Why were Joseph and Mariam poor?

The evidence then is that Jesus was of royal descent, a status he must have received from Joseph. But if so, why does Luke record that Joseph presented at Jesus's dedication only two doves, the poorest offering allowed by the law? (Luke 2:24; Lev. 12:6–8) There are two reasons.

First, there is the condition of the Israelite patrician families of David's line in the early first century. They had great status—everyone still believed the Messiah would come from their line. And those who could claim descent from David, even matrilineally, like Hillel and his sons, made the most of it.[20] But their former wealth and power was gone.

After the return from the Babylonian Exile, the house of David, from Zerubbabel on, still governed Jerusalem, but under Persian and

[18] Kloner, 'Did a Rolling Stone Close Jesus' Tomb?', pp. 23–29, 76.
[19] Mark 15:46; 16:3 and parallels.
[20] For Hillel's descent from David, see Y. Kil. 9:3; Y. Ta'an 4:2; B. Ket. 62:2.

Greek sovereignty. They sat as *nasi* over the Great Assembly, the *Knesset Ha-Gedolah*, which governed Israel in the Persian period (c. 516–330 BC). But, in 165 BC, the Zadokite Hasmoneans led a successful uprising against the Greek Seleucid dynasty. They ruled with increasing autonomy until John Hyrcanus I proclaimed himself both king and high priest of Israel. His claim to be king was widely resisted. Everyone else held that the title belonged to the house of David. But the Hasmonean response was predictable. They excluded the descendants of David from influence in the Sanhedrin, and eliminated those who spoke out. We saw earlier how Alexander Jannai purged those who denied the legitimacy of his rule. And some of them would have been of Davidic descent.

But a worse storm than the Hasmoneans was brewing. Under the reign of John Hyrcanus II, Antipater the Edomite wormed himself into power. Then, appointed by Julius Caesar as Roman Procurator of Judea, he made his sons, Phasael and Herod, governors of Jerusalem and Galilee respectively.

When John Hyrcanus was seized and carried away by the Parthians, at the instigation of his nephew, Antigonus, it was Herod who came to the rescue. He defeated Antigonus and handed him over to Mark Antony in 37 BC for a shameful execution. Then Herod brought Hyrcanus back to Jerusalem, but took the throne for himself.

Then, as Josephus relates, Herod killed and plundered forty-five leading men of the Jewish nation who objected to his seizing power from Antigonus. He married Hyrcanus's grand-daughter, the lovely Mariamme. He then drowned Mariamme's brother, Aristobulus, and, on charges of treason, dispatched old Hyrcanus. Finally, weary of her objections, he slew Mariamme herself (*Ant.* 15:2, 6, 7).

Herod then put to death all the members of the Sanhedrin, save Shemaiah the *nasi.* This was in revenge for their former impudence in calling him to trial, when he was first appointed governor of Galilee at the age of fifteen, for the unlawful killing of a Galilean guerilla leader, when Hyrcanus was king. The blood-chilling tale is told by Josephus.

> Hyrcanus was so moved by these complaints, that he summoned Herod to come to trial for the charges against him. Accordingly, he came. But his father persuaded him to come not like a private man, but with a guard, for the security of his person; and that, when he had settled the affairs of Galilee in the best manner he could for his own advantage,

> he should come to his trial, but still with a body of men sufficient for his security on his journey, yet so that he should not come with so great a force as might look like terrifying Hyrcanus, but still such a one as might not leave him defenceless. However, Sextus Cæsar, president of Syria, wrote to Hyrcanus, and desired him to clear Herod, and dismiss him at his trial, and threatened him beforehand if he did not do it. This letter of his was the reason why Hyrcanus delivered Herod from suffering any harm from the Sanhedrin, for he [Sextus Caesar] loved him [Herod] as his own son.
>
> But when Herod stood before the Sanhedrin, with his body of men about him, he terrified them all, and none of his former accusers dared to bring any charge against him, but there was a deep silence, and nobody knew what was to be done. When affairs stood thus, one whose name was Sameas [Shemaiah], a righteous man he was, and for that reason above all fear, rose up, and said, "O you that are judges with me, and O thou that art our king [Hyrcanus], I neither have ever myself known such a case, nor do I suppose that any one of you can name its parallel, that one who is called to take his trial by us ever stood in such a manner before us. Rather, every one, whoever he be, that comes to be tried by this Sanhedrin, presents himself in a submissive manner, and like one that is in fear of himself, and that endeavours to move us to compassion, with his hair dishevelled, and in a black and mourning garment: but this admirable man Herod, who is accused of murder, and called to answer so heavy an accusation, stands here clothed in purple, and with the hair of his head finely trimmed, and with his armed men about him, that if we shall condemn him by our law, he may slay us, and by overbearing justice may himself escape death. Yet I do not make this complaint against Herod himself; he is to be sure more concerned for himself than for the laws; but my complaint is against yourselves, and your king, who gave him a licence so to do. However, take you notice, that God is great, and that this very man, whom you are going to absolve and dismiss, for the sake of Hyrcanus, will one day punish both you and your king himself also."
>
> Nor was Sameas wrong in any part of this prediction; for when Herod gained the kingdom, he slew all the members of this Sanhedrin, and Hyrcanus himself also, except Sameas, for he had a great honour for him on account of his righteousness, and because, when the city was afterward besieged by Herod and Sosius, he persuaded the people to admit Herod into it; and told them that for their sins they would not be able to escape his hands. (*Antiquities*, 14:9:2–4)

Those Herod executed—the Sanhedrin members and Antigonus's supporters—surely included many of the patrician heads of Jerusalem who claimed descent from David. Indeed, after the rise of Herod, it is a wonder that any of David's seed survived at all or that any of them still held any property. It is no surprise that Joseph was not rich.

Yet, Joseph and Mariam still seem awfully poor. One would think an artisan from a land-owning family could bring the proper sacrifices for the birth of a child. But there is one more thing to consider.

Joseph's decision to take Mariam as his wife would have appalled his family. He had initially planned to divorce her when he learned of her pregnancy. He clearly knew the child she carried was not his. Now, as we shall see, he was not a youth when these things happened. But he was young enough that his parents or other family elders would still have been alive. His family would have been aware of his plan to divorce her.

Then Joseph decided to proceed with the marriage on the advice of an angel. But his family, without the benefit of angelic counsel, would have deplored his intention to take to wife this woman impregnated by who-knows-whom. Why are you doing this? Are you mad? She deserves death! Will you bring shame upon us all? Upon the royal name you bear?

There was no sympathy for his decision to take her to wife. They swiftly enacted the *k'tsatsah*, spilling the fruit and declaring, 'Brethren of the House of Israel, give ear, our brother Joseph has married an unsuitable woman and we are afraid lest his seed mingle with our seed.' And they dispossesed him.

And so, Joseph, disinherited and impoverished, and Mariam, cast off by her own family, found themselves fallen from princedom to poverty, from honour to shame. With nothing but the work of his hands, he laboured to support his family. Like many others, before and since, he bore his portion of disgrace for the sake of the Messiah.

7

Two Good Genealogies

GENEALOGY was vital in Israel. So it is no surprise that Matthew begins his gospel, just like that, with the declaration, *This is the book of the genealogy of Jesus the Messiah.* His choice of words is significant. They mean, for a start, that Matthew is working from a written record of Jesus's genealogy, not simply from hearsay. But, more, the words echo Genesis 2:4 and 5:1: *This is the book of the genealogy of the heavens and the earth / of Adam.* Matthew seems to be presenting Jesus as the culmination both of the Genesis creation narrative and of Adam's line. Finally, Matthew calls Jesus *son of Abraham, son of David.* An Israelite, writing in Hebrew for Israelites, he is telling his readers that this is the fulfilment of the promise of the Messiah given to the fathers. Then he traces the line of descent from Avraham, through the kings of Judah, to Joseph of Nazareth.

Luke also presents a genealogy. But, in showing Jesus as the saviour of the world, he traces Joseph's descent all the way back to Adam. Yet, despite this, Luke's gospel describes Israelite rites absent from the other gospels. He is the only one to mention Jesus's circumcision, his mother's postpartum ritual purification, Jesus's presentation in the temple, and his implied Bar Mitzvah when he visited the temple at the age of twelve.

The reason why Luke gives these details is because the one to whom Luke gospel addressed his gospel was, it seems, Theophilus ben Annas, *kohen gadol* from AD 37 to 41. Luke's salutation to Theophilus as 'excellency' was not just flattery. It was a form of address reserved for kings or high priests. And, since the Jewish high-priest kept his title for life, and since Theophilus is likely to have been alive when Luke wrote his gospel in the late 50's or early 60's AD, this Theophilus, the son of Annas and brother-in-law of Joseph Caiaphas, is by far the best candidate for dedicatee of Luke's gospel.[1] This view is supported by Luke's praise of the righteous *kohen* Zechariah, his lack of direct criticism of the Zadokites (Sadducees), and his frequent remarks on Zadokite belief on issues like divorce, angels, demons, and resurrection. Luke aimed to show Theophilus that the teacher sentenced to death by Theophilus's father and brother-in-law was Israel's Messiah and the saviour of the world.

So there are differences in the agenda underlying Matthew's and Luke's genealogies. But when we turn to the details, it gets more interesting still. Luke's account of the descent from Adam to Abraham is fairly easy. It is the same as the genealogy of Genesis chapters 5 and 10, except that Cainan appears between Arphaxad and Shelah, as he does in the Septuagint (3:36; cf. Gen. 10:24; 11:12–13; see Appendix 1).

Luke's genealogy having brought us to Avraham, the father of Israel and other peoples of the east, Matthew's genealogy chimes in. Then things begin to get complicated. The two genealogical lines or stirps run parallel from Abraham to David. Then, from David to the exile, they diverge down two different stirps—Matthew through Solomon, Luke through Nathan (1 Chr. 3:5). Then they converge again in the persons of Shealtiel and Zerubbabel. Then they diverge again. Then they converge again in Joseph of Nazareth.

Luke 3:33-38

1. God
2. Adam
3. Seth
4. Enosh
5. Kenan
6. Mahalalel
7. Jared
8. Enoch
9. Methuselah
10. Lamech
11. Noah
12. Shem
13. Arphaxad
14. Cainan
15. Shelah
16. Eber
17. Peleg
18. Reu
19. Serug
20. Nahor
21. Terah

[1] This view, first proposed by Theodore Hase (1725), has received attention in recent decades; cf. Anderson, 'Theophilus'. Josephus, *Ant.* 19:6:2 gives Theophilus's genealogy. Evidence for his existence came to light in the 1980s, in the ossuary of 'Johanna granddaughter of Theophilus, the High Priest' (Barag and Flusser, 'Ossuary'). Although Luke is usually seen as a gentile (Col. 4:11–14), some argue otherwise (Strelan, *Luke the Priest*). Such a scenario would explain his access to Theophilus.

Matthew 1:1–16

1. Abraham
2. Isaac
3. Jacob
4. Judah
5. Perez
6. Hezron
7. Ram
8. Amminadab
9. Nahshon
10. Salmon
11. Boaz
12. Obed
13. Jesse
14. David
15. Solomon
16. Rehoboam
17. Abijah
18. Asa
19. Jehoshaphat
20. Jehoram

a. Ahaziah ben Jehoram omitted

b. Jehoash ben Ahaziah omitted

c. Amaziah ben Jehoash omitted

21. Uzziah
22. Jotham
23. Ahaz
24. Hezekiah
25. Manasseh
26. Amon
27. Josiah

d. Jehoiakim ben Josiah omitted

28. Jeconiah
29. Shealtiel
30. Zerubbabel
31. Abiud
32. Eliakim
33. Azor

Luke 3:23–38

22. Abraham
23. Isaac
24. Jacob
25. Judah
26. Perez
27. Hezron
28. Aram
29. Amminadab
30. Nahshon
31. Salmon
32. Boaz
33. Obed
34. Jesse
35. David
36. Nathan (1 Chr. 3:5)
37. Mattatha
38. Menna
39. Melea
40. Eliakim
41. Jonam
42. Joseph
43. Judah
44. Simeon
45. Levi
46. Matthat
47. Jorim
48. Eliezer
49. Joshua
50. Er
51. Elmadam
52. Cosam
53. Addi
54. Melki
55. Neri
56. Shealtiel
57. Zerubbabel
58. Rhesa
59. Joanan
60. Joda
61. Josech
62. Semein
63. Mattathias
64. Maath

34. Zadok
35. Akim
36. Eliud
37. Eleazar
38. Matthan
39. Jacob
40. Joseph
41. (Mary)
42. Jesus

65. Naggai
66. Esli
67. Nahum
68. Amos
69. Mattathias
70. Joseph
71. Jannai
72. Melki
73. Levi
74. Matthat
75. Heli
76. Joseph

77. Jesus

The descent from Abraham to David is the same in both gospels, except for Hezron to Amminadab. There Matthew gives one name, Ram, which agrees with the best texts of Luke which have Aram, the Greek name for the same person.[2] But other texts of Luke give two names, Arni and Admin, and there are other minor variants.[3] It doesn't make a lot of difference. Allowing Arni and Admin makes Luke's genealogy seventy-seven generations until Jesus, rather than including Jesus. Nor is there any genealogical problem. Even if a generation is omitted, Hezron is still the progenitor of Amminadab. So from Abraham to David, both gospels have essentially the same stirps.

But the genealogies from David on—diverging, converging, and diverging again—are trickier altogether. The patrilineal offspring of two brothers, Solomon and Nathan, cannot normally lead to a single individual a thousand years later. Much less can stirps converge, diverge, and then converge again. That is why some simply dismiss one or both genealogies as hopelessly corrupt. Brown, for instance, says that Matthew's and Luke's genealogies of Jesus 'tell us nothing certain about his grandparents or his great-grandparents'.[4] And Flusser says,

> We should keep in mind that the two genealogies agree only from Abraham down to David. The internal problems of both lists and their considerable differences leave us with the impression that both

[2] Cod. Alexand. and Bezae, Vulgate and Peshitta. For *Aram*, see LXX 1 Chr. 2:10.

[3] The second correction to Codex Sinaiticus and Papyrus P4. Other early Greek texts, and the Bohairic Coptic and Ethiopic texts, have Joram and Aram.

[4] Brown, *Birth of the Messiah*, 94.

genealogies were constructed *ad hoc*, so to speak, in order to prove descent from David.[5]

But I am less sceptical. As we saw, Israel's genealogical records were kept in the temple. And the patrician families of David and Zadok kept their own independent records. Such records were available for consultation by any serious enquirer, for these families were proud of their descent. So Matthew and Luke would both have had access to them. Indeed, Luke—whose genealogy might be most suspect, as diverging from the royal line—claims to have investigated thoroughly. And indeed he must have done so if he were presenting genealogies to Theophilus. The *kohen gadol* had the temple genealogies to hand. Any alternative line of descent would need to be well-grounded.

So I think the genealogies are not fictional. But reconciling them is no simple matter. Any attempt to do so must answer the following questions.

1. Why does Matthew omit names from his list?
2. Was Shealtiel's father Jeconiah or Neri?
3. Was Zerubbabel the son of Shealtiel, as in Matthew and Luke, or of Pedaiah, as in 1 Chronicles 3:19?
4. Why do Matthew and Luke give Zerubbabel's sons as Abiud and Rhesa, yet 1 Chronicles 3 lists them as Meshullam and Hananiah?
5. Was Joseph's father Jacob or Heli?
6. Does Luke's genealogy represent the descent of Mariam?

Why does Matthew omit names?

Matthew traces Joseph's descent through Solomon and the royal house of Judah. He follows the genealogy of the kings of Judah from David to the 6th century BC, as given in 1 Chronicles 3:10-19, then continues through the period after the Exile in Babylon.[6] At the end, he states that it consists of three times fourteen generations (1:17). To this, some reply that he cooked the books by omitting names and, anyway, he couldn't count, since he gives only forty generations in his list.

We will deal with the omissions shortly. But Matthew clearly had a numerological agenda. Yet he was not alone in this. Luke's genealogy

[5] Flusser, *Jesus*, 7.
[6] Jehoram is Joram (2 Kgs 8:20–24); Uzziah is Azariah (2 Kgs 15:1–2; 2 Chr. 26:1–2).

falls into a pattern of eleven times seven generations from Adam to Jesus: that is, three sevens from Adam to Abraham, two sevens from Isaac to David, three sevens from Nathan to Shealtiel, three sevens from Zerubbabel to Jesus.[7] In fact, Luke's genealogy seems to follow the Book of Enoch which has seventy-seven generations from creation till the messianic age.[8] Likewise, Josephus gives twenty-one generations—three sevens—for the house of David to the exile (Ant. 5.9.4). And the early medieval *Seder olam zutta* (The lesser book of the world), has five sets of ten generations from Adam to Jehoiakim. So numerology was something genealogists did. One of the reasons may have been to aid the memory.

But why fourteen? The number is important for several reasons. First, it is the number of David. In Hebrew, as in Latin, the letters of the alphabet have numerical value. David's name in Hebrew has three letters: *daleth-vav-daleth* (d-v-d). *Daleth* has a numerical value of four and *vav* a value of six, and so the three letters add up to fourteen.

But fourteen also symbolizes royal power. The letters for writing the number fourteen are *yodh* and *daleth*, with numerical values of ten and four respectively. Written in Hebrew, right to left, they form the word *yad*, 'hand', the organ of human power and control. For instance, we read that God delivered David from Saul's hand or that he delivered David's enemies into his hand; the same is said of Abraham, Moses, Joshua, and others.[9] Sennacherib boasted, 'Ashur and Ishtar...have opened my hand for the destruction of the enemies of Ashur.'[10] So fourteen represents the name of David and his hand of royal power.

But why three times fourteen? Threefold repetition signifies completeness. *Holy, holy, holy!* cry the seraphim, for YHVH is all holy (Isa. 6:3). *O land, land, land, hear the word of YHVH!* says Jeremiah, for all the land must hear (Jer. 22:29). *Overturn, overturn, overturn!* says Ezekiel, for the reversal will be complete (Ezek. 21:27). So

[7] Or, if we follow those texts of Luke 3:33 which insert Admin after Aram-Arni, then the count begins with Adam (not God). The groups of 7 still fall more or less in place, *ie*, Abraham ends the third seven rather than beginning the fourth.

[8] Uriel tells Enoch the fallen angels will be bound for 70 generations till the judgement (1 Enoch 10:15). Adding the seven generations from Adam to Enoch makes 77 generations from creation to judgement, after which follows the golden age.

[9] Ps. 18:1; 1 Sam. 30:23; Gen. 14:20; Exod. 23:31; Deut. 7:24; Josh. 2:24; etc.

[10] From the Sennacherib stele in Istanbul. Isa. 10:14 represents him saying, As one reaches into a nest, so my hand reached for the wealth of the nations.

Matthew's three times fourteen generations point to the Messiah being the complete fullness of the promises and the power of David.

But three times fourteen is significant for one more reason. Three fourteens equal six sevens, that is, one seven short of a Jubilee, the year of favour and release which followed seven times seven years.[11] Matthew's three fourteens may be saying that the Great Jubilee draws near in the coming of the one who is the completeness of David's kingdom and power.

So Matthew's numerology encodes important messages. Yet it is true that Matthew does omit four individuals: Ahaziah, Jehoash, Amaziah, and Jehoiakim. (He also omits three rulers not in the royal succession: Athaliah, Jehoahaz, and Zedekiah.) Is he ditching historical accuracy for the sake of his numerological structure?

The abbreviation of genealogy was always acceptable, as long as the line continued correctly (cf. Ezra 7:3 with 1 Chr. 6:7–10). And, if an individual were in some way unworthy or disqualified for kingship, then his exclusion might be expected. And this, as we shall see, is exactly why Matthew does omit some individuals.

Seven generations after David, three kings, Ahaziah, Jehoash, and Amaziah are omitted. They were the offspring to four generations of Ahab of the northern Kingdom of Israel who, for his idolatry and wickedness, was cursed by Elijah.

> Behold, I will bring evil upon you, and will utterly sweep away your posterity, and will cut off from Ahab everyone who urinates against a wall [every male], both bond and free, in Israel (1 Kgs 21:21).

Athaliah, the daughter of Ahab and Jezebel, married King Jehoram ben Jehoshaphat of Judah. Yet Jehoram, though led into idolatry by Athaliah, was not excluded from Matthew's genealogy, for he was not a child of cursed Ahab. But Jehoram's offspring by Ahab's daughter did inherit Ahab's curse (2 Kgs 8:18).

The curse was manifest in their own wicked lives. Jehoram's son Ahaziah walked in the ways of the house of Ahab and was slain in the first wave of Jehu's purge (2 Kgs 8:26–9:29; 2 Chr. 22:1–9). Ahaziah's son Jehoash (Joash) forsook the Holy One and slew Zechariah the son of Jehoiada the *kohen* who brought him to the throne. He was wounded

[11] McCarthy says the three fourteens are one and a half lunar phases, from Abraham (new moon) to David (full moon) to Captivity (darkness) to Messiah (full moon).

by the Arameans and slain by his officials (2 Kgs 12:1–21; 2 Chr. 24:1–27). Amaziah served the gods of Edom, spurned a prophet's counsel, launched a disastrous war against Israel, and, like his father, was slain by his own people (2 Kgs 14:1–20; 2 Chr. 25:1–8). Thus the curse on Ahab's seed was fulfilled in four generations, as Moses taught (Exod. 20:3–6). They were extirpated in the northern kingdom of Israel (2 Kgs 9:8; 10:1–11) and discounted from the royal line of Judah.[12]

The curse being complete, Matthew takes up his list again with Amaziah's son, Uzziah. Then, seven generations later, he omits King Jehoiakim from his genealogy.

Jehoiakim (born Eliakim), the second son of Josiah, was appointed king by Pharaoh Necho and ruled for eleven years. *He did evil in the eyes of YHVH* and *detestable things* and *filled Jerusalem with blood* (2 Kgs 23:36–24:7; 2 Chr. 36:5–8). When Judah was groaning under Egyptian tribute, he embarked upon a palace-building spree, forcing the people into slave labour (Jer. 22:13–23). When presented with Jeremiah's prophecies of the doom of Jerusalem and Judah, he burned them. Ezekiel and others add more crimes to his record—blasphemy, incestuous relations with his mother, daughter-in-law, and stepmother, murdering men to seize their wives and property.[13] For all this, Jeremiah cursed him and his offspring in the name of YHVH and foretold his shameful end at the hands of Nebuchadnezzar.

> Thus says YHVH about Jehoiakim king of Judah: He will have no one to sit on the throne of David; his body will be thrown out and exposed to the heat by day and the frost by night (Jer. 36:30).

But quite apart from Jehoiakim's moral failings, there was another reason for his omission from Matthew's list. He was unlawfully raised to the throne. For he was appointed by Pharaoh Necho, not by Israel's *kohanim.* So, in truth, Jehoiakim was never a true king of Israel at all.

But, if that is so, why does his son, Jeconiah (Jehoiachin, Coniah), appear in Matthew's list? If his father was not lawfully king, how did Jeconiah inherit the throne? The answer is that, when the Babylonians

[12] Some of these points are noted by Jerome, *Comm. on Matt.*; Chrysostom, *Comm. on Matt.*, homily 1; Hilary of Poitiers, *Comm. on Matt.*; Augustine adds that Jehoram's name was not removed from the genealogy because, just as Solomon was spared for the sake of his righteous father, David, so Jehoram was spared for the sake of his righteous father, Jehoshaphat (*De quaestionibus*, 85).

[13] Ezek. 22.6–12, 25; Sanh. 103a; Lev. R. 19:6.

removed his father, Jeconiah was appointed to the throne by the temple *kohanim.* No one says otherwise (2 Kgs 24:8; 2 Chr. 36:9). And so he was a lawful king, even though he too merited Jeremiah's curse.

So, in summary, all those individuals whom Matthew omitted were either cursed by the prophets, or disqualified from legitimate kingship in Israel, or both. And Matthew listed only those kings that sat lawfully upon the throne.

Finally, there is the issue of why Matthew claims that there were three times fourteen generations when he gives only forty names. Perhaps *Abraham to David...David to the exile...the exile to the Christ* means that David and exiled Jeconiah should be counted twice. Or, perhaps more likely, Mariam and Jesus, mentioned at the end of the list (1:16), should be reckoned in the number; that is, there are really two separate genealogies—Abraham to Joseph, and Mariam to Jesus—making forty-two generations. But, either way, a close examination of Matthew's genealogy does not give the impression of dyscalculia, but of a careful account of the Judean king-list, omitting those who were in some way disqualified.

Was Shealtiel's Father Jeconiah or Neri?

But there are weightier enigmas in Matthew's and Luke's genealogies. Matthew says Shealtiel was the son of Jeconiah. Luke says he was the son of Neri. This looks like the same Shealtiel, for they both live at the same time, and both are followed by Zerubbabel. But how can a son have two fathers?

Jeremiah, who pronounced the curse on Jehoiakim, reiterated it over Jehoiakim's son Jeconiah:

> Record this man childless [in the royal genealogies], a man who will not succeed in his days, for none of his seed will succeed to sit on the throne of David or rule in Jerusalem (22:30).

But when we compare Jeremiah's curse with the king-list of 1 Chronicles 3, we find something surprising. It records Jeconiah first as having one son, Zedekiah: *The descendants of Jehoiakim: Jeconiah his son, Zedekiah his son* (v. 16). Throughout the list, the tag 'his son' (*b'no*) serves to announce the royal heir of the next generation. So

Zedekiah is Jeconiah's son and Jehoiakim's grandson. He was named, one imagines, after his great-uncle Zedekiah, the younger brother of Jehoiakim, placed on the throne by the Babylonians and so cruelly punished for his disloyalty.[14]

Yet the very next verse of the king-list says Jeconiah had seven sons. And Zedekiah is not mentioned. The heir (*b'no*) is now Shealtiel.

> And the sons of Jeconiah captive, Shealtiel his son (*b'no*), and Malkiram and Pedaiah and Shenazzar, Jekamiah, Hoshama and Nedabiah (1 Chr. 3:17).

Note that Jeconiah is now called 'captive' or 'imprisoned', meaning that these seven became his sons after he was taken prisoner to Babylon. From Pedaiah then issued Zerubbabel (1 Chr. 3:18). And from Zerubbabel, in turn, issued two stirps within the king-list—Hananiah and Meshullam (1 Chr. 3:19)—and two more, if Matthew and Luke are right, in Abiud and Rhesa.

How can one who is declared to be childless have so many sons? One solution is to soften Jeremiah's curse. Some render it, 'Write this man down *as if* childless' (NIV). They mean Jeconiah may have children, but they won't sit on David's throne or rule in Jerusalem. Now, it is true that the sons of David never again ruled in Jerusalem as they had before. Yet from Meshullam sprang the Tobiad and Oniad dynasties of the post-exilic *nasi* of Jerusalem. And from Hananiah sprang the Resh G'lutha or Exilarch, the Jewish kings of David's line who ruled over the large Jewish community in Babylon. Meanwhile, Matthew and Luke record his descendants to many generations through Abiud and Rhesa. For Jeconiah to have so many offspring seems in flat denial of Jeremiah's prophecy.

One imaginative solution is to say that Jeconiah repented in captivity and found grace with heaven and was granted seven sons.

> But R. Joshua ben Levi argued as follows: Repentance sets aside the entire decree, and prayer half the decree. You find that it was so with

[14] Zedekiah (Mattaniah), Josiah's fourth son, was enthroned by the Babylonians after they took Jeconiah captive. He ruled eleven years and *did evil in the eyes of the Lord*, opposing Jeremiah and presiding over national apostasy. Turning to Egypt, he broke his oath to Babylon. Ezekiel foretold that all his house would be overthrown until the coming of the Messiah (21:25–27). When the Babylonians took Jerusalem, they slew his sons, blinded him, and took him in chains to Babylon (2 Kgs 24:18–25:7; 2 Chr. 36:11–14; Jer. 32:3–5; 34:1–3, 21–22; 39:1–7; 52:1–11; Ezek. 12:12–13).

> Jeconiah, king of Judah. For the Holy One, blessed be he, swore in his anger, *As I live, says HaShem, though [Je]Coniah the son of Jehoiakim king of Judah were the signet on my hand, yet by my right hand*—note, as R. Meir said, that it was by his right hand that God swore—*I would pluck thee hence* (Jer. 22:24). And what was decreed against Jeconiah? That he die childless. As it is said, *Record this man as childless* (Jer. 22:30). But as soon as he avowed penitence, the Holy One, blessed be he, set aside the decree, as it is said, The sons of Jeconiah captive: *Shealtiel his son,* etc. (1 Chr. 3:17). And it says further: *In that day... will I take thee, O Zerubbabel...the son of Shealtiel...and will make thee as a signet* (Hag. 2:23). Behold, then how penitence can set aside the entire decree! (Pesikta Rabbati 47)[15]

Yet there is no hint at all of Jeconiah's repentance in the Bible. In fact, a careful look at 1 Chronicles 3 shows that he was indeed childless.

> [10]And the son of Solomon, Rehoboam; Abijah his son; Asa his son, Jehoshapat his son.
> [11]Joram his son, Ahaziah his son, Joash his son.
> [12]Amaziah his son, Azariah his son, Jotham his son.
> [13]Ahaz his son, Hezekiah his son, Manasseh his son.
> [14]Amon his son, Josiah his son.
> [15]And the sons of Josiah: Johanan the firstborn, the second Jehoiakim; the third Zedekiah, the fourth Shallum.
> [16]And the sons of Jehoiakim: Jeconiah his son, Zedekiah his son.
> [17]And the sons of Jeconiah captive: Shealtiel his son, and [18]Malkiram and Pedaiah and Shenazzar, Jekamiah, Hoshama, and Nedabiah.

In each case, the word 'his son' (*b'no*) follows the name of the heir to the throne. But the first notable exception is Johanan, the firstborn of Josiah (v. 15). Mentioned only here in the Bible, Johanan never came to the throne. (He may have died with Josiah in the battle with Pharaoh Necho at Megiddo.) And so he is called 'firstborn' but not 'his son'.

Then, after the deaths of Josiah and Johanan, Josiah's fourth son Shallum (Jehoahaz) ruled for three months until he was deposed and taken to Egypt by Necho. Necho then set Jehoiakim on the throne. As we see, 'his son', that is, his heir, was Jeconiah; and 'his son', Jeconiah's heir, was Zedekiah (v. 16). But after Zedekiah, no one else is called 'his son'. Instead the line of succession begins anew with 'Jeconiah captive', who has now obtained another seven sons. And, of

[15] Cf. Lev. R. 19:6: R. Shabbethai said: He [Jeconiah] did not move thence until the Holy One, blessed be He, pardoned him all his sins, as it is said: *Thou art all fair, my love, and there is no blemish in thee* (Song 4:7). Cf. B. Sanh. 37–38a; Num. R. 20:20.

these seven, Shealtiel is now 'his son', that is, the heir to the throne.

These verses conceal the clue to understanding Matthew's and Luke's genealogies. But how are we to understand it?

First, we must take Jeremiah's curse seriously. If his prophecy on Jehoiakim's seed had not come true, later generations would have judged him a false prophet and would not have preserved his prophecy. Since his prophecy was preserved, we must expect that the curse of childlessness was fulfilled in the sight of all Israel.

And so the answer, consistent with Jeremiah's curse and the king-list above, is that Jeconiah's son Zedekiah, the heir apparent, died young and without issue, fulfilling Jeremiah's prophecy. Thereupon Jeconiah, captive in Babylon, obtained another seven sons, of whom Shealtiel inherited David's throne. But if Jeremiah's prophecy were to stand, then these seven sons were not Jeconiah's seed. They must have been the seed of another, who became Jeconiah's heirs by adoption.

Adoption was widespread in ancient times. It was necessary for protection and survival at a time when heirs might die young, leaving the aged without a protector. In such cases, the bereaved adopted a clan member to whom they passed on their title and wealth in return for protection and upkeep from the adoptee.

The adoption of these seven sons by Jeconiah explains the biblical texts. It happens that it also has textual support in the ancient genealogy or 'tree' preserved by the Loeb family.[16] It states,

> King Jeconiah, called 'the captive', married Tamar, his cousin, her second marriage, the daughter of the late crown-prince, Johanan, his uncle, and begot Zedekiah, the crown-prince. The early death of the crown-prince [Zedekiah] was the fulfillment of 'Coniah's Curse', placed on King Jeconiah's offspring by Jeremiah the prophet. The king adopted his stepsons, the sons of his wife, Tamar, by a previous marriage, since they too were of the royal seed; that is, her first husband was a Davidic prince. They are: Shealtiel, who became the new crown-prince, Malchiram, Pedaiah, Shenazzur (Sin-ab-Usur), Jekamiah, Hoshama, Nedabiah, father of Shemphat, the ancestor of the Bagratids of the Caucasus (§51).

And it also states,

> Johanan, the crown-prince, was father of a daughter, Tamar, who, according to the judicial ruling made by Moses (Num. 27:8) and its

[16] The Loeb genealogy can be found at www.loebtree.com/kings.html.

conditional clause (Num. 36:8), was technically the heiress. Her first husband was Prince Neri, representative of a major Davidic descent-line; and her second husband was King [Je]Coniah (§49).

Figure 4. From David to Abiud and Rhesa

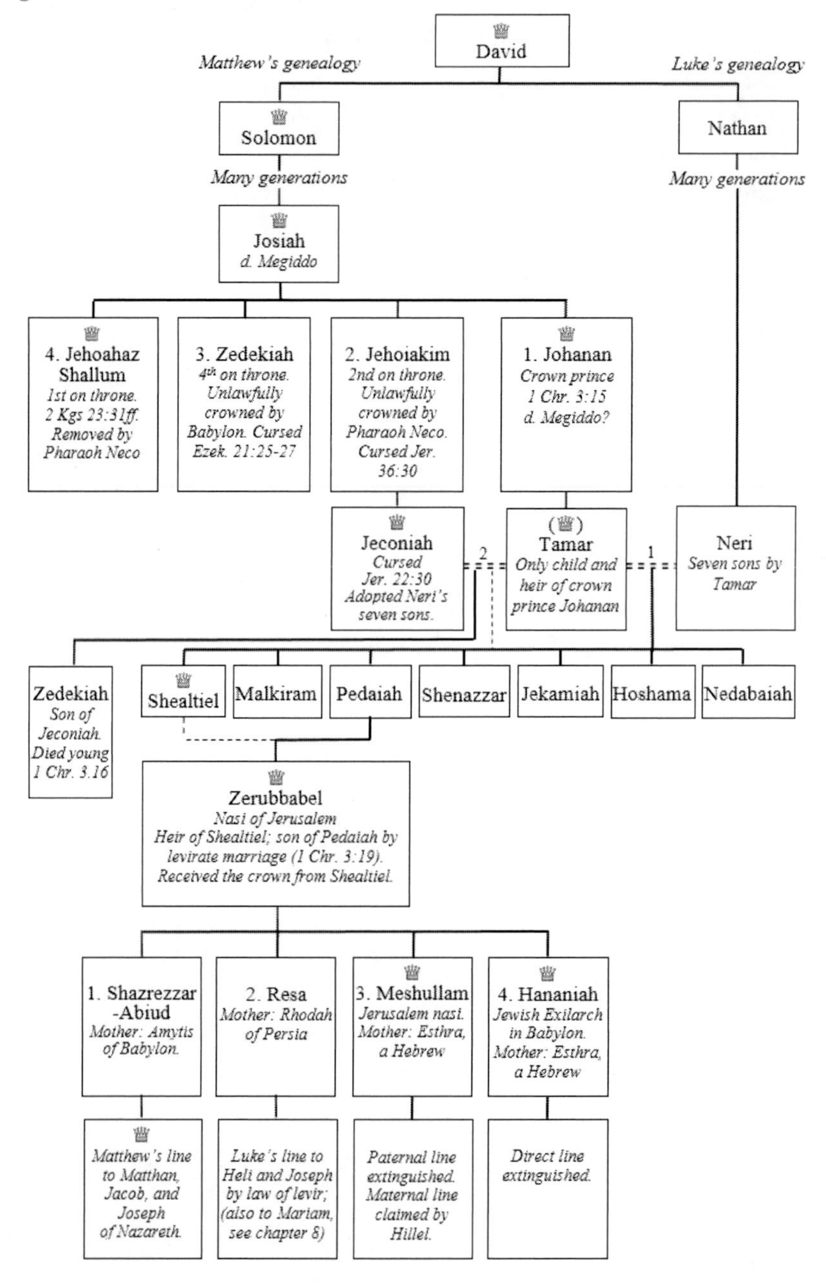

Now this Loeb genealogy is not from any Roman-period manuscript. But it is authenticated by a nineteenth-century affidavit attesting to a sixteenth-century attestation by seven rabbis, including Rabbi Mosheh Alshekh of Safed. Yet the best witness to its authenticity is how it sheds light on these genealogies as no other source does.

Since 1 Chronicles 3:16–17 does indeed point to the extinction of Jeconiah's line, then Shealtiel must have been adopted by Jeconiah, but, for the sake of the succession, he must also be the genetic offspring of another branch of David's line. And so the Loeb tree and the gospels agree. The Loeb tree gives the name of the pivotal matriarch, Tamar, the daughter of Johanan the firstborn of Josiah, who joined the two dynasties. As the only child of Johanan, Josiah's firstborn, she passed on the succession to her own firstborn son, Shealtiel. Luke and Loeb both give the name of Shealtiel's genetic father, Neri, from the house of David through the line of Nathan. And Matthew gives the line of succession as far as Jeconiah who, being set on the throne by Israel's *kohanim*, was a legitimate king. Thus Shealtiel received the crown both from his mother and his adoptive father, but the patrilineal descent of the royal line was now entirely from Nathan and Neri, not Solomon.

There is a final confirmation of this in Zechariah's vision of the royal families of Jerusalem bewailing the death of their pierced king. He says the house of David and the house of Nathan will mourn, but says nothing of Solomon or any other Davidic line (12:12). Zechariah knew the house of Nathan was now the chief Davidic line.

So, while the antiquity of the Loeb genealogy cannot be proven, it upholds Jeremiah's curse, explains 1 Chronicles 3:16 and Zechariah 12:12, and reconciles Luke with Matthew. And that is remarkable.

WAS ZERUBBABEL THE SON OF SHEALTIEL OR PEDAIAH?

The next question—perhaps of lesser importance but still worth addressing—is whose son was Zerubbabel? Matthew and Luke say he was the son of Shealtiel. So do most other Bible texts (Ezra 3:2, 8; 5:2; Neh. 12:1; Hag. 1:1, 12, 14; 2:23). But the Hebrew texts of 1 Chronicles 3:19 say he was the son of Shealtiel's brother Pedaiah.

> [19] The sons of Pedaiah: Zerubbabel and Shimei; and the son[s] of Zerubbabel: Meshullam and Hananiah and Shelomit their sister.

This reading is found in the two Masoretic codices of the Bible—that is, the Aleppo and Leningrad codices—and in the Aramaic Peshitta, the Targum of Chronicles, and the Lucian Greek text.

On the other hand, most ancient Greek and Latin texts of the Bible—Septuagint, Aquila, Symmachus, Theodotion, Vulgate—make him the son of Shealtiel, as in Matthew and Luke. So there are two options.

a) Zerubbabel was the son of Pedaiah, as recorded in the Hebrew and Aramaic texts and Lucian of 1 Chronicles 3:19. In that case, we must explain why Matthew and Luke call him the son of Shealtiel.
b) Zerubbabel was the son of Shealtiel. In that case, Matthew, Luke, and the ancient Greek and Latin texts are correct, and the Hebrew and Aramaic texts are wrong.

If the answer is (a), then the explanation would be levirate marriage, a custom in ancient Israel where, if a man died without issue, his brother took the dead man's wife to father a child to inherit the dead man's name and property. This practice was required in the law of Moses (Deut. 25:5–6). But it was customary among the Hebrews long before Moses's time, as with Onan and Tamar (Gen. 38:8–10).

In such a scenario, Shealtiel died without issue and his brother Pedaiah took Shealtiel's wife to beget children in his brother's name.

Answer (b), on the other hand, is simpler. It only involves saying that the Aleppo, Leningrad, Peshitta, targum, and Lucian texts are wrong. Now errors are possible in some of these texts. Lucian, a church father, was probably not subject to rigorous inspection. The same may be true of the medieval targum text. As for the Leningrad text, Shmuel ben Ya'akov, who wrote and punctuated it in the early eleventh century, was an avowed follower of Aharon ben Asher's Aleppo text. So the Leningrad text is largely a copy of the Aleppo text.

But there is rather more difficulty allowing for an error in the Peshitta, for it was an early translation from the Hebrew. And there is the greatest difficulty of all in allowing that there might be an error in the Aleppo Codex. No text ever written is as meticulous and perfect as the Aleppo Codex. As Menachem Cohen of Bar Ilan University says, "It is flawless, like the work of an angel."

The Aleppo Codex was written by two men. One wrote the Hebrew consonants. The other inserted the vowel points and cantillation marks into the consonants. We know just who they were for the colophon to the Codex gave their names. Although the colophon was lost in the second half of the twentieth century, it was copied by Professor Umberto Cassuto in 1943. It said:

> This is the complete codex of the twenty-four books, written by our teacher and rabbi Shlomo known as Ben Boya'a, the swift scribe, and the spirit of the Lord guided him, and it was vocalized and transmitted with great meticulousness by the great scholar and wise sage, the lord of scribes and the father of sages, the chief of scholars, swift in his deeds, whose understanding of the work was unique in his generation, Rabbi Aharon ben Rabbi Asher, may his soul be bound in life with the prophets and pious and righteous.

So Shlomo ben Boya'a wrote the Hebrew consonants *pdyh.* And Aharon ben Asher, "the great scholar and wise sage, the lord of scribes and the father of sages" added the vowel points, making *Pedayah.* Now, all the evidence is that the Aleppo text was Ben Asher's master text. He checked it over and over again for decades. He scratched out tiny errors in the vowels and cantillation marks and rewrote them. It is hard to believe that, among all these checkings, Aharon ben Asher came to Shlomo ben Boya'a's 'mistake' and just added the vowels and cantillation to it without noticing that it was the wrong name.

Further, this 'mistake' is consistent over 800 years or so among the texts which rely on a Hebrew source. The earliest is probably the old Syriac texts, translated from the Hebrew, which lay behind the Peshitta. Then Lucian, living in Antioch, probably worked from the Aramaic text. Later still, the Targum on Chronicles was translated from the Hebrew. And finally, Ben Asher's Aleppo Codex, appearing in the early 10th century, but based on ancient manuscripts, gives the same reading as the others. This all looks very much like the 'Pedaiah' reading is a very ancient Hebrew reading and not a mistake at all.

So, in the end, deciding between these two options is not easy. The Hebrew reading for 1 Chronicles 3:19 is supported by the best texts. Yet it seems to disagree with Ezra, Nehemiah, Haggai, Matthew and Luke. Meanwhile, the Greek and Latin translations, on the other hand, do not present any such difficulty, but they are inferior texts.

My inclination is to accept the Hebrew tradition and Pedaiah's levirate marriage to Shealtiel's widow. This is because of my great respect for the Aleppo text. But, in the end, all these texts, including

Matthew and Luke, are correct. For the purpose of levirate marriage was to produce an heir from the seed of the brother's clan, bearing the brother's name. And so Zerubbabel, even if begotten by Pedaiah, was rightly recorded as Shealtiel's son everywhere else in the Bible.

Who were Abiud and Rhesa?

Matthew records a stirps descending from Zerubbabel through Abiud and Luke another through Rhesa. But 1 Chronicles 3:19–20 gives Meshullam and Hananiah as Zerubbabel's sons, as well as Hashubah, Ohel, Berekiah, Hasadiah and Jushab-Hesed. So who were Abiud and Rhesa? The only source that gives any answer is the Loeb genealogy (§ 54). It says that Zerubbabel:

- married Amytis, a Babylonian princess, called a 'foreign wife', and begot Shazrezzar, a Babylonian name, the ancestor of a major Davidic line. Shazrezzar was an ancestor of Joseph, the husband of Mary, from the Christian bible.
- married Rhodah, a Persian princess (who later remarried a Persian prince) and begot Reza (Rhesa), a Persian name, the half-brother through his mother of the Persian shah, the ancestor of a major Davidic line.[17] Reza was an ancestor of Mary from the Christian Bible.
- married Esthra, a Jewish princess, and begot Meshullam, Hananiah, and Shelomith (the wife of Elnathan, Governor of Judea, c. 500 B.C.E.)

If we seek to reconcile this with Matthew and Luke, then Shazrezzar would be Matthew's Abiud. Meanwhile Reza would be Luke's Rhesa, as the Loeb tree suggests. The Loeb tree also suggests Reza was the ancestor of Mariam the mother of Jesus, which, as we shall see in the next chapter, is also correct.

1 Chronicles 3:20 also attributes other sons to Zerubbabel, namely, Hashubah, Ohel, Berekiah, Hasadiah and Jushab-Hesed and numbers them 'five'. Two of them may perhaps be other names for Abiud and Rhesa, while the other three would be the offspring of other wives or

[17] Reza is indeed a Persian name. It means 'contentment' and was popular among the erstwhile royal family. But its popularity springs from the Eighth Imam, Ali ibn Musa al-Ridha (in Persian, Reza) (AD 766–818) who, being the only Imam to reside and die in Persia, is popular there. The name may have existed earlier, but I am not aware of any evidence for it. On the other hand, Zerubbabel's son might equally have been called *resha*, Aramaic for 'chief', as Bauckham suggests (*Jude*, 330–333). An Aramaic name would have been understood equally by the Jewish and Persian communities.

concubines. Or, alternatively, following the Loeb tree, these 'five' may actually be the offspring of Meshullam, who is otherwise childless.

That Zerubbabel should marry into the highest class of Babylonian and then Persian society is not inconceivable. Amel-Marduk (Evil-Merodach) released Zerubbabel's grandfather, Jeconiah, from prison, and spoke to him favourably, so that he ate bread before the king—that is, his household were fed from palace provisions—and received a royal pension throughout his life (2 Kgs 25:27–30). And 1 Esdras 3–4 tells how Zerubbabel, when he was the young bodyguard of Darius Hystaspes, won the king's favour by his wisdom and gracious speech, and persuaded him to finance the rebuilding of Jerusalem. Some imagine the story is mythical. But it must have a core of truth. For the rebuilding of Jerusalem was of no benefit to Darius. Someone must have prompted him to fund it so generously. And if it was not Zerubbabel, he who later led the returnees to Jerusalem, then who was it?

But if the Loeb genealogy is correct about Zerubbabel's offspring from three wives, then why do the lines of Abiud and Rhesa not appear more fully in the Bible?

The answer, as the Loeb genealogy also says, is Ezra's reform. Ezra, seeking to purify Israel's genealogies, effectively introduced the rule that to be Israelite both your father and your mother must be Israelite. This broke with former practice, which required only the father to be of Israelite descent. And so, in Ezra's time, those returnees to Jerusalem who wished to continue as part of the Israelite community had to put away their foreign wives and children. This would have included Zerubbabel, who would have divorced his non-Jewish wives and their children would have been discounted from his genealogy. Indeed, the Loeb tree confirms this, saying, 'Ezra "The Prophet", during his reforms (458 BC), ruled in favor of the descendants of Zorobabel by his Jewish wife' (§ 54). It adds that his Persian wife remarried.

Zerubbabel's sons by his Jewish wife, Esthra, were Meshullam and Hananiah. They were the progenitors of the two post-exilic dynasties of Judean kings—the prince or *nasi* who ruled under the Persians as governor in Jerusalem, and the Resh G'lutha or Exilarch who ruled over the Jewish exiles in Mesopotamia. Meanwhile Abiud and Rhesa and their offspring lived their lives in relative obscurity.

However, the lineages of the Jerusalem *nasi* and the exilarch finally dwindled into silence. Hillel and his descendants, from the late first century BC into the first and second centuries AD, made much of their maternal descent from David, but there was no corresponding claimant for the paternal line from Meshullam. It is likely that many of them were extinguished in the purges of the Hasmoneans and Herod.

Perhaps the last member of Meshullam's patrilineal line was the messianic claimant Simon of Perea, who crowned himself king, with popular support, and conquered Jericho and its region, burning and plundering Herod's palaces there. But his troops were defeated and he was slain by the commander of the opposing Roman army.[18] Josephus calls him a 'royal slave' and 'bandit' who thought himself more worthy of kingship than anyone else, and crowned himself king. But 'bandit' was Josephus's term for anyone who rose against his Roman patrons.[19] It is likely that this Simon was of royal blood, as Tacitus implies, saying he took to himself the title of king (*regium nomen invaserat*) without Roman consent.[20] For it is unlikely that he would have found any Judahite support unless he had some valid claim to David's throne.

As for the exilarchate, the best record—the Loeb tree—is uncertain on dates and names throughout this period, giving only fifteen rulers from the fifth century BC to the third century AD.

It therefore seems that, by the late first century BC, the lines of Meshullam and Hananiah had expired and the only surviving paternal lines of the house of David were those of Abiud and Rhesa, begotten through foreign wives. Yet, according to the Loeb genealogy, these two lines, though discounted in Ezra's reform, actually had the better claim to the throne. Abiud was the firstborn, from Zerubbabel's first wife, and thus, according to the law of Moses (Deut 21:15–17), the lawful heir to the throne. And Rhesa, Zerubbabel's second son, born of his second wife, had precedence over Meshullam and Hananiah, the sons of his third wife.

[18] Josephus lists Simon's uprising among events after Herod's death. This agrees with Tacitus (*Hist.* 5:9) who says Simon rebelled at Herod's death and was subdued by Quintilius Varus. But Josephus says it was quelled by Gratus 5 (*Ant.* 17:10:6), who looks like Valerius Gratus, Prefect of Judah from 15 to 26 AD. The best solution is to place Simon early, and assume an earlier Gratus or Josephus's confusion of Varus and Gratus. The other option, that Tacitus is wrong, is less likely, for both writers point to Simon's uprising taking place after Herod's death.

[19] Josephus, *Ant.* 17:10:6; *War* 2:4:2.

[20] Tacitus, History 5:9.

JOSEPH'S TWO FATHERS

When we arrive at the end of the New Testament genealogies, we again meet one person, Joseph, who seems to have two fathers, Jacob and Heli. This is usually explained in one of two ways: either by levirate marriage—as with Shealtiel and Zerubbabel—or Marian genealogy.

Levirate marriage is by far the older explanation. It derives from Sextus Julius Africanus who was born in Jerusalem around AD 160. He said that the descendants of James the brother of the Lord told him how they had preserved their own genealogical records when Herod burned the temple records. They explained Joseph's two fathers to him as follows:

> Matthan and Melchi, having taken the same woman to wife in succession, begot children who were uterine brothers, as the law did not prevent a widow, whether such by divorce or by the death of her husband, from marrying another. By Estha, then—for such is her name according to tradition—Matthan first, the descendant of Solomon, begets Jacob; and on Matthan's death, Melchi, who traces his descent back to Nathan, being of the same tribe but of another family, having married her, as has been already said, had a son Heli. Thus, then, we shall find Jacob and Heli uterine brothers, though of different families. And of these, the one Jacob having taken the wife of his brother Heli, who died childless, begot by her the third, Joseph—his son by nature and by account. Whence also it is written, And Jacob begot Joseph. But according to law he was the son of Heli, for Jacob his brother raised up seed to him.
>
> Matthan, descended from Solomon, begot Jacob. Matthan dying, Melchi, descended from Nathan, begot Heli by the same woman. Thus Heli and Jacob are uterine brothers. Heli dying childless, Jacob raised up seed to him, begetting Joseph, his own son by nature, but by law the son of Heli. Thus Joseph was the son of both (Africanus, *Letter to Aristides* 3:6).

Africanus's account was influential among the church fathers.[21] But it has its own challenges. It makes Melchi the father of Heli, whereas Luke makes Matthat the father of Heli and Melchi the great-grandfather. But this can be explained if we allow that Matthat bore his grandfather's name, Matthat-Melchi. Papponymics—taking one's grandfather's name—were not uncommon. Meanwhile, the fact that Africanus's list is not a carbon copy of Luke's supports his claim that

[21] Eusebius, *History* 1:7; 7:15; Augustine, *Harmony of the Gospels*, 2.

he got his information elsewhere. And again, the information that the wife both of Matthan and of Melchi was named Estha could only have come from a genealogical source in the Holy Land. So, all in all, even after eighteen centuries, Africanus's account is still the best we've got.

Figure 5. Zerubbabel to Joseph according to Africanus

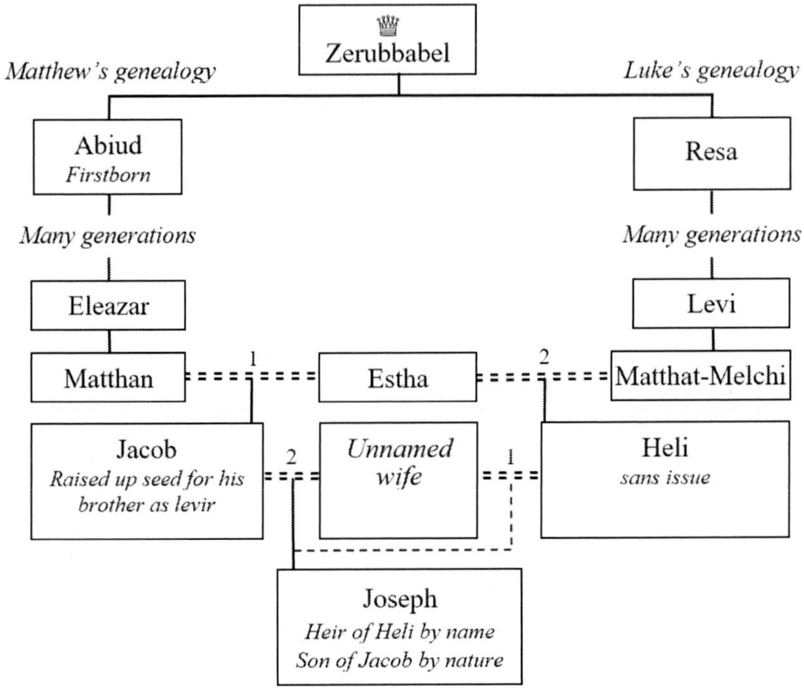

Zerubbabel

Matthew's genealogy

Luke's genealogy

Abiud
Firstborn

Resa

Many generations

Many generations

Eleazar

Levi

Matthan

1

Estha

2

Matthat-Melchi

Jacob
Raised up seed for his brother as levir

2

Unnamed wife

1

Heli
sans issue

Joseph
Heir of Heli by name
Son of Jacob by nature

Marian genealogy is the view that Luke's genealogy is that of Mariam. We hear of something like it in the fourth century when Hilary of Poitiers says, in his commentary on Matthew, 'Many are of the opinion that the genealogy which Matthew lists is to be ascribed to Joseph and the genealogy listed by Luke is to be ascribed to Mariam.' But he does not say who these 'many' are or in what sense they ascribe Luke's genealogy to Mariam. It is likely that they held a view like that of John of Damascus, as we shall see. But, for Hilary himself, both Matthew and Luke give Joseph's genealogy.

John of Damascus, in the early eighth century, does say that Luke gives Mariam's genealogy. But he does not mean by this that Luke's genealogy is that of Mariam alone. He states clearly that both evangelists give genealogies of Joseph, not Mariam.

> That Joseph is descended from the tribe of David is expressly demonstrated by Matthew and Luke, the most holy evangelists. But Matthew derives Joseph from David through Solomon, while Luke does so through Nathan; while over the holy Virgin's origin both pass in silence. One ought to remember that it was not the custom of the Hebrews nor of the divine Scripture to give genealogies of women; and the law was to prevent one tribe seeking wives from another (4:14).[22]

He then endorses Africanus's account of the divergent genealogies. But he adds a detail absent from Africanus, namely, that Melchi was the brother of Panther who was an ancestor of Mariam.

> And of the line of Solomon, the son of David, Matthan had a wife of whom he begat Jacob. Now on the death of Matthan, Melchi, of the tribe of Nathan, the son of Levi and brother of Panther, married the wife of Matthan, Jacob's mother, of whom he begat Heli.

Then after describing Joseph's descent, just as in Africanus, he adds:

> Born then of the line of Nathan, the son of David, Levi begat Melchi and Panther: Panther begat Bar Panther, so called. This Bar Panther begat Joakim. Joakim begat the holy Mother of God.

So John does not say that Luke is giving only Mariam's genealogy. Rather, he says that Luke's genealogy is Mariam's insofar as her paternal descent from David is the same as Joseph's until Levi ben Melchi, then they diverge. We will look at this in the next chapter.

Annio's Marian genealogy. A quite different view altogether is that Luke's genealogy is exclusively a genealogy of Mariam, and so Luke's Heli was Mariam's father, not Joseph's. This view first appears in the writings of the Dominican friar Annio da Viterbo in 1502. Annio produces an entirely new reading of Luke 3:23. Until Annio's time, Heli was seen as Joseph's father, and *being supposed* meant virgin-conceived Jesus was thought to have come from Joseph and Heli.

> Jesus...being (as supposed) son of Joseph, son of Heli...

[22] *The Orthodox Faith* 4.14. Jerome too says, 'Since Joseph is not the father of our Lord and Saviour, how does a genealogy coming down to Joseph pertain in any way to our Lord? To this we reply, first, that it is not the custom of the Scriptures that the category of women be woven into genealogies; secondly, that Joseph and Mary were from one tribe: whence by law he was obliged to receive her as a near relative, and they were registered together in the census in Bethlehem, as having sprung from one tribe.' (On Matt. 1:18 [PL, 26:24])

But Annio said Heli was Mariam's father and Jesus his grandson.

> Jesus...being (as supposed a son of Joseph) the-[grand]son-of Heli, *etc.*

Now this is an odd reading of the Greek by any standard. But it came easily to Annio, for he was no linguist.

Annio then says Heli is the same person as Joakim, Mariam's father in the Protoevangelium of James. Joakim, says Annio, was otherwise called Eliakim, the divine name (Jo/Yo) being substituted for the generic word for God (El), as with King Eliakim-Jehoiakim (2 Kgs 23:34). Then Eliakim in turn became Eli who became Heli.

But while Eli and Heli may be swappable in Annio's Renaissance-period Latin, they are not remotely so in Hebrew. In fact, Annio is confusing two quite distinct Hebrew words.

1. *ᵉli* (אֱלִי) 'my God', a prefix to names like Elijah, Elisha, and Eliakim, but never a name in itself. It begins with the consonant *alef* and the short *e*-vowel *ḥataf seghol.* It enters the Septuagint as HΛI (*ēli*)—Elijah (Eliyahu), for instance, is HΛIOY (*ēliou*)—and becomes ELIAS in the Latin Vulgate which Annio read.
2. *'ēli* (עֵלִי) 'Ascent', the name of the rejected priest of Shiloh (1 Sam. 1–3). It begins with the consonant *ayin* followed by the long *ē*-vowel *tsere.* In Luke's Greek, which has no sound equivalent to *ayin*, it is again written HΛI (*ēli*). Then it enters the Latin Vulgate as HELI, the H being an attempt to represent Hebrew *ayin.*

So Annio thinks Joakim was otherwise Eliakim, which became Eli. But no Hebrew would ever call anyone Eli (אלי) as a short form of Eliakim. Eli, beginning with *alef*, means 'my God'. To call a person such a name would be unthinkable. Annio is confusing it with 'Eli (עלי), beginning with the quite different consonant *ayin.* That is certainly a name. But it is quite different. The initial Hebrew consonant and vowel sound different. It is not a contraction of Eliakim or anything else. It is impossible that Heli should come from Eliakim.

Meanwhile, Luke confirms elsewhere the plain sense of Luke 3:23, tracing Jesus's descent from Joseph. For he speaks repeatedly of Joseph being of the house of David and says nothing of Mariam's ancestry.

> In the sixth month the angel Gabriel was sent from God to a city of Galilee named Nazareth, to a virgin betrothed to a man whose name was Joseph, of the house of David. The virgin's name was Mariam (Luke 1:27–28).

> And Joseph also went up from Galilee, from the city of Nazareth, to Judea, to the city of David, which is called Bethlehem, because he was of the house and lineage of David (Luke 2:4).

It's not that Luke has nothing to say about Mariam's origins. He says she is related to the priesthood (Luke 1:5, 36). But she is not the subject of his genealogy. As John of Damascus said, 'It is not the custom of the Hebrews to give genealogies of women.' Or as Didon said,

> All Jewish genealogies are constructed by the succession of heirs male, and nothing could be more improbable than the notion that Matthew, the Evangelist of Palestine, and Luke, the Hellenic Evangelist, should, in drawing up a Jewish genealogy, have discarded the usage of their nation from which they were borrowing their tables.[23]

Apart from his theory of Marian genealogy, Annio's scholarly output—marked by forgeries and fabrications—is discredited. It is a pity that his theory of Marian genealogy should still be so widespread.

SUMMARY

The divergent genealogies of Matthew and Luke both pertain to Joseph, the husband of Mariam.

Matthew first traces the line of royal succession from Solomon. But, since Solomon's descendants, Jehoiakim and his son Jeconiah, were cursed by Jeremiah (22:30; 36:30), the Messiah could not be a genetic descendant of that royal line.

Luke traces the line of genetic descent, from Nathan, through the marriage of Neri and Josiah's granddaughter, Tamar. In their offspring, adopted by Jeconiah, the genetic line of Nathan became the line of royal succession. From this line sprang Joseph of Nazareth. From this line too, as we shall see, sprang Mariam on her father's side.

Thus the words of the prophets were fulfilled. Even before the first reproaches fell on Solomon's line (1 Kgs 11.1–13), a promise was given to preserve a lamp (*ner*) for David (Ps. 132.17;[24] 1 Kgs 11.36), a promise later fulfilled in Neri ('my lamp' or 'lamp of YHVH').[25] Isaiah,

[23] Didon, *Jesus Christ*, 2:429.

[24] For the date of Ps. 132, see my *Songs of Ascents*, chap. 4, where I show it must date from not later than the early years of Solomon's reign.

[25] Neri is perhaps short for Neriah, *i.e.*, 'Lamp of Yah (YHVH)'.

foreseeing the fall of Solomon's tree, foretold a shoot to spring from Jesse's stump (Isa. 11:11); that is, new growth sprung from another son of the same root, from Nathan. The Lord raised up, in place of the cursed tree of Jeconiah and Jehoiakim, a righteous branch for David (Jer. 23:5–6; cf. 22:30; 36:30). The signet ring plucked off in Jeconiah (Jer. 22:24) became the signet ring put on in Zerubbabel (Hag. 2:23), who was not a patrilineal descendant of Solomon or his cursed kings, but of Nathan.

There are many complexities in unravelling these genealogies. But we need not conclude, as some do, that they are fictional or hopelessly corrupt. The Evangelists had access to genealogical tables. They were preserved not only by James and Jude and the family of Joseph, but also by Mariam and her relatives. The evangelists must have been in a position to justify these genealogies, for their readers were knowledgeable and jealous of their pedigrees.

The two genealogies are reconciled by two premisses. First, that Jeconiah married the widow of Neri and adopted Neri's children as his own. Second, that Africanus's account is correct in the matter of the levirate marriage leading to the birth of Joseph of Nazareth.

Jacques Masson, in his detailed research on the genealogies of Matthew and Luke, deduced, without the Loeb genealogy, that the solution to Zerubbabel's two fathers must be a princess of Solomon's line marrying into Nathan's line. But taking the Loeb genealogy into account reveals the identity of this pivotal woman who joined two dynasties: she was Tamar, the daughter of Johanan ben Josiah.

Genealogy is always complex, just as truth is stranger than fiction. (Fiction is from the mind of man, but truth from the mind of God.) But, for those willing to accept, the genealogies of Matthew and Luke are not only reconcilable, but contain the solution as to how the Messiah's descent bypasses the prophets' curses on the kings of Solomon's line.

8

Princess Mariam

MARIAM too, like her husband and her son, gets tarred with the 'peasant' brush. Even by the faithful. R.C. Sproul wrote of the Holy Spirit 'overshadowing a peasant virgin'.[1] John White, a British-Canadian evangelical, wrote of 'God coming into the world through the uterus of a Jewish peasant girl.' Even five hundred years ago, Luther said of her, in his sermon on the Annunciation, 'Among the downtrodden people she was one of the lowliest, not a maid of high station in the capital city, but a daughter of a plain man in a small town.'

Nor are these charges new. They were voiced, at least by pagans, as far back as the second century, when lowly birth meant lowly worth. Then Celsus wrote, 'It is not likely that God would have fallen in love with her since she was neither wealthy nor of royal birth. For nobody knew her, not even her neighbours', for she was 'a poor woman of the country, who gained her subsistence by spinning'.[2]

But Mariam was no more a peasant than Joseph. This is plain enough if we accept Matthew's genealogy of Joseph. Princes don't usually marry peasants. Rarely even now. And more rarely still back then. Joseph's betrothal to Mariam, as recorded by Matthew and Luke (Matt. 1:18; Luke 1:27), would have been sanctioned on all sides before the appearance of her pregnancy. Joseph's clan thought Mariam a suitable match for the apparent heir of the house of David. Mariam's

[1] Sproul, *Glory of Christ*, 31.
[2] Origen, *Contra Celsum*, I:28.

family were of a status that could secure such a match. She was not a peasant but a princess.

PRINCESS MARIAM OF THE HOUSE OF DAVID

Mariam, unlike Joseph, does not have her genealogy recorded in any systematic manner. It was not Hebrew custom to record women's genealogies. But evidence for her genealogy can still be found.

It is found, first, in those New Testament passages which speak of Jesus being born of Mariam alone—that is, virgin-born—yet also of the seed of David. So, for instance, Luke says Gabriel tells Mariam that the son she is to conceive by the Holy Spirit will inherit the throne of his father David. Since the child is to be conceived without human father, his descent can only be through Mariam herself, making her a descendant of David.

Paul doesn't speak directly of Jesus being virgin-born. Yet he did say Jesus was the pre-existent, firstborn son of God, co-creator of all things, enthroned on high, God's son sent forth, *born of a woman*, to save the world, like the 'seed of the woman' of Genesis 3:15, the promised saviour, who is not of the seed of man.[3] With such a view, he must surely have believed Jesus's conception was no human matter. And so when he says Jesus was born *of the seed* (ek spermatos) *of David according to the flesh* (Rom. 1:3; cf. 2 Tim. 2:8), he too is implying Jesus's descent from David via Mariam.

The author of Hebrews shares the same high view of Jesus as Paul does. He calls Jesus the pre-existent son of God, maker of all things, exalted in heaven (Heb. 1:1–3), implying a miraculous conception. Then he says *Our Lord descended from the tribe of Judah* (7:14), which again must imply Judahite descent from Mariam.

Early Christian writers are explicit about this. The Protoevangelium of James tells how Mariam was chosen from 'the undefiled virgins of the house of David' (§10). Ignatius wrote, 'Jesus Christ, was, according to the appointment of God, conceived in the womb by Mariam of the seed of David, but by the Holy Ghost' (Eph. 18). Justin Martyr (100–165) speaks of his birth by the virgin who was 'of the family of David, and Jacob, and Isaac, and Abraham' (*Dial.* 100). And Irenaeus (c. 140-

[3] 1 Cor. 8:6; Phil. 2:5–10; Col. 1:15–20; Rom. 8:3; 1 Cor. 15:25–7; Gal. 4:4.

202) says that when God promised David he would raise up from the fruit of his belly an eternal King (cf. Ps. 132:11), it 'is the same one who was born of the Virgin, herself of the lineage of David' (*Adv. Haer.* 3:21). Tertullian (155–240) says 'the root of Jesse is the family of David, and the stem of the root is Mariam descended from David, and the blossom of the stem is Mariam's son, who is called Jesus Christ' (*Flesh of Christ* 21; cf. *Adv. Jud.* 9). Augustine (354–430) says 'The evangelists assert that Christ was born of a woman of the seed of David' (*Contra Faustum* 5:4). Eusebius (c. 263–339), followed by John of Damascus, took a different tack. He states that, since the Israelites were to marry within their tribe, Joseph's descent from David proves Mariam's too.[4]

Eusebius perhaps overstates the case. Except when the inheritance fell to daughters, the Israelites were free to marry with other tribes. It was the confines of Iron Age life that curbed inter-tribal marriage. Josephus insists that it was the practice of the *kohanim* to marry only within their own clan. But, in reality, the *kohanim*, scattered among Israel, without family lands, did intermarry. Aaron took the daughter of the Judahite chief Amminadab. And, in temple times, when Judahites and Levites lived in Jerusalem, such marriages were not unusual. The priest Jehoiada, for instance, married the daughter of King Jehoram.[5] Later, the Hasmonean priest-kings had a settled policy of intermarriage with the tribe of David so as to cement their claim to the throne.

Yet, one way or another, the idea that Mariam descended from David was well established in the early church.

Mariam's Davidic Lineage

If we seek more detail about Mariam's genealogy, our earliest source is the Protoevangelium of James. Since the Protoevangelium was known to Origen, in the early third century, its date of composition is usually given as the mid-second century. However, as we shall see in the next chapter, it may well be earlier.

The Protoevangelium says Mariam was 'of the house of David'. She

[4] Eusebius, *History*, I:7; John of Damascus (676–749), *Orthodox Faith*, 4:14.

[5] B. Ber. 10a, cf. 2 Kgs 21:1; 2 Chr. 22:11. Cf. also 2 Chr. 27:1 for Uzziah.

was the only child of her father, a wealthy and pious man called Joakim, and of her mother, Anna, and she was born to them in their old age, in the town of Sepphoris, six kilometres north-west of Nazareth, before Sepphoris became the playground of Herod Antipas.

More information on Mariam's Davidic lineage is found in two later texts, a seventh-century Jewish text called *The Teaching of Jacob* and the eighth-century testimony of John of Damascus. Taken together their testimony is significant.

The *Teaching of Jacob* (*Didaskalia Iakobou*) is a debate between a group of Jews in Byzantine Palestine. One of them, Jacob, says he thought Mohamed was the promised prophet, until he saw the destruction wrought by him. At that point he felt that Jews had indeed missed the Messiah. He confided to his fellows that he was inclined to believe the Christian faith, though he still had doubts. On the basis of internal historical references, the text is thought to date from about AD 634. Jacob's remarks include an account of Mariam's ancestry.

> But why do Christians extol Mariam so highly, calling her nobler than the cherubim, incomparably greater than the seraphim, raised above the heavens, purer than the very rays of the sun? For she was a woman, of the race of David, born to Anne her mother and Joakim her father, who was the son of Panther. Panther and Melchi were brothers, sons of Levi, of the stock of Nathan, whose father was David of the tribe of Judah.[6]

Some think the *Teaching of Jacob* was a Christian work designed for Jewish proselytization. They imagine perhaps that no Jews ever leaned to the Christian faith in the seventh century, nor ever spoke Greek in Byzantine Palestine. But to me it looks Jewish. I cannot imagine that its comments on Mariam came from the hand of a Byzantine patriarch. They seem to reflect the lower Jewish view of women. But, whoever wrote it, they spoke as if they knew about Mariam's genealogy.

The confirmation of this genealogy appears in John of Damascus. After citing Africanus's account of Joseph's dual descent from Jacob and Heli, John too says that Mariam descended from Joseph's ancestors Levi and Panther.

> Born then of the line of Nathan, the son of David, Levi begat Melchi and Panther: Panther begat Barpanther, so called. This Barpanther

[6] Text in Dagron and Déroche, 'Juifs et Chrétiens'; Bonwetsch, 'Doctrina Iacobi'.

> begat Joakim: Joakim begat the holy Mother of God. (*On the Orthodox Faith*, 4:14)

So the *Teaching of Jacob* and John of Damascus present pretty much the same genealogy. There is just one difference. The *Teaching of Jacob* says Joakim is the son of Panther, in which case, Joakim is Bar Panther. But John of Damascus says Joakim is the grandson of Panther, via his father, Bar Panther. If John is right, then Joseph and Mariam share a great-grandfather, Levi, and they are levirate second cousins. But if the *Teaching of Jacob* is right, then Levi is Joseph's great-grandfather and Mariam's great-great-grandfather and they are levirate second cousins once removed.[7]

Following these sources, here then is the genealogy of Mariam and Joseph from Zerubbabel. To follow John of Damascus, rather than the *Teaching*, one must insert Bar Panther between Panther and Joakim.

Figure 6. The patrilineal descent of Mariam from Zerubbabel

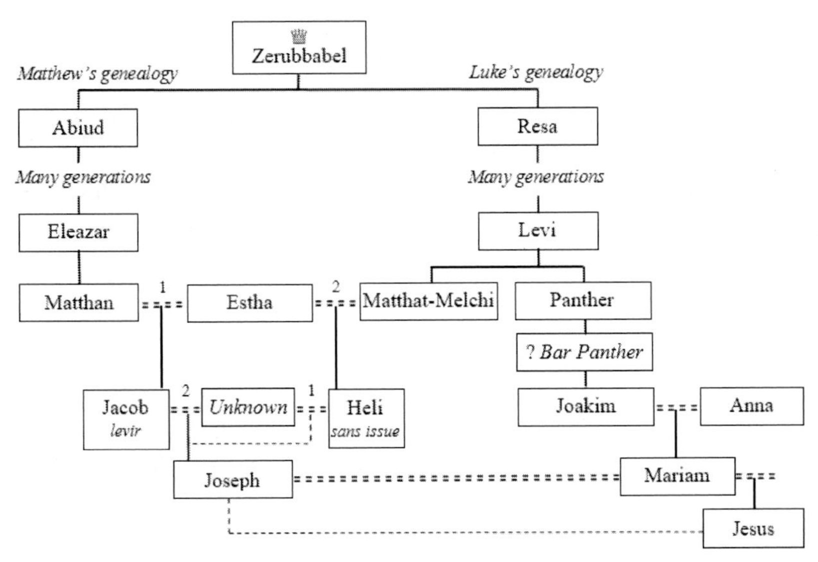

Did John of Damascus know the *Teaching of Jacob*? I think not. For if he drew his genealogy directly from the Teaching, why did he omit Bar Panther as the intervening progenitor? I suspect that both John and

[7] Jerome also says, 'Joseph and Mary were from one tribe: whence by law he was obliged to receive her as a near relative, and they were registered together in the census in Bethlehem, as having sprung from one tribe.' (On Matt. 1:18 [PL, 26:24]).

the *Teaching* drew independently from traditions about Mariam's family that still existed in the east. But, certainly, the *Teaching of Jacob* refutes any notion that John of Damascus fabricated his genealogy of Mariam.

Princess Mariam of the House of Aaron

But Luke says that Mariam is also related to the house of Aaron. She was a blood-relative of Elizabeth who was a descendant of Aaron (Luke 1:5, 36). So Mariam had Zadokite as well as royal blood.

But what exactly was her kinship with Elizabeth? Well, Elizabeth and her husband Zechariah were getting on in years. But Zechariah was still in priestly service, and so must have been less than fifty (Num. 8:25). His wife was probably some years his junior. So we can place Zechariah in his mid to late forties and Elizabeth maybe around forty when she gave birth to John Baptist. Yet teenage Mariam and older Elizabeth were close enough that Mariam felt she could share with her, of all people, the news of her most surprising conception. One suspects then that she was no distant relative, but either her aunt or older cousin. So if Mariam was descended from David on her father's side, then it must have been by her mother that she was related to her Zadokite kinswoman Elizabeth. And so Mariam's mother was a Zadokite.

Mariam's Nephew: Yohanan ben Zavdai ha-Kohen

More New Testament evidence for such a view is found in John the son of Zebedee and his family. We learn, from the gospel accounts of the women at the cross (Matt. 27:56; Mark 15:40; John 19:25), that Mariam's sister, Mariam-Salome, was the wife of Zebedee and the mother of John son of Zebedee.[8] Now John seems to have been of Zadokite lineage. Nothing else can explain how he, a Galilean, was *known to the high priest*, how he got himself and Peter into the high priest's house, and how John himself was even given access to the council chamber during Jesus's trial (John 18:15–16). It also looks like

[8] Pseudo-Matthew §42 relates that the parents of Mariam-Salome gave her the same name as her sister to console them after devoting Mariam to the temple service.

John's family, like most priestly clans, had a house in Jerusalem (John 19:27). So John too, though Galilean, was no peasant.

John's Zadokite lineage is spoken of by Polycrates (*fl:150*–196). Speaking of the church leaders who taught and were buried in Asia, he says:

> And again there is John, who leant back on the Lord's breast, who became a priest (*hiereus*) wearing the diadem (*petalon*), a martyr and a teacher: he too sleeps in Ephesus (Eusebius, *History*, 3:31; 5:24).

Here *hiereus* must refer to a Jerusalem temple *kohen*. If Polycrates were speaking of a Christian 'priest' he would certainly have called him a presbyter (*presbuteros*). But, more importantly, the *petalon* was the golden diadem or frontlet of the *kohen gadol*. This requires discussion.

In everyday Greek, *petalon* was a leaf or petal or, by analogy, a thin metal plate. But in Hebraic Greek, it meant the golden plate inscribed 'Holiness to YHVH' worn on the turban of the *kohen gadol*. We first meet it in Exodus 28:36–38 where it is called the *tzitz* in Hebrew and *petalon* in the Greek Septuagint. Josephus says it was worn only by the high priest and that only one was ever made from antiquity to his own time.[9] The *tzitz* or *petalon* was said to shine on those penitents who had found acceptance with God.

> Come and hear. For what does the *tzitz* propitiate? For the blood, and for the meat, and for the fat that became impure, whether unwittingly or intentionally, whether beyond control or wilfully, whether of an individual or of a community (B. Pes. 16b).

This is similar to what we find in the Protoevangelium of James:

> And on the following day he brought his offerings, saying in himself: If the Lord God has been rendered gracious to me, the plate (*petalon*) on the priest's forehead will make it manifest to me. And Joakim brought his offerings, and observed attentively the priest's plate (*petalon*) when he went up to the altar of the Lord, and he saw no sin in himself (§5).

So when Polycrates says that John wore the *petalon* he seems to be saying that John was a *kohen gadol*. But this is hardly credible. Josephus lists all the high priests until the destruction of the temple in AD 70, and there is no John in the first century. We do meet a John in

[9] *Ant.* III.vii.6; VIII.iii.8.

the retinue of Annas in Acts 4:6. But since that John was prosecuting John son of Zebedee, they cannot be the same person.

It would be easy to conclude that Polycrates just got it wrong. Yet Epiphanius says James the Just was 'permitted to wear the *petalon*', something as hard to understand as the claim of Polycrates.[10] And Hegesippus, in the second century, says James had access to the temple sanctuary, something forbidden to all except the *kohanim.*[11]

Therefore, since Polycrates and Epiphanius both make the same claim, we must at least concede that they knew what they meant. I suspect they are saying that John and James were of a family associated with the high-priestly office. There is a parallel in the way that first-century writers refer to all males of the high-priestly family as *archiereis* or 'high priests'.[12] In other words, John and James were from the highest-ranking Zadokite families.

Now, if John was a *kohen*, he could have received the *k'hunah* only by virtue of his descent. It is likely that both his father, Zebedee, and his mother, Salome, were descendants of Aaron. For, by this period, matrilineal descent had become essential. And since his mother was Mariam's sister, this would again suggest Mariam's Zadokite lineage.

As to how James the Just received *k'hunah* status and access to the temple, who can say? It was not through his father, Joseph of Nazareth, who was of the house of David. Yet access to temple privileges was never hermetically sealed. The Nethinim, of Canaanite stock, worked there.[13] The Recabites, of Kenite descent, 'stood before' the Lord there (1 Chron. 2.55; Jer. 35:19). There was even a *goy* who passed himself off as a *kohen* to gorge on the temple sacrifices, until he was discovered and put to death (Pes. 3b). So perhaps James's royal descent allowed him access to the temple, the more so if his mother, Joseph's first wife, of whom nothing is known, was of Aaronite stock.

Mariam's Zadokite Lineage

Another surprising testimony to Mariam's Zadokite lineage comes from the fourth-century Manichaean bishop Faustus. Manichaeism was

[10] *Panarion* 29:4:4.
[11] So Eusebius, 2:23.
[12] BDAG, p. 139.
[13] On the Nethinim, see Chapter 9 of my *Songs of Ascents.*

a form of Christianized Zoroastrianism first propounded by Mani in third-century Persia. It was influential in its time, though it is now remembered more as the former faith of Augustine of Hippo. Augustine wrote a polemical tract directed against Faustus in which he represents Faustus speaking as follows:

> Moreover, the Virgin herself appears to have belonged not to the tribe of Judah, to which the Jewish kings belonged, and which all agree was David's tribe, but to the priestly tribe of Levi. This appears from the fact that the Virgin's father Joakim was a priest; and his name does not occur in the genealogy. How, then, can Mary be brought within the pale of relationship to David, when she has neither father nor husband belonging to it? Consequently, Mary's son cannot possibly be the son of David, unless you can bring the mother into some connection with Joseph, so as to be either his wife or his daughter. (*Con. Faust.* 23:4)

The question of Joakim's descent is one we investigate in the next chapter. But Faustus had evidently heard of Mariam's priestly descent.

Later, the eastern Fathers relate the Zadokite lineage of Mariam's mother Anna. Hippolytus of Thebes, in the seventh century, wrote:

> For there were three sisters of Bethlehem, daughters of Matthan the priest and of Maria [*sic.*] his wife, in the reign of Cleopatra and Casparis of Persia, before the kingdom of Herod son of Antipater. The first was Mariam, the second Sobe, and the name of the third was Anna. The first, Mariam, married in Bethlehem and gave birth to Salome the midwife. And then the second, Sobe, married in Bethlehem, and bore Elizabeth. Last of all, the third, Anna, married in the land of Galilee, and brought forth Mariam, the Mother of God, from whom sprang forth to us Christ the Truth.[14]

This teaching dates from six centuries after New Testament times. Yet the historical note about the reigns of Cleopatra, 'Casparis'—probably Mithridates the Great or Pharnaces II—and Herod argues in its favour. These names would have meant little to Hippolytus's seventh-century Theban hearers, but would have been important to first or second century Jews. Their preservation here suggests that this derives from an old Palestinian teaching. Likewise, the name of Sobe (Σόϐη) looks

[14] The original text of Hippolytus' *Chronicle* is lost. The passage is cited in Nicephorus Callistus (*fl.* 1300–1320), *Historia Ecclesiastica* II.3 (*Patrologiae Graeca* [*PG*] 145:760). Cf. Andrew of Crete (c. 650–c. 725) (*PG* 97:1325); Epiphanius Monachus (8th–9th C.) (*PG* 120:189); Andronikos Komnenos (*fl.* 1150–1180) (*PG* 133:860).

genuine. It is an unusual name altogether, not figuring in the Greek Bible or anywhere else I know of.[15] If Hippolytus had just invented this tradition, he would surely have chosen a more obvious name.

If we extract the historical details, the three sisters grew up in the reign of Cleopatra (51–30 BC), before Herod became king of Judah (40 or 39 BC), that is, in the period 51–40 BC. If this was when they grew and married, they would have been born the decade before. Luke records that Elizabeth was a mature primagravida (1:7, 18). The Protoevangelium of James says the same of Anna and adds that Mariam gave birth to Jesus at the age of sixteen. Meanwhile, a rather later work, the *Infancy Gospel of Matthew* (*The Book About the Origin of the Blessed Mary and the Childhood of the Savior*), based on the Protoevangelium of James, says Anna give birth after 20 years of marriage. We can therefore estimate their dates very roughly as follows.

- Mariam, born 61 BC, gave birth at age 30, in 31 BC, to Salome the midwife. Salome married Zavdai (Zebedee) and gave birth at age 30 to James, in 1 BC, and then to John, in AD 1.
- Sobe, born 60 BC, gave birth to Elizabeth at age 17, in 43 BC. Elizabeth married Zechariah and gave birth, at age 40, to John Baptist, in 3 BC.
- Anna, born 58 BC, gave birth to Mariam at age 40, in 18 BC. Mariam gave birth to Jesus at age 16, in 2 BC.

If these dates are roughly correct, then we may suppose that Matthan, the father of the three sisters, was born between 90 and 80 BC. The name Matthan—and its variants, Mattathiah, Matthai, Matthat, Matthias—was popular among the Hasmonean *kohanim*, in honour of their progenitor, Mattathias the *kohen* of Modi'in. Josephus records four people called Matthias in his own Hasmonean genealogy, namely, his brother, his father, and two ancestors, Matthias Curtus and Matthias Ephilas.[16] The last of these married the sister of Judah Maccabee, whose brothers, Jonathan and Simon were high priests. It is likely, as we shall see, that Mariam's maternal descent was from the same Zadokite aristocracy.

[15] If Hebrew, its origin might be *tsvi* (צבי), 'gazelle', or perhaps *so<u>b</u>a'* (שבע) 'abundance'. In Greek, Σόϐη means 'horse-tail' (Liddell & Scott, *Lexicon*, p. 1367). Noble Greek names often allude to horses—Archippus, Hippocrates, Hippolytus, Philippos, Xanthippe—but Sobe remains unusual.

[16] *Ant.* 1:1:1–2.

We can therefore represent Mariam's descent, from David on her father's side, and from Aaron on her mother's, in a genealogical chart as follows.

Figure 7. Mariam's Descent from David and Aaron

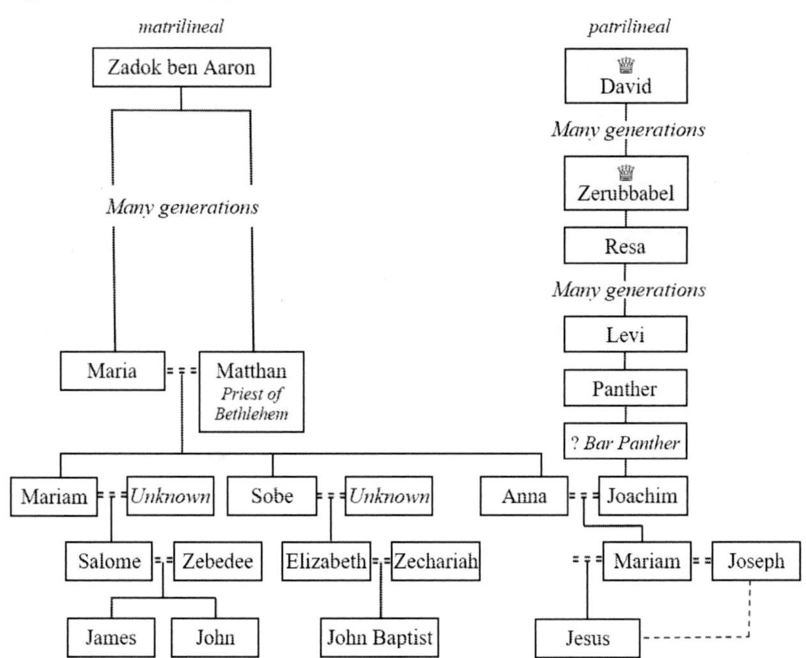

Princess Mariam of David and Aaron in the Twelve Testaments

What we have seen so far suggests that Mariam was descended both from David's tribe of Judah and from Aaron's tribe of Levi. A couple of texts confirm this more clearly. One is from an old Hebrew compilation, The Testaments of the Twelve Patriarchs. The other is from the Talmud.

The Testaments of the Twelve Patriarchs is a compendium of twelve discourses spoken in the persons of the twelve sons of Jacob. The best texts of the Testaments are in Greek. But incomplete Hebrew and Aramaic texts also exist, showing that they are of Israelite origin and were probably first written in Hebrew.

There is much dispute over when the Testaments were written. They used to be seen as second-century BC Jewish texts.[17] But, in the mid-twentieth century, the idea arose that they are Christian texts from the second century AD, loosely based on Jewish material.[18] This new view has become popular. But there are many who still accept the older view.[19] For there is simply too much in the Testaments that doesn't look Christian, while even some passages that are labelled Christian are quite explicable as later Jewish ideas. It is a debate we cannot resolve here. But let us allow two passages from the Testaments to speak for themselves. In this first passage, the bracketed words are sometimes regarded as Christian interpolation.

> And now, my children, obey Levi and Judah, and be not lifted up against these two tribes, for from them shall arise unto you the salvation of God. For the Lord shall raise up from Levi as it were a High-priest, and from Judah as it were a King [God and man]. He shall save all [the Gentiles and] the race of Israel. (T. Simeon 7:1–2)

From Levi and Judah shall arise *the salvation of God*, a frequent title for the Messiah.[20] This *salvation of God* is a high-priest and a king. But both figures are spoken of with a singular pronoun—*He shall save.* And so the one Messiah is both priest and king, from Levi and from Judah.

The Testament of Joseph makes the same point more clearly still.

> And I saw that a virgin was born from Judah, wearing a linen stole. And from her was born a spotless lamb...Honour Levi and Judah, because from their seed will arise the Lamb of God who will take away the sin of the world, and will save all the nations, as well as Israel. (T. Joseph 19:8, 11).

Both texts speak of the Messiah's descent from Levi and Judah. But the Testament of Joseph says that both lines are from his mother.

Of course, given the complex question of dating the Testaments, we cannot say for sure whether these are pre-Christian texts looking forward or early Christian texts looking back. My view is that they are the former and that the Israelites, on the basis of biblical prophecy,

[17] Following Charles 1908 and 1913, though the origins of the Testaments had been disputed since the 17th century.

[18] So de Jonge 1953; 1964; 1991; cf. Hollander 1985: 73–74; VanderKam 2001:100.

[19] De Bruin 2015; Toepel 2005; Kugel 1995; Kee 1983; Thomas 1969; Philonenko 1958–59; van der Woude 1957; Dupont-Sommer 1952; Bickerman 1950 regard the Testaments as essentially Jewish.

[20] See chapter 13.

foresaw the dual lineage of the Messiah before he was born. But, for those who prefer the latter view, the text testifies to early Christian belief in Mariam's dual descent from David and Aaron.

PRINCESS MARIAM OF DAVID AND AARON IN THE TALMUD

Finally, lest anyone imagine that Mariam's descent from Judah and Levi is only Christian fantasy, the Talmud comes to our defence. Rav Pappa, a fourth-century sage, head of the *yeshivah* in Nehardea by Babylon, knew about Mariam's genealogy.

> R. Pappa observed: This is what they say, '[The child] of *segans* and rulers, she played the harlot with carpenters.' (B. Sanh. 106a).

The passage appears amidst a discussion about Balaam ben Beor—the diviner of Numbers 23 and 24—who led Israel astray. But there is good reason to think that 'Balaam' here means Jesus. The rabbis often hid the identity of their opponents by referring to them in the persona of a foe they were thought to resemble. Rome, for instance, was routinely called Edom, for the two names look similar in Hebrew and the Romans destroyed the second temple as the Edomites helped to destroy the first.[21] In the same way, Jesus is called Balaam, for Balaam was a seducer of Israel—leading them astray with Moabite women—and Jesus was said to have led Israel from the path of rectitude.[22]

We see this confirmed earlier on the same page of Talmud. R. Shimon ben Lakish says of this 'Balaam', 'Woe to him who makes himself live (*še-m'ḥayeh 'atsmo*) by the name of God.' Some argue that this means that Balaam the sorcerer made himself a living by the sacred name.[23] But that completely understates the force of *m'ḥayeh*—'cause to live'. It's a Bible word. It first appears in Hannah's prophecy of the resurrection of the dead.

> YHVH kills and makes live (*m'ḥayeh*)
> He brings down to Sheol and raises up. (1 Sam. 2:6)

Later, the Levites pray,

[21] Roma (רומא) and Edom (אדום). Cf. Ps. 137:7; Obad. 1–20.

[22] See Herford, *Christianity in the Talmud*, 48.

[23] See the William Davidson Talmud. The Soncino translation is more accurate: 'Woe unto him who maketh himself alive by the name of God.'

> You alone are he, YHVH. You made the heavens, the heaven of heavens, and all their host, the earth and all upon it, the seas and all within them. You give life (*m'ḥayeh*) to all, and the host of heaven worships you. (Neh. 9:6)

In other words, *m'ḥayeh* means to give life to something that has no life, things dead or not-yet-existing. The medieval rabbi Rashi recognized this. His commentary on the passage says: 'He made himself live by the name of God, making himself God like Pharaoh and Hiram.' But since the real Balaam neither made himself live nor made himself God, Rashi understands that this 'Balaam' is Jesus.[24]

So R. Shimon is speaking of Jesus. Of course, the rabbis never doubted Jesus's miraculous powers. The rabbinic anti-gospel, the Toldot Yeshu, tells how he performed sorcery and raised the dead by the power of the sacred name. But here, in the Talmud, R. Shimon is confessing that Jesus revived himself by the sacred name. And so is Rashi. Surely this is remarkable. Here is the core text of Rabbinic Judaism and the foremost medieval Jewish interpreter both agreeing that Jesus made himself come alive by the power of the divine Name.

Later on the same page of Talmud, a *min* (a Jew-Christian) asks R. Ḥanina, who lived in Sepphoris in Galilee, how old Balaam was.[25] Ḥanina replies that since 'bloody and deceitful men will not live out half their days' (Ps. 55:23), he must have been thirty-three or thirty-four. The *min* replies that Ḥanina is right, for he has read in 'Balaam's Chronicle' that Balaam was thirty-three years old when Pinḥas the Robber (*Pinḥas ha-lista'ah*) slew him. Now there is no 'Balaam's Chronicle' giving Balaam's age at death. Nor is there much reason why two Galileans would discuss the age of Balaam ben Beor. And although Pinḥas (Phineas) ben Eleazar ben Aaron slew Balaam, such a hero would never be described as 'Pinḥas the Robber'. This is all about Jesus and the gospels. Balaam is Jesus who died around the age of thrity-three. 'Pinḥas' is a rabbinic word-play on 'Pontius' and *lista'ah* on the slightly-assonant 'Pilatus'. R. Ḥanina is having his little joke: as Pinḥas slew Balaam, so Pinḥas-Pontius slew Balaam-Jesus.

[24] See likewise the comments of Herford, *Christianity in the Talmud*, p. 76.

[25] A *min* denotes, in theory, any sectarian Jew. But in practice it usually means a Jew-Christian, for this was the form of *minut* (heresy) best known to the rabbis. A *min* is never a non-Jew, as Rav Naḥman said, 'There are no *minim* among the gentiles' (Hul. 13b). In the Talmud, the *min* often debates with the rabbinic sage about the Christian faith.

So it's clear enough. In both these passages, 'Balaam' means Jesus. And so we can assume the same meaning when, on the same page of Talmud, Rav Pappa speaks of 'Balaam' whose mother was a child of *segans* and rulers and played the harlot with carpenters.

Segan is an Aramaic term. It originally meant any viceroy or vizier. Nehemiah and Daniel, for instance, use it for Persian government officials. But in second temple Judaism, it meant the *Segan ha-kohanim*, the deputy *kohen gadol.* This official oversaw the ministering *kohanim* and performed high-priestly functions if the *kohen gadol* became unfit for duty. In rabbinic literature, any reference to a *segan* denotes this temple high official. So Rav Pappa is speaking of a woman from the leading families of the Zadokite priestood.

She is also a child of 'rulers'. The word here is *shilton.* It's Aramaic again, and is related to the Arabic word *sultan.* It denotes a governor or ruler, as it does in Daniel 3:3. It is a word which well describes the line of David, from the kingship the whole way through the period of the Davidic princes who ruled under Persian and Greek oversight.

So the woman of whom R. Pappa speaks is certainly not the mother of Balaam ben Beor. The scriptures know nothing of Balaam's mother, nor of her relationships with carpenters, nor was she the child of *segans.* But the rabbis know all about the lineage of this woman of whom Rav Pappa speaks. So, from the context, the reference is surely to the mother of Jesus.[26]

Why then did Rav Pappa speak in such a disparaging way about Joseph? After all, as we saw in the last chapter, the rabbis knew that Jesus's family were of the royal blood. Presumably, he wished to denigrate Joseph's lineage so as to refute Jesus's messianic claim. Yet, nonetheless, he seems to regard Jesus as the son of Joseph the carpenter.

And why did he speak this way about carpenters? Pappa, like all his colleagues, praised manual work. He himself was a brewer and taught that no one in an honest profession should be snubbed: 'If you wish to talk to a wool-washer, do not be ashamed to call him at the town gate [the public meeting-place] and sit down beside him' (Yeb. 118b). So why did he condemn what he elsewhere commends? Perhaps his desire to vilify the woman overruled his better nature. And perhaps the great

[26] 'The mother of Jesus may be alluded to, which theory is strengthened by the statement that she mated with a carpenter.' (Soncino Talmud footnote).

wealth he made from brewing and sharp credit made him look down on others (Pes. 113a; B.M. 65a).

And why did he say of the woman that 'she played the harlot with carpenters'? If, as he suggests, Mariam bore Jesus to Joseph the carpenter, why was she a harlot? Did Pappa not know the law? A wife was legitimately acquired by cohabitation and sexual intercourse, even without dowry or contract (M. Kid. 1). But Pappa is determined to demean her. Denying any legitimacy to her marriage with Joseph, he imputes to her harlotry by suggesting she coupled with many men. He intends the smear of illegitimacy to pass to her child.

So Rav Pappa said Jesus was fathered by a no-name carpenter on a harlot. It's not a charitable assessment. But it was characteristic of Rav Pappa. For even his colleagues spoke of his hard and mean spirit.[27] But, in all of this, he was unwilling or unable to deny that Jesus's mother was of royal and priestly descent. The reason must surely be that her lineage was widely known in rabbinic circles. And Pappa's testimony must surely be true. For he would not willingly have credited noble birth to one he so sought to demean.

Summary

So we conclude that the evidence of the New Testament—limited though it be—suggests that Princess Mariam descended on her father's side from the royal line of David and on her mother's side from the Zadokite line of Aaron. This is confirmed by patristic writers, by the Testaments of the Twelve Patriarchs, and by the Talmud. Irenaeus sums it up nicely, saying, 'From Levi and Judah he was descended according to the flesh, as King and Priest.' (Fragment 17)

The Protoevangelium of James gives Mariam's father's name as Joakim and her mother's name as Anna (Hannah). Joakim's descent from David, according to the *Teaching of Jacob* and John of Damascus, was through David's son, Nathan, and finally through Levi, the great-grandfather of Mariam's husband Joseph.

Her mother's descent from Aaron, according to Hippolytus of Thebes, is from the priest Matthan and his wife Maria, after whom the younger Mariam, her granddaughter, was named. This couple lived in

[27] B. Git. 73a Ket. 85a; B.B. 9a, 10a.

the first half of the first century BC, before Herod came to power. Matthan would perhaps be one of the *segans* that Rav Pappa finds in Mariam's genealogy.

One may reflect that from this one couple, Matthan and Mariam, sprang John the Evangelist, John the Baptist, and Jesus the Messiah. One must surely be amazed at such fruit, which Matthan and his wife never lived to see. But, sowing in faith, they brought up their children in the fear and instruction of the Lord. Peacemakers who sow in peace reap a harvest of righteousness.

9

The Temple Virgin

IF WE WANT to know more about Mariam and Joseph than is in the gospels, we must look to the Protoevangelium of James. This Protoevangelium (or Infancy Gospel) should not be confused with other non-biblical texts like the Gospels of Thomas or Peter. These are Gnostic texts, and present a Jesus quite unlike the Jesus of the New Testament gospels.[1] But the Protoevangelium is earlier and more credible.

The Protoevangelium was always a popular text in the churches both of east and west. There are over one hundred and fifty ancient manuscripts in Greek, plus others in another dozen tongues.

Some think the text dates from the third century. But Clement of Alexandria (AD 198–203) asserts Mariam's perpetual virginity, as taught in the Protoevangelium.[2] Another Alexandrian, Celsus, calls Mariam 'a poor woman who gained her subsistence by spinning'.[3] The only known source for such an idea is again the Protoevangelium, which suggests it was circulating in Egypt in Celsus's time.[4] And a little later, Justin Martyr, in Ephesus and Rome, taught that Jesus was born in a cave (Trypho §78), another idea known only from the Protoevangelium. So it is likely that the Protoevangelium dates from the early second century or before.

[1] See Evans, 'Extracanonical Works', for the date of these texts.

[2] Clement, Stromata 7.16. For the date, see Ferguson, *Clement of Alexandria*, 17.

[3] Origen, *Cont. Celsum* I:28.

[4] Origen says Celsus 'lived in Hadrian's time and later' (*Cont. Celsum* I:8). Hadrian ruled from 117–138. For other views, see Chadwick, *Contra Celsum*, xxiv–xxix.

It claims to have been written by 'James in Jerusalem', presumably meaning James the Just, the son of Joseph, the brother of Jesus. This is often doubted. Origen declared it spurious, as did Jerome, Pope Innocent III, and Aquinas. Yet their reasons for rejecting it are not cogent. Jerome rejects it on the ground that it speaks of midwives at Jesus's birth, which he finds at odds with the gospels; Aquinas parrots Jerome and dismisses the book as 'apocryphal ravings'.[5] Meanwhile, modern writers dismiss it on the ground that it speaks of temple virgins in Jerusalem, something they claim never existed.

Yet much about the work seems to fit the time of James. For a start, although the Jerusalem temple and its rites are the backdrop to the whole book, there is not a word about the destruction of the temple in AD 70. This is striking, especially if we compare it to books written after the destruction, like 4 Ezra or the Apocalypse of Baruch. They are fixated with the question of why God allowed his temple to be destroyed. But the Protoevangelium's picture of peacefully-proceeding temple rites and its complete silence on the temple's fate suggest it was written before the destruction.

In fact, its descriptions of temple protocol look like they were written by someone familiar with temple life from the inside, as James was. There are accurate details of temple architecture. And there is its description of the virgins who lived in the temple precincts, spinning and weaving fabric for the temple.

Further, the Protoevangelium does not look at all like it is directly derived from the gospels. Jesus is born in a cave, something not mentioned in any of the gospels, yet not inconsistent with them. And it is unclear whether Joseph is engaged to Mariam to take her to wife, or simply to be her guardian. This too can be resolved with the gospels, but it certainly does not derive from them. The text purports to have been composed by an eyewitness of the events, an eyewitness who cannot possibly have been any of the other four evangelists. Indeed, it claims that Joseph's sons were present at the birth. If that is so, James was uniquely placed to give the account of the birth which the Protoevangelium records.

My view then is that the Protoevangelium deserves more credence than it has often received. Let's look at it in more detail.

[5] Jerome, Adv. Helvid. 4; Aquinas, Summa Theologica, Ques. 35, Art. 6.

THE PROTOEVANGELIUM OF JAMES

For now, I will summarize the Protevangelium. Then we can ask how much of it is credible. But I advise you to read it in full. It takes about fifteen minutes to read and is easily found online. Walker's translation is excellent.[6]

> Joakim (Ιωακειμ) and Anna were wealthy but childless, which brought them disgrace. They fasted and prayed for divine intervention on their behalf (§1–3). Angels appeared to them, saying they would have a child. Anna promised that the child would be dedicated to the Lord (§4). Mariam was born. When she was three years old, she was taken to the temple. She was received by the priest, who foretold that through her the Lord would send redemption to Israel. She danced on the altar steps before the Lord, and dwelt in the temple, beloved by all (§7).
>
> When she reached her twelfth year, the priests decided she must leave the temple lest, at the onset of menstruation, she defile the sanctuary. The high priest was instructed by an angel to send out heralds asking the widowers of Israel to bring their staffs to the temple, whereupon a sign would be given as to whose wife she should be (§8). Joseph brought his staff, and it gave forth a dove, showing the maiden was to be given into his safe-keeping. He, being already a father and elderly, demurred, fearing ridicule. But the priest said he should obey lest he incur divine punishment. So Joseph took Mariam into his keeping and she dwelt in his home, while he pursued his daily labour as a builder (§9).
>
> Later, after Zechariah had been struck dumb, she was summoned, from among the undefiled virgins of the house of David, to spin purple and scarlet thread for the curtain in the holy place. She took the thread home, where she spun it (§10). One day, going to draw water from the well, she was hailed by the voice of an invisible speaker. She returned home in fear. Then the archangel Gabriel appeared to her and told her she would conceive by the power of the Lord and bear the son of the Most High, who would be called Jesus (§11).
>
> She returned the spun thread to the priest, who pronounced her ever-blessed. Then she went to see Elizabeth. During her three months there, Mariam grew bigger and secluded herself from the Israelites. She was sixteen at the time (§12).
>
> She returned home. In the sixth month, Joseph saw she was big with child and suspected her of promiscuity. She insisted on her innocence (§13). Joseph made plans to put her away secretly, but was told by an angel in a dream that the child was from the Holy Spirit (§14).

[6] From *Ante-Nicent Fathers*, vol. 8. https://www.newadvent.org/fathers/0847.htm

> Annas, a scribe, noticed Mariam's condition and reported it to the priest. The priest accused Joseph of defiling the temple virgin and marrying her by stealth. But they both asserted their innocence (§15). They were given the water of ordeal to drink (cf. Num. 5:14–22), but both were unharmed by it (§16).
>
> In response to Caesar's decree, Joseph went to Bethlehem with his sons and Mariam, who rode the ass (§17). When she went into labour, he left her in a cave outside Bethlehem with his two sons, while he went to seek a midwife. In a cave just outside the city, she gave birth. At that moment—Joseph relates—all nature was still (§18). He tells the midwife that Mariam is his betrothed, obtained by lot as his wife, but the child is from the Holy Spirit (§19). Upon the midwife's inspection, Mariam was found to be a virgin after the birth of the child (§20). The Magi visited and left, as recorded by Matthew (§21). Then Herod, seeking not only Jesus but also John the son of Zechariah, slew Zechariah when he refused to reveal John's whereabouts (§22).

Such is the narrative. The question is: How far might it be true? To answer that we must first address objections. Then we can proceed to see how it might match with Matthew and Luke.

The Temple Virgin

The Protoevangelium says Mariam lived in the temple until the onset of puberty, then she continued to spin thread for the temple at home. Some say that Judaism had no role for girls living in the temple. If they are correct, then the Protoevangelium looks like a hoax. But if they are wrong, then the author had inside knowledge of temple routine.

Temple virgins were a feature of other ancient cults. In Rome, virgins were chosen from patrician families as priestesses of Vesta, goddess of the hearth, to maintain her sacred fire. Seven in number, the Vestal Virgins were chosen before their tenth year and took a vow of celibacy. Their prayers were said to have great power and they were accorded great privileges. When they left the service of the goddess, usually in their thirties, their high status enabled them to marry well.

Likewise, the Pythia of Delphi, in early times, was a young virgin, as Diodorus Siculus records (16.26.6). But when their charms proved too much for the more muscular worshippers, they were later replaced with ladies of maturer years.

Of course, Israelite belief in the defilement of menstruation barred women of child-bearing age from the sanctuary area. But prepubescent and menopausal women might have served in the sanctuary. And pubescent, unmarried girls might have served the sanctuary from home. We may assume that, as in Rome, such girls would be chosen from eminent families.

Several Bible passages point to women having just such a role at the sanctuary. Exodus 38:8 and 1 Samuel 2:22 both speak of women who 'attend' or 'serve' at the door of the tent of meeting, the same verb (*tsava*) as describes the practical service of the Levites (Num. 4:23; 8:24). Presumably then, these women also had a practical role, perhaps looking after the curtains and vestments, just as the yarn for them had originally been spun by women (Exod. 35:25–26). Nothing is said in the Hebrew text about their age. But Hophni and Pinhas's illicit activity with them suggests they were young, attractive, and unmarried, for no-one was punished for adultery (1 Sam. 2:22). Meanwhile, the targum on Exodus 38:8, says that the women at the tabernacle in Moses's time were *ts'ni'uta* or 'chaste', that is, virgin.

> He made the laver of bronze and its base of bronze, from the bronze mirrors of the chaste women, who at the time when they came to pray at the door of the tabernacle of appointment, stood beside their oblations, giving thanks and confession. And going to their husbands, they became the mothers of righteous children, when they were purified from the uncleanness of their blood. (Targum Yerushalmi Exod. 38:8)

The Septuagint adds that these young women fasted and prayed at the entrance to the tabernacle.

> He made the brazen laver, and the brazen base of it of the mirrors of the women that fasted, who fasted by the doors of the tabernacle of witness, in the day in which he set it up. (LXX Exod. 38:26 [=MT 38:8])

Later, 2 Maccabees 3 records how, when the Syro-Greek general Heliodorus invaded the temple and demanded its treasures, all within the temple cried out in prayer.

> And also the encloistered virgins (*katakleistoi tôn parthenôn*) ran forth, some on the gates, and some on the walls, and others looked out of the windows. And, all holding up their hands towards heaven, made supplication. (2 Macc 3:19–20)

Clearly, the virgins here are not all the virgins of Jerusalem, but a special category, the 'enclosed' (*katakleistoi*) ones. And these virgins saw the events unfolding in the temple courts below. But, since the temple's high walls meant its courts were not visible from the city, the girls must have been looking from the windows, gatehouses, and walls within the temple precincts. So we may conclude that they lived in the temple precincts.

The Apocalypse of Baruch, describing the destruction of the temple in AD 70, addresses first the temple priests, and then the virgins, suggesting that the virgins, like the priests, were part of the temple personnel.

> You priests, take the keys of the sanctuary and cast them into the height of heaven, and give them to the Lord and say: 'Guard your house yourself, for, behold, we are found false stewards.'
>
> And you virgins, who weave byssus and silk and gold from Ophir, in haste pick it all up and throw it in the fire that it may return it to its Author, and that the flame may take it back to its Creator, lest the enemy seize it. (2 Baruch 10:18–19)

A Mishnah text tells how the temple veil was woven by young girls.

> The veil of the Temple was a palm-length in width. It was woven with seventy-two smooth stitches each made of twenty-four threads. The length was forty cubits and the width twenty cubits. Eighty-two damsels wove it.[7] Two veils were made each year and three hundred priests were needed to carry it to the pool. (M. Shek. 8:5–6)

Tosefta Shekalim confirms the same thing.

> The women were weavers of the curtain of the house and they made the bread of the Presence. Those of the house of Abtinas made the incense bought from contributions to the [Temple] treasury (2:6).[8]

The Talmud refers to 'women who made the curtains for the Temple...and baked the showbread'.[9] And Pesikta Rabbati tells how,

[7] There are variant readings. One says 82 "damsels" (ריבות) and the other 82 "thousands" (ריבוא). The latter is taken to mean that the curtain contained 82,000 (threads) or was worth 82,000 (denars). But '82,000' without a noun is unintelligible. "Damsels" is by far the preferable reading.

[8] The House of Abtinas were the priestly clan in charge of preparing the temple incense (M. Yoma 3:11; 1:5).

[9] B. Ket. 106a.

when the Romans sacked Jerusalem, 'the virgins who were weaving threw themselves in the flames' so as not to be abducted by the Romans (26:6). The same passage says that these virgins lived in the three-storey building inside the Temple area.[10]

A later Christian text, the Gospel of Pseudo-Matthew, summarizes all the above quite nicely. The high priest, named Abiathar, announces,

> Ever since this temple was built by Solomon, there have been in it virgins, the daughters of kings, and the daughters of prophets, and of high priests and priests; and they were great and worthy of admiration. But when they came to the proper age they were given in marriage, and followed the course of their mothers before them, and were pleasing to God. (Ps.-Matt. 8)

So there is plenty evidence that women—especially nimble-fingered young girls—did do work for the temple service. They made and repaired vestments and fabrics, like the temple curtain. They perhaps took part in the temple prayers. Like the Vestal Virgins of Rome they would have been of patrician families. And their formative years as temple virgins would enable them later to make favourable marriages. Like a finishing school, the guild of temple virgins produced young women for the ruling class of Israel. They lived in the temple cloisters, overseen by matrons, until puberty. Then they left the temple to marry.

It follows that the author of the Protoevangelium does not misrepresent temple practice. Rather, he is familiar with aspects of it that have been overlooked. He knows of the virgins who wove the temple veils. He also knows, as we saw in the last chapter, how the high-priestly diadem or *petalon* was said to shine on those who are forgiven. He knows of the bitter water ordeal, apparently in a form practised in later temple times.[11] He knows there are twelve bells on the *kohen gadol's* robe. Whoever he was, he appears to have been Jewish and very well acquainted with first-century temple protocol.

So there is no ground for dismissing the Protoevangelium as historically inaccurate. We may now ask far it might actually be true when it speaks on matters where Matthew and Luke are silent, namely, on Mariam's postpartum virginity, on Joseph's children by an earlier marriage, and on his mature age.

[10] Josephus tells of cloisters in the temple (War 5:5:2) without stating their purpose.
[11] For more, see Nutzman, 'Mary In The Protevangelium Of James', 556-559.

Mariam and Joseph

The Protoevangelium is the earliest source of the idea that Mariam remained a virgin after the birth of her child. Indeed, what seems to be implied is the idea of her perpetual virginity. This leads inevitably to questions about her relations with Joseph.

Matthew says Joseph was betrothed to Mariam with the intention that they should ultimately 'come together' in marriage (1:18). That, as we saw, was the usual course of events for consecrated virgins. But the Protoevangelium seems unclear whether Mariam is betrothed to Joseph for marriage or merely entrusted to him as a ward. It says, on the one hand, that the widowers' staffs were to show whose wife she should be (§8), and Joseph tells the midwife that Mariam is his betrothed (§19). But, on the other hand, she is committed into his 'safe-keeping' (§9). And when she is found to be pregnant in his house, he is accused of defiling her and both must submit to the temple ordeal (§15–16). Yet, if they were indeed betrothed, her pregnancy would be no matter for enquiry, for the consummation of the marriage would be lawful.

If there is an answer to this apparent conflict within the Protoevangelium, it is in the matter of Mariam being chosen 'from among the undefiled virgins' to spin yarn. In other words, we are perhaps to understand that Mariam, being of an age where menstruation might begin, must leave the temple, yet she might still spin yarn for the temple while living as an undefiled virgin elsewhere. At the beginning of this period, she was only twelve years old (§8)—too young for marriage. So we are to understand that she was to live with Joseph, but apart—a bit like the wife captured in war (cf. Deut. 21:13)—and the marriage was not to be consummated until an agreed time, when Mariam was older and would have ceased spinning yarn for the temple.

Such a scenario would reconcile the conflicts within the Protoevangelium and permit it to harmonize with Matthew and Luke.

Jesus's Siblings

But that leads on to the matter of Mariam's subsequent relations with Joseph, which leads in turn to the question of who were Jesus's brothers and sisters.

The gospels speak of Jesus having four brothers—James, Joseph, Simon, and Jude—and at least two sisters, Salome and Mariam. In the early church, this gave rise to three distinct views—now called Helvidian, Hieronymian, and Epiphanian, after their respective champions—which persist to this day.

1. The Helvidian view was named after Helvidius who, in the late fourth century, denied the perpetual virginity of Mariam, saying Jesus's brothers and sisters were the offspring of Joseph and Mariam. This view first arose among the Eunomians and Apollinarists, then spread in Arabia, before it was brought to Rome by Helvidius.

Helvidius's tract is lost, but his arguments can be reconstructed from Jerome's rebuttal. Helvidius says that Mariam was found to be pregnant 'before they came together' (Matt. 1:18), which implies that at some future point they did come together. He adds that since Joseph had no sexual relations with Mariam 'until' Jesus was born (Matt. 1:25), it implies that he did have such relations with her thereafter. He says further that virginity is not superior to marriage, for procreation is necessary for the human race, including virgins, to exist. He claims that his view was also held by Tertullian.[12]

2. The Hieronymian view is named after Jerome, who published a refutation of Helvidius. Jerome says Jesus's brothers and sisters were actually his cousins, the children of Joseph's brother, Clopas. He says that 'before' (Matt. 1:18) can describe an action that was planned but not fulfilled. He explains that 'until' (Matt. 1:25) need not imply that they ever had sexual relations. (He asks, by way of mockery, whether 'until' means that Joseph coupled with Mariam as soon as her child was delivered.) For Jesus tells his disciples that he will be with the disciples 'until' the end of the age, but that does not mean he will leave them at that point (Matt. 28.20). This use of 'until' is standard in Hebrew (Gen. 28.15). He adds that, if Mariam had other sons and daughters who could have taken care of her, Jesus would not have entrusted her to John's care at the cross (John 19:27). He says the view of Tertullian is worthless because he was not a priest. Finally, he adds that Joseph, like Mariam, was a perpetual virgin. He highly extols virginity.

3. A little later, Epiphanius, Bishop of Salamis in Cyprus, says Jesus's brothers and sisters were rather Joseph's children by an earlier

[12] The reference is perhaps to Tertullian, *Flesh of Christ* 23, who says Mariam was a mother before she was a wife. But that does not imply her sexual relations with Joseph.

marriage. He notes that Jesus's brothers behaved haughtily toward him, which they would not have done if they were younger. Like Jerome, he says that Mariam's being entrusted to John shows that Mariam had neither husband nor sons to take care of her (John 19:27). He calls those who hold the Helvidian view Antidicomarians or 'enemies of Mariam'.

The Helvidian view was a minority view in the early church, and was opposed also by Ambrose and Basil. Yet in modern times, it has become widespread among Protestants. This is surprising, since it was not a view held by Luther, Calvin, Zwingli, or any other Protestant leader of Reformation times. One imagines that it arises from modern Protestant opposition to what they see as excessive Catholic reverence for Mariam.

It seems to me that John's account of Jesus confiding Mariam to his care is conclusive proof that she had neither husband nor other child. If she had, why would Jesus have done this, and why would Mariam and John not have objected? It is true too that Jesus's brothers act like elder rather than younger siblings. They seek to constrain him, as a threat to the family, saying he has lost his mind (Mark 3:21, 31). They tick him off for seeking public acclaim (John 7:3–5). It is also true that the Greek of Matthew 1:18 and 1:25 does not imply sexual relations between Joseph and Mariam. The latter text should be read as *He had no sexual relations with her right up until the time she brought forth a son.* That is, Matthew's point is not what happened after the birth, but rather what did not happen before it: Joseph had no relations with her at any time before the birth, and so the child was not his. Likewise, Bauckham is surely right when he says that belief in Mariam's perpetual virginity arose early in the Palestinian church, and this would hardly have happened if it were known that she had borne seven children. All this supports the view that Mariam had only one child and had no sexual relations with Joseph either before or after Jesus's birth.

We should also reflect on how Mariam's conception by the Holy Spirit was seen by Mariam and Joseph. They would surely have reasoned that such a conception made her the bride of the Most High. From such a bridegroom one could never be divorced nor widowed. And he was known for jealousy. One imagines that they would both have regarded the thought of their having sexual relations as adultery against the Most High. Joseph, I imagine, would have been afraid to touch her, both out of holy reverence and genuine fear.

But what of Jesus's siblings? Were they cousins, as Jerome says, and as Catholic tradition still maintains? Or were they half-siblings, as Epiphanius and the Protoevangelium say, and as the Orthodox churches maintain?

Jerome's view is unlikely. The Greek word for brother or step-brother (*adelphos*) cannot normally mean a cousin. There is a perfectly good Greek word for 'cousin' (*anepsios*). It is used for the relationship between Barnabas and Mark (Col. 4:10). Likewise, Hegesippus, who calls James and Jude the 'brothers of the Lord', calls Simeon ben Clopas the 'cousin of the Lord'.[13] If Jesus's brothers were actually cousins, one would expect the gospels to use the right word.

Epiphanius's view, that Jesus's brothers were Joseph's sons by an earlier marriage, is much more reasonable. Greek—like Aramaic and Hebrew—has no separate word for step-brother or step-sister. So New Testament references to Jesus's brothers and sisters as *adelphoi* and *adelphai* are quite consistent with their being his step-siblings.

Further, the Epiphanian view, though it appeared last of the three views mentioned in the fourth-century, is surely the oldest of the three. For it is the same view found centuries before in the Protoevangelium. There Joseph, a widower, takes Mariam to Bethlehem together with his sons, who are present at the birth of her firstborn, Jesus.

The Epiphanian view has been held by the churches of the east from ancient times. It was held too by prominent Anglican scholars like Lightfoot. Even Jerome, it seems, came round to it in the end.

There is one consequence to it, which does not apply to the other two views. It is this. If Jesus was not Joseph's first son, albeit by adoption, then he did not inherit Joseph's title as *nasi* of the house of David. In that case, he was not the direct heir to David's throne. James was. And the law taught that the right of the firstborn was inalienable (Deut. 21:15–17).

Nevertheless, we do see just such a pattern throughout the Bible. Neither Isaac nor Jacob nor Joseph nor Ephraim were their fathers' firstborn, yet all received the title due to their older siblings. More particularly, Joseph was his mother's firstborn, though not his father's. And perhaps David was the same.[14]

[13] Eusebius, *Hist. Eccl.* 2:23; 3:20 (James and Jude); 3:11; 4:22 (Simeon).

[14] David's words, *In sin my mother conceived me* (Ps. 51:5) suggest that his mother was not the mother of his elder brothers. It was not a case of adultery or of forbidden

So we may conclude that, in the case of Jesus, as in his great prototypes Joseph and David, the will of the Most High overruled the claim of paternal primogeniture. Joseph's brother Judah led his own clan but Joseph became ruler of Israel in Egypt. David's brother Eliab inherited the clan headship in Bethlehem, but David received the throne. And Jesus's brother James inherited the rule of the believing community in the Holy Land, but Jesus became king in a higher realm altogether.

How Old Was Joseph?

The Protoevangelium shows Joseph as older than Mariam. Later traditions, taking the spur from this, make him very old indeed. The *History of Joseph the Carpenter*, from the late sixth century, makes him ninety when he took Mariam in.

These old Syriac stories made their way, by the hand of Crusdaers, to England and gave rise to the ancient Joseph that we meet in English Christmas carols.[15] The fifteenth-century *Cherry Tree Carol* says,

Joseph was an old man,
And an old man was he,
When he wedded Mary
In the land of Galilee.

Another carol, *The Angel Gabriel*, tells how, when visited by the angel, Mariam laments,

Mary anon looked him upon,
And said, "Sir, what are ye?
I marvel at these tidings
Which thou hast brought to me.
Married I am unto an old man,
As the lot fell unto me."

Another carol, *Righteous Joseph*, sympathizes with old Joseph's distress at discovering his young wife's pregnancy.

kin-relations, for in that case both father and son would have been outcast. The apparent solution is that he was the offspring of his father's union with a young unattached woman—and so her firstborn—without the consent of her family.

[15] *The Oxford Book of Carols* (Oxford: University Press, 1964), pp. 72, 143, 80.

Fear not, old Joseph, she's thy wife;
She's still a spotless maid.

But how old is Joseph in the Protoevangelium? On the one hand, we read that he is a widower and does not want to become an object of mirth by marrying a young girl (§9, 17). Yet he is strong and active enough to pursue his daily trade as a builder. And he is young enough that his sons must travel to Bethlehem with him rather than remaining at home. Such a scenario makes James perhaps ten years older than Jesus, which fits well with the apparent age of James when he was killed in the mid-sixties AD. Further, Joseph was the brother of Clopas, who was capable of walking to Emmaus and back in one day in the mid 30s AD, whose wife was Mariam's companion, and whose son became bishop of Jerusalem after James's death.[16] So it looks like the age difference between Joseph and Mariam was not so very great. In other words, the description of Joseph in the Protoevangelium is consistent with Joseph being a widower perhaps in his forties; not young, but still strong and active and well able to protect and provide for Mariam and her child.

It is clear from the gospels that Joseph had died by the time of Jesus's ministry. If not, Jesus would not have committed his mother to John's care from the cross. But the History of Joseph the Carpenter tells us that Joseph exits this world in the embrace of Jesus. And that's a good place to end.

[16] Acts 24:18; John 19:25; Eusebius, History 4.22.

10

A Question of Paternity

IN EXPLORING Jesus's origins, we must now turn to his paternity. There are traditional Christian and Jewish views of this question. But a review of the history will show us that the discussion was not all black and white all the time.

JESUS THE SON OF JOSEPH

One possible view in Jesus's own time, was that he was the legitimate son of Joseph and Mariam. It is likely that those New Testament figures who call him 'Son of David' did think he was patrilineally descended from David via Joseph of Nazareth. That would surely have been a possible belief when all attention was on his miracles and the rumours of his irregular birth and his denials of Davidic descent—in Matthew 22 and John 8—were less widely known.

It was a view that was never quite eclipsed. It continued, according to Eusebius, among the Ebionites—in Hebrew, the *evyonim* or 'poor ones'—who were Torah-observant Jews who held that Jesus was the son of Joseph and a prophet (*Hist.* 6.17). The Ebionites prayed in the synagogue on Shabbat, in the *ecclesia* on the next day, and treasured a version of Matthew's gospel that omitted the first three chapters with their birth narrative.

Apparently, some Pharisees shared the view that Jesus was Joseph's son, but they were less inclined to allow the legitimacy of his birth. Such a view was apparently held by Rav Pappa, whom we met earlier.

But such views were a minority. The New Testament writers agree that Jesus was a heavenly man conceived in the womb of Mariam the virgin by the power of the Holy Spirit. Meanwhile, the usual Pharisaic view is that he was not the son of Joseph, but the son of another.

JESUS AS *MAMZER*

It is clear, even in the New Testament, that the Judahite elite accused Jesus of being illegitimately conceived, a *mamzer*. In the heated debate in John chapter eight, his opponents say to him: '*We* were not born of fornication' (John 8:41). (The *we* is emphatic in the Greek.) They thought Jesus was indeed so born. The same thing is found in Mark where the people of Nazareth call him 'Mariam's son' (Mark 6:3). It was a deliberate slur. In Israel a man was called by his father's name—Judah ben Gamliel, Mosheh ben Maimon. To call him by his mother's name was tantamount to saying that his father was unknown. Evidently, Jesus's paternity was much disputed while he was alive.

These accusations continued. Justin Martyr reminds Trypho how, after the resurrection, the Judahites sent out correction squads to defame Jesus and his followers to all people, even to those who had not yet heard of him.

> For after that you had crucified him, the only blameless and righteous man, through whose stripes those who approach the Father by him are healed, when you knew that he had risen from the dead and ascended to heaven, as the prophets foretold he would, you not only did not repent of the wickedness which you had committed, but at that time you selected and sent out from Jerusalem chosen men through all the land to tell that the godless heresy of the Christians had sprung up, and to publish those things which all they who knew us not speak against us. So that you are the cause not only of your own unrighteousness, but in fact of that of all other men. (*Dialogue with Trypho* §17)

And later:

> You have sent chosen and ordained men throughout all the world to proclaim that a godless and lawless heresy had sprung from one Jesus, a Galilæan deceiver, whom we crucified. But his disciples stole him by

> night from the tomb, where he was laid when unfastened from the cross, and now deceive men by asserting that he has risen from the dead and ascended to heaven. Moreover, you accuse him of having taught those godless, lawless, and unholy doctrines which you mention, in order to condemn those who confess him to be Christ, and a Teacher from and Son of God. (*Dialogue with Trypho* §108)

Shaye Cohen thinks Justin's testimony here is 'Christian invention'. He reasons,

> I find it impossible to believe that the office of the Jerusalem high-priest commanded sufficient support and exerted sufficient authority so as to be able to control, or even attempt to control, Jewish religious life in the diaspora. The high priest could not control Jewish religious life in Judaea – how could he control Jewish religious life in the diaspora?[1]

Well, yes. The high priest's authority was not absolute. No leader's ever is. But that does not mean that the high priest did not do all in his power to overturn the growing influence of the Nazarene community. And it was well within his power to fund a smear campaign.

Of course, some dispute the authenticity of Justin's *Dialogue* more generally. Its critics rightly note that Justin had complete authorial control of his Trypho. Yet many details of his record ring true to life. Trypho is surrounded by his *talmidim.* He comes across as reasonable and courteous, sometimes more than Justin. Justin confesses to Trypho that, yes, Christians do disagree on keeping the law of Moses (§47). And, as Judith Lieu says, there are even two different Judaisms visible in the speech of Justin and Trypho.

> Justin's Judaism is a near-monolithic entity of unbelief...the Jews occupy a special place. They alone...possess potentially the true philosophy, a potential never fulfilled by them; they alone are culpable for that failure. Trypho's Judaism is something very different: a viable religious alternative, pursuing its own piety in obedience to God's law.[2]

So, all in all, Justin's Dialogue does look the record of his discourse with a Jewish sage, Trypho—whom I take to be R. Tarfon ha-Kohen—in second-century Ephesus, where Trypho and his *talmidim* had fled the aftermath of the Second Jewish Revolt in Judea (AD 132–135).

[1] Cohen, 'The ways that parted', 10.
[2] Lieu, *Image and Reality,* 148.

Justin's claims about the 'chosen men' sent from Jerusalem to slander Jesus and his followers agree, of course, with the testimony of Saul-Paul, who said he had been sent with letters from the high priest to suppress the growing Nazarene movement. He would have been well funded in this, for, as he said, 'Who serves as a soldier at his own expense?' (1 Cor. 9:7) The killing of Stephen, of James the son of Zebedee, of James the Just, and the attempts on the life of Peter and Paul witness to the same hostile reaction of the Judahite élite to the Jesus movement. So too does the Talmudic record of the trial of Jesus's disciples at Sanhedrin 43a, which we read earlier.

Justin's claim is that these anti-Jesus manifestations were no sporadic business. They were part of a systematized campaign, funded by the Zadokites and the Sanhedrin, to refute the Nazarene claims about Jesus. And it seems that, like Saul in his day, these messengers set about their work briskly.

Sefer Toldot Yeshu

One early evidence of Justin's claim of a sustained campaign to refute the gospels is the *Sefer Toldot Yeshu* (Book of the Generations of Yeshu). *Toldot* is a Hebrew word that means 'begettings', that is, conception and genealogy. We see it, for instance, in Gen. 25:19: *These are the generations* (toldot) *of Isaac.* In the same way, the *Sefer Toldot Yeshu* offers an account of Jesus's conception, birth, and life. But it is quite the inverse narrative of the one found in the gospels. It knows many of the details of Jesus's life: his irregular conception, his birth in Bethlehem, his childhood sojourn in Egypt, his Bar-Mitzvah debate with the sages in the temple, his power to work miracles, even to raise the dead and ascend into the air. But his conception is ascribed to adultery and his powers to sorcery. Here is the birth narrative.[3]

> In the year 3671 in the days of King Jannaeus, a great misfortune befell Israel, when there arose a certain disreputable man of the tribe of Judah, whose name was Joseph Pandera. He lived at Bethlehem in Judah.
>
> Near his house dwelt a widow and her lovely and chaste daughter named Miriam. Miriam was betrothed to Yohanan, of the royal house of David, a man learned in the Torah and God-fearing.

[3] Text from Goldstein 1950: 148.

At the close of a certain Sabbath, Joseph Pandera, attractive and like a warrior in appearance, having gazed lustfully upon Miriam, knocked upon the door of her room and betrayed her by pretending that he was her betrothed husband, Yohanan. Even so, she was amazed at this improper conduct and submitted only against her will.

Thereafter, when Yohanan came to her, Miriam expressed astonishment at behavior so foreign to his character. It was thus that they both came to know the crime of Joseph Pandera and the terrible mistake on the part of Miriam. Whereupon Yohanan went to Rabban Shimon ben Shetah and related to him the tragic seduction. Lacking witnesses required for the punishment of Joseph Pandera, and Miriam being with child, Yohanan left for Babylonia.

Miriam gave birth to a son and named him Yehoshua, after her brother. This name later deteriorated to Yeshu. On the eighth day he was circumcised. When he was old enough the lad was taken by Miriam to the *bet ha-midrash* to be instructed in the Jewish tradition.

One day Yeshu walked in front of the Sages with his head uncovered, showing shameful disrespect. At this, the discussion arose as to whether this behavior did not truly indicate that Yeshu was a *mamzer* and the son of a *niddah* [a woman unpurified from menstruation]. Moreover, the story tells that while the rabbis were discussing the Tractate *Nezikin*, he gave his own impudent interpretation of the law and in an ensuing debate he held that Moses could not be the greatest of the prophets if he had to receive counsel from Jethro. This led to further inquiry as to the antecedents of Yeshu, and it was discovered through Rabban Shimon ben Shetah that he was the illegitimate son of Joseph Pandera. Miriam admitted it. After this became known, it was necessary for Yeshu to flee to Upper Galilee.

The narrative continues at some length. It tells how Jesus acquired magical powers by his unlawful use of the Ineffable Name which he carried from the temple in an incision in his flesh, of his ascent into the air, and of his aerial battle with Judas, of his being crucified on a cabbage stalk, and of the body being stolen by his disciples.

The origins and the date of *Toldot Yeshu* are unclear. Yet many of its claims about Jesus's conception are echoed by Celsus who lived in the first part of the second century, probably in Alexandria. He spoke of Jesus as the illegitimate son of a Roman soldier called Panthera, and of his visit to Egypt where he acquired magical powers.[4] This suggests that a version of the *Toldot* was circulating around the Mediterranean in Celsus's time, and may well date from the first century.

[4] Celsus's writings survive in citation in Origen's *Contra Celsum*. See 1:28–32.

As with any document so ancient, there are variant readings of certain passages. Nonetheless, *Sefer Toldot Yeshu* looks like it began as a single text. Nor does it appear to be a folk-type composition. Its point-by-point comparison with details of the gospels suggests it was consciously composed to refute the gospel narratives.

One might say that the *Sefer Toldot Yeshu*, at least in the version above, does not present Mariam in too bad a light. She is a chaste maiden of noble character, forcefully used. Celsus says worse things of her. But the *Sefer Toldot* is hinting more than it says. Her impregnation takes place in a darkness so deep that she cannot even recognize the voice of her betrothed. It is all, not accidentally, quite farcical. Her guilt is implied just as surely as it is proclaimed by Celsus. However, in this version of the *Toldot*, her violator is Jewish and so her son has a claim to being a *mamzeri* Jew.

JESUS AS *MAMZER* IN THE TALMUD

A more explicit claim of Jesus's *mamzerut* is found in Bavli Shabbat 104b. The Mishnah passage under discussion is about what form of writing is permitted on Shabbat. The Talmud gives an old oral tradition or *baraitha* of Rabbi Eliezer ben Hyrcanus who, here as elsewhere, seems not unsympathetic to Jesus. He seems to know the *Toldot Yeshu* tradition that Jesus carried spells scratched in his flesh. And he tries to advance this as a halakhic precedent that writing on one's flesh is perhaps permissible.

> MISHNAH: *One who writes in his flesh* [during Shabbat] is liable [to bring a sin offering].
> GEMARA: *One who writes in his flesh.* It was taught that Rabbi Eliezer said to the sages, 'And did not Ben Stada bring spells from Egypt in a cut in his flesh?'
> They said to him, 'He was a fool, and there is no taking of precedent from a fool.'
> [Then follow various redactoral views on the name.] Ben Stada is Ben Pandira. R. Ḥisda said, 'The husband was Stada, the paramour was Pandira.' The husband was Pappos ben Yehuda, the mother was Stada [and he was named after her]. The mother was Miriam, a dresser of women's hair, as we say in Pumbeditha, 'She strayed from [*satath-da*] her husband.' (B. Shab. 104b; see too B. Sanh 67a)

His colleagues reject Eliezer's view. They say Jesus was a fool and *mamzer,* the adulterously-conceived son of Pandira. We also learn that Ben Stada, whom we meet elsewhere, is another name for Ben Pandira/Pandera.

The allegation that Jesus was a *mamzer* appears elsewhere in rabbinic literature. In the Mishnah, we find the following discussion:

> Who is a *mamzer*?...R. Joshua says: [The offspring of any union] for which one deserves to die by the judgement of a court. R. Shimon b. Azzai said: I found a roll of pedigrees in Jerusalem, and in it was written 'So-and-so (*ish p'loni*) [was] a *mamzer* of a married woman.' This was to confirm the words of R. Joshua. (M. Yeb. 4:13)

Joshua ben Ḥananiah, a former temple singer, was a favourite disciple of Rabban Yoḥanan ben Zakkai (Abot 2:8), a contemporary of Jesus. They were among the leading teachers of the first century. Joshua is known elsewhere for his opposition to the Nazarenes (Hag. 5b).

His argument implies that a *mamzer*, even if he escaped death at birth, would naturally deserve death later on. Joshua's disciple, Rabbi Shimon, agrees. He says he knew about just such a person, but avoids the mention of his name. But, as Herford says, 'Unless some well-known man were intended, there would be no point in referring to him; and unless there had been some strong argument for avoiding his name, the name would have been given in order to strengthen the argument.'[5] So it is likely that the reference is to Jesus but that his name was taboo.

So rabbinic literature speaks of Jesus being illegitimate. Sometimes his father is said to be a lawless Jew. Elsewhere, we find what Boyarin calls 'the Jewish slander tradition, known at least as early as Celsus, that Jesus was the bastard son of a Roman soldier named Panthera.'[6] Either way, the purpose of these accounts was not only to blacken Jesus and his mother, but also to undermine the genealogies that tied her son to the house of David.

Rabbis and Nazarenes

Relations between Pharisees and Nazarenes remained polarized. In time, Christianity became the faith of the Roman power. And, with the

[5] Herford, Christianity in Talmud, p. 44.
[6] Boyarin, *Dying for God,* 104.

codification of the Talmuds in the middle of the first millennnium, Pharisaism became Rabbinic Judaism. There were times of open conflict. The Jewish contingent of the Persian army, led by the Exilarch Nehemiah ben Hushiel, sacked Byzantine Jerusalem in 614, killing some 100,000 souls of its Christian population. Then Crusaders massacred the Jews of the Rheinland and Mamluk Jerusalem.[7]

But there were times of discourse too, even in the early period. Here, it is worth spending a little time on the story of Rabbi Eliezer ben Hyrcanus and his Pharisaic contemporaries of the first and second century AD. Their story may help us understand a little better the relations between Christianity and proto-Judaism in the first and early second century.

In his youth, Eliezer studied in the *yeshiva* of Rabbi Yoḥanan ben Zakkai in Jerusalem. When the city was besieged and its dire end was drawing nigh, Eliezer and his fellow-student, Joshua ben Ḥananiah, smuggled Ben Zakkai through the siege in a coffin and took him to the Roman general Vespasian just before the city's destruction.[8] Yoḥanan hailed Vespasian as king. That was a dangerous thing to say, and Vespasian threatened to kill him. But, at that moment, news arrived that Vespasian had indeed been appointed emperor. Vespasian, in his joy, invited Ben Zakkai to ask him for a boon. Ben Zakkai asked him to spare the lineage of David—that is, the matrilineal line from Hillel to Gamliel II—and 'the sages and scholars of Yavneh', which was a centre of Torah study in the coastal plain, just south of Jaffa. Why Ben Zakkai did not beg mercy for the holy temple has been a matter of wonder for two millennia. But perhaps the answer lies in his deep-seated hostility to the temple Zadokites and all they stood for.

Vespasian granted Ben Zakkai's wish and he and his disciples went to Yavneh with Gamliel II. There they set up a *yeshiva* with their little group of scholars. Thus Yavneh become the new centre of Pharisaic Judaism and the seat of their Sanhedrin, over which they duly appointed Gamliel II as *nasi.* This Gamliel was the great-great-grandson of Hillel and the grandson of Rabban Gamliel (or Gamaliel) the Elder, who was Paul's teacher and who features in the New Testament (Acts 5:34; 22:3).

[7] Horowitz, 'Vengeance', 1–39; Avni, 'Persian Conquest', 35–48; Reich, 'Ancient Burial Ground', 111–18.

[8] As related in B. Gittin 56a/b. For R. Joshua as a temple singer, see B. Arak. 11b.

Eliezer was of priestly lineage, and he became one of the leaders of the small community of rabbis. He was appointed assistant to Gamliel as co-president of the little Sanhedrin, and he married Gamliel's sister, Ima Shalom. Indeed, Eliezer, his colleagues, and his disciples, are at the centre of much of the narrative of the Mishnah and Talmud.

Eliezer taught Akiva and Tarfon—whom Justin called Trypho. They, in turn, taught the foremost sages of the next generation: Rabbi Judah the Prince, Rabbi Meir, Judah bar Ilai, Shimon ben Yoḥai, and Jose ben Ḥalafta. Eliezer was part of the high-level deputation that travelled to Rome with Gamliel and Joshua.[9]

Hillel-Gamliel tree

1. Hillel (d. AD 10)
2. Shimon ben Hillel (d. c. AD 20)
3. Rabban Gamliel the Elder (c. 50 BC–AD 52), first half of the 1st century, son of (2)
4. Rabban Shimon ben Gamliel (10 BC–AD 70), son of (3).
5. Rabban Gamliel II ben Shimon, of Yavneh (c. 55–118), son of (4).
6. Rabban Shimon II ben Gamliel (c. 95–180), son of (5).
7. Rabbi Judah ha-Nasi (the Prince) (135 to 217), editor of the Mishnah, son of (6).
8. Rabban Gamliel III beRabbi (c. 177–225), son of (7).

But later Eliezer fell out with his colleagues. It all came to a head over the question of the ritual purity of an oven—the Oven of Akhnai—as the story is told in Bavli Bava Metzia 59. Eliezer declared that the oven was ritually pure, while his colleagues disagreed. It is said that Eliezer's judgement was approved by miracles of nature and by a heavenly voice. But Joshua ben Ḥananiah declared that authority for the decision was 'not in heaven' since heaven had delegated authority to their Sanhedrin.[10] Yet Eliezer obstinately refused to change his opinion. So they duly declared him a heretic and ostracized him, burning all the things he declared to be pure. When their judgement was conveyed to him by Akiva, Eliezer was heart-broken and wept. Thus persecuted for conscience, he retired to his own house, either in Lydda or Caesarea.[11]

[9] B. Hag. 5b; Y. Sanh. 7 (end; 25d); Deut. R. 2:24.

[10] 'It is not in heaven' (*lo ba-shamayim hi*) is from Deut. 30:12, where it means that the divine law has been revealed on earth. But Joshua's midrashic appropriation of the words took them to mean that rabbinic sages have authority over the interpretation of the Torah. To this day, the phrase serves as the basis for halakhic jurisprudence, see Rambam, Mishneh Torah, Foundations 9:1–4.

[11] He had a school in Lod (Lydda) but retired to Caesarea (B. Sanh. 36b; 68a).

But, as we saw, Eliezer was not unsympathetic to the Nazarenes.[12] And one day, he was arrested by the Roman authority as a suspected Christian. The story goes as follows:

> Our Rabbis taught: When R. Eliezer was arrested for [*or* of] *minut*, they brought him to court to be tried. The judge [*hegemon*] said to him: 'Does a man of your mature years busy himself with such nonsense?'
>
> Eliezer replied: 'I trust the judge.' The judge thought that he was speaking of him, but he spoke only of his Father in heaven.
>
> The judge said: 'Then I trust you. Case dismissed. You are free.'
>
> Now when Eliezer came home, his disciples came to console him, but he accepted no consolation.
>
> Then R. Akiva said to him: 'Rabbi, permit me to tell you something of what you taught me.'
>
> He said: 'Speak.'
>
> He said to him: 'Rabbi, maybe some *minut* came before you. And you delighted in it. And so you were held liable (by heaven).'
>
> He said: 'Akiva, you remind me that once I was walking in the upper market of Sepphoris and I met one of the disciples of Yeshu the Nazarene, one Yaakov of Kfar Sakhniya. He said to me: 'It is written in your Torah, *You shalt not bring the hire of a prostitute [or the price of a dog into the house of your God]* (Deut. 23:19). What is the *halakhah*? May one make a privy for the high priest [of such gifts]?' I said nothing. He said to me: 'Thus Yeshu of Nazareth taught me: *Of the hire of a prostitute she has gathered them, and to the hire of a prostitute shall they return* (Mic. 1:7). From the place of filth they came; to the place of filth let them go.' This interpretation pleased me. And that is why I was arrested for *minut*, for I transgressed what is written in the Torah: *Remove your way far from her*—this is *minut. And do not come near the door of her house* (Prov. 5:8)—this means the government.' (Prov. 5:8).[13]

So Eliezer was in Sepphoris, the capital of Galilee, just six kilometres from Nazareth. There he met Yaakov from the village of Sakhniya in western Galilee. This may have been the Nazarene patriarch Yaakov (James), the grandson of Jude the brother of Jesus.[14] Eliezer said Yaakov taught him a halakhic decision—said to have been taught by Jesus—about what to do with the wages of a prostitute brought to the temple. It's not very savoury, nor respectful of the high priest. (One does not speak of the intestinal functions of high dignitaries.) But

[12] See too T. Yeb. 3:3-4 where Eliezer seems to avoid questions denigrating Jesus.
[13] B. Avodah Zarah, 16b–17a. The story is told also in T. Ḥullin 2:6.
[14] So Bauckham, *Jude*, 116–117.

Eliezer thinks it is a neat ruling and comes to respect Jesus as a Torah teacher. And this, he agrees, is why he ended up before the Roman tribunal, for he had cherished the teaching of Jesus in his heart.

But why were the Romans concerned to arrest Rabbi Eliezer as a Nazarene? After all, this wasn't Nero's Rome. Herford thinks it took place during Trajan's 'persecution' in AD 109. But Trajan's execution of Symeon ben Clopas was not so much a persecution as a simple response to the threat of Symeon's descent from the house of David.[15]

The fact is that there was harsh Roman scrutiny of the Nazarenes quite apart from Trajan. In fact, Trajan's correspondence with Pliny shows that, if Pliny routinely tortured and killed them, Trajan sought rather to abate Pliny's zeal in seeking them out. But the root of this persecution was the status of Judaism as a *religio licita* or 'permitted religion' and Judaism's relation to the Nazarene movement.[16]

Within the first-century *pax romana*, the Jews had worked hard to negotiate a *modus operandi* with the Roman power. Deputations had been sent, favours promised, quid pro quos negotiated, palms greased, the network worked, all so that the Jews might be free to worship without having to pay divine honours to the Roman gods or emperors. Philo had led such a deputation a century before. Eliezer knew all about it too. He had been part of a Yavneh deputation to Rome. The Jews had achieved this freedom by much labour and at no small cost. And all was going fine until the Nazarene movement began to spread.

It wasn't Jewish Nazarenes that were really the problem, although they were unpopular enough. The real issue was that non-Jews were becoming Christians. For the Jews, this was huge. They heard about the goings-on in Antioch: Jews worshipping together with pork-eating Syrians, uncircumcised men rubbing shoulders with Jewish maidens, menstruating women sitting in the congregation. It was beyond belief. But worse still, it would bring to an end their hard-won concessions with Rome. If every Greco-Roman pagan could now claim the Jewish exemption from sacrificing to the emperor, the concession would be withdrawn and all Jews would be forced to comply on pain of death.

[15] Herford, *Christianity*, 141–143; Bauckham, *Jude*, 111; Eusebius, *Hist.* 3:31–33.

[16] The phrase appears only in Tertullian's *Apologeticum* 21:1. There is no evidence of it in Roman law. Yet, practically, the Roman governance did recognize some religions, including that of Judah, as exempted from worship of the emperor. Tertullian is appealing to the rulers of the Roman empire (1:1) that Christians, being persecuted to death, should be granted the same tolerance.

Something had to be done. Exclusion from the synagogue was the first step. This was already done in the time of Jesus (John 9:22; 12:42; 16:2). But Gamliel II and the sages of Yavneh took it one step further by introducing the Birkat ha-Minim—the 'Blessing on the Heretics'—into the recitation of the Amidah daily prayer.

> For the *minim* let there be no hope. And let the arrogant government be speedily uprooted in our days. Let [the Nazarenes and] the *minim* be destroyed in a moment. And let them be blotted out of the Book of Life and not be inscribed together with the righteous. Blessed art thou, O Lord, who humblest the arrogant.[17]

This Blessing effectively drove out of the Jewish community any Nazarene unwilling to curse himself and those who shared his faith.

The next step was for the Pharisaic party to persuade Rome that the Nazarenes were no longer to be reckoned as Jews. This they did. It wasn't for nothing that Eliezer, Gamliel, and Joshua went to Rome and stood before the emperor debating with a Jewish Christian whether the divine favour still rested on Israel.

> Rabbi Joshua ben Ḥananiah was standing in the house of Caesar. A certain *epikoros*[18] gestured to him, that his was the nation whose Master had turned his face from it. He [Joshua] gestured to him: His hand is outstretched over us [in protection]. Caesar said to Rabbi Joshua: What did he gesture to you? [He replied, That mine is] the nation whose Master turned his face from it, and I gestured to him that his hand is outstretched over us.
>
> They said to that *min*: What did you gesture to him? [He said] The nation whose Master has turned from it. [They asked:] And what did he gesture to you? [He said:] I don't know. They said: A man who does not know what others gesture to him gestures in the presence of the king? They took him out and killed him. (B. Ḥagigah 5b)

But the Nazarenes had, of course, no wish to be excluded and forced to worship Roman gods. They were Israelites, after all. They wanted to

[17] The curse was composed by Shmuel haKatan at the request of Gamliel II (B. Ber. 28b-29a). Since early versions do not mention the Nazarenes, some say these *minim* were another Jewish group. Flusser thought it was perhaps the Sadducees. But the Sadducees were no longer a recognizable group in Gamliel's time. They were effectively obliterated in the conflagration of the Temple, while their remnant, like Eliezer, Tarfon, and Eleazar b. Azariah, joined the Pharisees at Yavneh. Justin had no doubt that the curse was directed against Christians (*Dial.* 16, 47, 96, 137).

[18] An *epikoros* (epicurean) is a general term of contempt, often for a pagan. But in the next paragraph the same individual is called a *min*, that is, an Israelite Christian.

remain within the Jewish fold and enjoy its immunity. They felt that if the Greco-Roman converts could be persuaded to be circumcised and eat kosher, then the taint of the Nazarene community would diminish and perhaps the hostility of the Jewish authorities might abate. This lies behind much of the New Testament debate on circumcision, as in Acts 15 and the epistles of Paul. The Nazarenes saw well enough that being Jewish was not essential to the new faith. But for them to be classed as non-Jews was not only a denial of their heritage, but an open door to Roman persecution.

Yet the Pharisaic party were not to be placated. The Nazarenes were to be driven out of Judaism. In time, they came to be regarded by the Roman authorities as not sharing in Jewish worship or privileges and became obliged to worship the emperor. And so, as Cohen says, 'by the early second century CE Christianity – even Jewish Christianity – became in Roman eyes a new thing separate from Judaism.'[19] And, one way or another, that is how Rabbi Eliezer, who had been part of the very deputation that sought to ban the Nazarenes, was called to answer to the Roman court as a suspected Nazarene himself.

Poor old Rabbi Eliezer. It was a tough time for him. Rejected by his brethren for honest adherence to his halakhic views, and drawn to Jesus as a true sage, someone ratted him to the *goyim* for being a Christian. Who would do such a thing? He came close to getting the life-or-death invitation to worship the emperor. He could have denied the charge and cursed Jesus. That was the standard recantation for a Jew. Yet he avoids doing so. Perhaps he was arrested by *minut* in more ways than one! The Talmud narrator—the *stamma*—even speaks of Eliezer's 'Father in heaven', a most un-Jewish expression altogether. Happily, Eliezer's astute answer saved his skin. But he and the rabbis were not reconciled during his lifetime. In bitterness of soul, he said of them:

> Warm thyself by the fire of the sages, but be cautious of their burning coals, that thou be not burned; for their bite is the bite of a jackal, their sting is of a scorpion, their hissing is of a snake, and all their words are fiery coals. (Avot 2:10)

Finally, they came to visit him on his deathbed, sitting afar from him, socially-distanced from the virus of his *minut*. Eliezer reproached them for their harshness. He foretold that Akiva, his *talmid* who so long

[19] Cohen, 'The ways that parted', 6–7.

forsook him, would die a dreadful death, as indeed he did, flayed alive for backing the failed rebellion of the savage messianic claimant, Bar Kokhba.[20] Then followed a halakhic discussion on purity and impurity. Eliezer muttered his last word—*tahor*, 'pure'—and passed away. This was taken as a good omen. R. Joshua revoked his excommunication, and they all chanted his praises at his funeral (Sanh. 68a).

Rabbi Eliezer had a contemporary, another Eliezer, who also knew Yaakov of Sakhniya. This was Eliezer ben Dama. When young, he asked his uncle, Yishmael ben Elisha, if he could study Greek philosophy now he had completed Torah studies. His uncle was not sympathetic. He said, 'Go, seek a time which is neither day nor night (cf. Josh. 1:8), and therein study Greek philosophy' (B. Men. 99b). But Eliezer still did not think the rabbinic community had a monopoly on truth. His tale ends as follows.[21]

> There was the case of Eliezer ben Dama, the son of the sister of R. Yishmael, who was bitten by a snake. And Yaakov of Kfar Sakhniya came to heal him. But R. Yishmael did not allow it. He said, 'You are not permitted, Ben Dama.'
>
> He said, 'I will bring you proof [from scripture] that he may heal me.' But he had not finished bringing a proof before he died.
>
> Said R. Yishmael, 'Happy are you, Ben Dama, for you have departed in peace, and have not broken through the fences of the sages. For on everyone who breaks through the fences of the sages punishment comes in the end, as it is said, *Whoever breaks a fence, a snake shall bite him.*' (Eccl. 10:8)

The context of the passage is about whether or not to receive medical aid from gentiles or *minim*. Yaakov of Kfar Sakhniya, in response to Eliezer's plight, came to heal him in the name of Yeshu. Apparently, neither Eliezer nor Uncle Yishmael doubted Yaakov's power to heal. But Yishmael declared it unlawful and would not allow Yaakov near. Eliezer was about to cite a scripture to show it was lawful, but died before he could do so. So this Eliezer too was sympathetic to the

[20] Bar Kokhba's deeds can be reconstructed from Seder Olam 30; Lam. R. 2.2§4; Y. Ta'an. 4.5, 8; B. Sanh. 93b. He tortured and slew those who refused to join his ranks. He said, 'Let God neither help nor hinder us.' He kicked to death his associate and maternal uncle, the priest Eleazar of Modein, on suspicion. Neusner, and Green say, 'The failed messiah of the second century, Bar Kokhba, above all, exemplifies arrogance against God.' (*Dictionary of Judaism* II:426)

[21] T. Ḥullin 2:6; cf. B. Abodah Zarah 27b; Y. Shab. 14d; Qohelet Rabbah 1:8:3.

Nazarenes. Too sympathetic for his own good, thought his uncle, whose final words suggest that the snake-bite was a punishment for Eliezer's infractions already incurred. Better, he said, that he is gone than he break any more fences.

It went otherwise with the grandson of Rabbi Yehoshua ben Levi, as recorded in Yerushalmi Shabbat 14d.

> The grandson [of R. Yehoshua ben Levi] had something stuck in his throat. There came one who whispered to him in the name of Yeshu Pandera and he recovered. When he [the healer] came out, he [R. Yehoshua] said to him, 'What did you whisper to him?' He said to him, 'A certain word.' He said, 'It had been better for him that he had died rather than this.'

A 'certain word', of course, replaces the words actually spoken by the Nazarene healer. (Perhaps they were something like in Acts 9:34.) Nor is it clear who called the healer to come, whether the boy's parents, with no objection to the healer's methods, or R. Yehoshua who sought the healing but objected to the words spoken. But, here again, the Talmud records the effectiveness of healing in the name of Jesus.

Finally, there is Rabbi Abahu. The discussion again is about whether or not to summon non-Jews or *minim* as healers. It is in Bavli Avodah Zarah 28a.

> But R. Abahu was an eminent man. Yaakov the *min* applied a potion to his leg. If it had not been for R. Ami and R. Asi, who licked [the potion off] his leg, he would have cut his leg off.

Within the discussion, we have just been told that exceptions to using non-Jewish physicians were permissible for eminent men. And so, since R. Abahu was an eminent man, it was permissible for him to call a *min* physician. Moreover, R. Abahu, in third-century Caesaria, must have mixed frequently with Christians, and he presumably called upon the best doctor he knew. Beyond that, the story is all a bit unclear. Apparently, two of his disciples licked the potion off his leg. But why he would have cut off his leg because of a potion administered by a physician of his own choosing was a secret the Yerushalmi redactor did not divulge. This Yaakov is, of course, not the Yaakov who visited the two Rabbis Eliezer more than a century before. It was a common Hebrew name, and popular among Christians in memory of the New Testament figures of the same name.

So the Talmud testifies to cases where Jews called on Christians to heal in the name of Jesus and the healing was effective. Despite the high-level opposition of the Rabbis to the growth of the Nazarenes, the divisions at ground level were not always hard and fast. Eliezer ben Hyrcanus admired Jesus as Torah teacher and did not deny being a Nazarene. Eliezer ben Dama thought healing could be had in Jesus's name, but did not obtain it. Yet others called in Nazarene physicians and were healed. The Talmud preserves the memory of some of these early Nazarene leaders and healers, providing a tacit witness to the sea of Nazarene Christianity that lapped at the shores of the little rabbinic community in Yavneh.

Yaakov ben Reuven

In the second millennium, the idea that Jesus is Joseph's son appears again in Jewish literature, in the *Sefer Milḥamot HaShem* (The Book of the Wars of the Lord), by the twelfth-century Andalusian rabbi, Yaakov ben Reuven ha-Rabbani. Yaakov had been embroiled in debate with the Jewish Christian, Petrus Alphonsi. As became customary with these disputations, each announced himself the winner, issuing his own account of the superiority of his own arguments.

Petrus called his book, *Dialogi contra Iudaeos*; its disputants are Christian 'Petrus' and Jewish 'Moyses'. Meanwhile Yaakov's *Sefer Milḥamot* has the 'Nazarene' and the 'Hebrew'.

In Yaakov's book, the Nazarene maintains that the parshat *Hinneh yaskil avdi* (Isa. 52:13–53:12) points entirely to Jesus. But his Hebrew opponent replies that this cannot be so, for Jesus, as a prince of Judah, was handsome and Isaiah's figure is not.

> He is said to be *despised and forlorn of men...without form or comeliness* (Isa. 53:3, 2). But he [Jesus] was handsome in person. Was he not one of the royal seed who assuredly were all goodly in form and well-favoured?[22]

So Yaakov believed that Jesus was of the royal seed of Judah. He does not specify patrilineal descent, of course. But we may assume that, being Jewish, he thought Jesus had a human father. And, if Jesus were

[22] From Driver and Neubauer. Hebrew at I:334; ET at II.389.

illegitimate, then he would not be 'of royal seed'. So Yaakov thinks Jesus was the son of Joseph.

Figure 8. The Dialogue of Petrus with his former self, Moyses. A 13th-century Belgian engraving from Petrus's *Dialogi contra Judaeos* (The Diaspora Museum, Tel Aviv).

It is, by the way, an interesting question whether Yaakov simply deduced Jesus's fine appearance from his royal descent, or whether he knew of a thousand-year-old tradition which actually spoke of Jesus's appearance.

Rambam

The next such comment on Jesus comes some fifty years later in the uncensored version of the *Mishneh Torah* of Rambam (Maimonides). He gives a very mixed appraisal of Jesus.

> Even Yeshua the Nazarene, who imagined that he was the Messiah and was put to death by the court, was foretold by Daniel, who said: *The sons of violence of your people shall assert themselves to establish the*

> *vision; but they shall stumble* (11:14). Was there ever a greater stumbling block than this? All the prophets said the Messiah was the redeemer of Israel and their saviour, the gatherer of their exiles and the strengthener of the commandments. But he caused Israel to be put to the sword, caused their remnant to be exiled and degraded, switched their Torah, and led much of the world to err and to worship a god other than HaShem.
>
> Nonetheless, the thoughts of the Creator of the World are beyond any man's understanding. For our ways are not his ways, and our thoughts are not his thoughts. And all the doings of Yeshua the Nazarene and of that Ishmaelite [*i.e.*, Mohamed] who came after him are nothing but to pave the way for the King Messiah and prepare the entire world to worship HaShem together, as it is said: *For then I will make the peoples pure of speech so that they all invoke the name of HaShem and serve Him with one accord* (Zeph 3:9).
>
> How is this so? The world is now already filled with matters of the Messiah and matters of the Torah and matters of the Commandments. Knowledge of these matters have spread to the distant islands and to the many nations of those with uncircumcised hearts.
>
> But when the true King Messiah will rise and succeed, and he will be lifted up and raised aloft, they all will immediately repent and confess that their fathers bequeathed them a lie, and their fathers and prophets led them astray (Kings and Wars 11:6–9).

It's a remarkable passage in many ways. For a start, Rambam lays the blame for Israel's destruction and exile squarely on Jesus. Since Jesus lived a generation before the destruction, one may ask if that is a fair accusation. Even the Talmud lays the blame for the destruction on the leaders of Israel, for their 'baseless hatred' (B. Yoma 9b). But Jesus did, of course, foretell the destruction (Matt. 24:2; Luke 21:6). If he was a false Messiah, did he prophesy truly? Or if he was the author of the destruction, some thirty-five years after his crucifixion, then what kind of a man was he? Rambam is silent on all of that. But he blames Israel's desolation on one who lived a generation before. Thus spake the philosopher.

He says that the true Messiah is yet to come. But Jesus has prepared the way for his coming by turning much of the world's population from idolatry and filling the world 'with matters of the Messiah and matters of the Torah and matters of the Commandments'. This has happened to such an extent that, when the true Messiah appears, all nations will be ready to acknowledge him. Is Rambam saying, howsoever unwillingly, that Jesus has the work of the Messiah? After all, the Messiah's task was to bring the knowledge of God to all lands: *I will also make you a light for the nations, that you may bring my salvation to the ends of the earth* (Isa. 49:6). Yet for Rambam, Jesus has filled the world 'with matters of the Messiah and matters of the Torah', but he has also led the nations to worship another god.

Rambam says nothing at all of Jesus's lineage. But the question arises: If Jesus has done a substantial portion of the Messiah's work, is he a bad man? Or, if he was a *mamzer* under an abiding curse, why did the Holy One, blessed be he, grant him the distinction of accomplishing so much of the Messiah's work?

Rabbi Yaakov ben Zvi of Emden

Six hundred years later, Rabbi Yaakov ben Zvi of Emden wrote his *Iggeret Shum* or 'Epistle to the Rabbis of the Four Lands' (1756) to counter the growing influence of the messianic pretender Shabbatai Zvi. In the epistle, he speaks of Jesus and the apostles at length. Echoing Rambam, he speaks of Jesus as having brought the knowledge of God to the nations. But he also praises Jesus as a strengthener of Torah. Jesus and his apostles, he says, were all Torah-observant Jews. They taught Torah-observance for all Jews, and made the Torah to be known and obeyed among the nations. His letter is worth quoting at length, particularly for its insights on the New Testament's legal obligations for Jews and Gentiles.

> Truly even according to the writers of the Gospels, a Jew is not permitted to leave his Torah, for Paul wrote in his letter to the Galatians (Gal. 5) 'I, Paul, say to you that if you receive circumcision, the Messiah will do you no good at all. You can take it from me that every man who receives circumcision is under obligation to keep the entire Torah.' Again, because of this, he admonished in a letter to the Corinthians (1 Cor. 7) that 'The circumcised should not remove the marks of circumcision, nor should the uncircumcised circumcise themselves.'
>
> Many have asked if Paul appears to contradict himself here. In the Acts of the Apostles (Acts 16), it is mentioned that Paul circumcised his disciple Timothy. And they found this very puzzling, for this act seems to contradict the later text which seems to indicate that he

considered circumcision a temporary commandment until the Messiah's arrival. But this took place after the time of the Nazarene! Therefore you must realize—and accept the truth from him who speaks it—that we see clearly here that the Nazarene and his Apostles did not wish to destroy the Torah from Israel. God forbid! For it is written in Matthew that the Nazarene said, 'Do not suppose that I have come to abolish the Torah. I did not come to abolish, but to fulfill. I tell you this: So long as heaven and earth endure, not a letter, not a stroke, will disappear from the Torah until it is achieved. If any man therefore sets aside even the least of the Torah's demands, and teaches others to do the same, he will have the lowest place in the Kingdom of Heaven, whereas anyone who keeps the Torah, and teaches others so, will stand high in the Kingdom of Heaven' (Matt. 5) This is also recorded in Luke (Luke 16). It is therefore exceedingly clear that the Nazarene never dreamt of destroying the Torah.

Similarly, we find Paul, his disciple, in a letter to the Corinthians (1 Cor. 5), accusing them of fornication, and condemning one who had lived with his father's wife. You may therefore understand that Paul doesn't contradict himself because of his circumcision of Timothy, for the latter was the son of a Jewish mother and a Gentile father (Acts 16), and Paul was a scholar, an attendant of Rabban Gamaliel the Elder, well versed in the laws of the Torah. He knew that the child of a Jewish mother is considered a full Jew, even if the father should be a Gentile, as is written in the Talmud and the Codes. He therefore acted entirely in accordance with the *halakhah* by circumcising Timothy. This would be in line with his position that all should remain within their own faith (1 Cor. 7). Timothy, born of a Jewish mother, had the law of a Jew, and had to be circumcised, just as he was enjoined to observe all commandments of the Torah, (Paul's condemnation of the man who lived with his stepmother is similarly understandable, as such an act is also forbidden to Noahides), for all who are circumcised are bound by all the commandments.[23] This provides a satisfactory reply to the question.

This also solves the apparent contradictions in the Nazarene's own statements. Christian scholars have assumed from certain passages in the Gospels that he wished to give a new Torah to take the place of the Torah of Moses. How could he then have said explicitly that he comes only to fulfil it? But it is as I said earlier, the writers of the Gospels never meant to say that the Nazarene came to abolish Judaism, but only that he came to establish a religion for the Gentiles from that time onward. Nor was it new, but actually ancient; they being the Seven Commandments of the sons of Noah, which were forgotten. The Apostles of the Nazarene then established them anew. However, those

[23] Noahides are Gentiles who worship the true God and should follow the seven laws of Noah; see later in the letter.

born as Jews, or circumcised as converts to Judaism (Exod. 12:49; one law shall be to him that is home-born, and unto the stranger) are obligated to observe all the commandments of the Torah without exception.

But for the Gentiles he reserved the Seven Commandments which they have always been obligated to fulfill. It is for that reason that they were forbidden pollutions of idols, fornication, blood, and things strangled (Acts 15). They also forbade them circumcision and the Sabbath. All of this was in accord with the law and custom of our Torah, as expounded by our Sages, the true transmitters from Moses at Sinai. It was they who sat upon his seat, as the Nazarene himself attested (Matt. 23). It was they (the Sages or Pharisees) who said that it is forbidden to circumcise a Gentile who does not accept upon himself the yoke of (all) the commandments. The Sages likewise said that the Gentile is enjoined not (fully) to observe the Sabbath. The Apostles of the Nazarene therefore chose for those Gentiles who do not enter the Jewish faith that instead of circumcision they should practice immersion (for truly immersion is also a condition of full conversion), and a commemoration of the Sabbath was made for them on Sunday.

But the Nazarene and his Apostles observed the Sabbath and circumcision as mentioned earlier, for they were born as Jews. They observed the Torah fully, until after a period of time a few of them decided to give up the Torah among themselves completely. They said that its observance was too difficult for them and agreed to remove its yoke from their necks (Acts 15).

But even here they did what is right as far as the Gentiles were concerned, for the Gentiles were not commanded to observe it. Nor is it proper to make it difficult for them, since they did not receive the Torah and are not enjoined to observe the 613 commandments. However, it is completely different as far as the Jews are concerned, for they became obligated to fulfill the Torah because God delivered them from the iron furnace (Egypt) to be the people of his possession. Therefore they and their children became subject to it forever. This, their covenant, will not be forgotten from their mouths, nor be discontinued from their children. For it they have given their lives throughout the generations, as the Psalmist has recorded: *All this is come upon us; yet have we not forgotten Thee, neither have we been false to Thy covenant.* (Ps. 44:18)

Certainly, therefore, there is no doubt that one who seeks truth will agree with our thesis, that the Nazarene and his Apostles never meant to abolish the Torah of Moses from one who was born a Jew. Likewise did Paul write in his letter to the Corinthians (1 Cor. 7) that each should adhere to the faith in which each was called. They therefore acted in accordance with the Torah by forbidding circumcision to Gentiles, according to the *halakhah*, as it is forbidden to one who does not accept the yoke of the commandments. They knew that it would be too difficult for the Gentiles to observe the Torah of Moses. They therefore forbade them to circumcise, and it would suffice that they observe the Seven Noahide Commandments, as commanded upon them through the *halakhah* from Moses at Sinai.

It is therefore a habitual saying of mine (not as a hypocritical flatterer, God forbid, for I am of the faithful believers of Israel, and I know well that the remnant of Israel will not speak falsehood, nor will their mouths contain a deceitful tongue) that the Nazarene brought about a double kindness in the world. On the one hand, he strengthened the Torah of Moses majestically, as mentioned earlier, and not one of our Sages spoke out more emphatically concerning the immutability of the Torah. And on the other hand, he did much good for the Gentiles (provided they do not turn about his intent as they please, as some foolish ones have done because they did not fully understand the intent of the authors of the Gospels. I have recently seen someone publish a book, and he had no idea about what he was writing. For if he had understood the subject, he would have kept his silence and not wasted the paper and ink. There are also found among us foolish scholars who know not their right from their left in the Written and Oral Torahs and cause the people to err with their pompous pronouncements. But there are true scholars among the Christians, just as there are the chosen few among Torah scholars; and there are few of the truly great.) [He did the Gentiles good] by doing away with idolatry and removing the images from their midst. He obligated them with the Seven Commandments [of Noah] so that they should not be as the beasts of the field. He also bestowed upon them ethical ways, and in this respect he was much more stringent with them than the Torah of Moses, as is well-known. This in itself was most proper, as it is the correct way to acquire ethical practices, as the philosopher [Maimonides] mentioned. We have written similarly in our Siddur. However, it is not necessary to impose upon Jews such extreme ethical practices, since they have been obligated to the yoke of Torah, which weakens the strength of the (evil) inclination without it. They have taken the oath at Sinai and are already trained in proper practice and nature. These are clear words that will not be rejected by a clear-thinking person.

If certain Christians who consider themselves scholars would understand this secret, who believe that they are commanded to abolish the Torah of Moses from the seed of Israel, they would not engage in such foolishness. The people listen to their self-conceived words, something which was never intended by the writers of the Gospels. Quite the opposite, they have written clearly that they intended the contrary.

> Because of these errant scholars, hatred has increased toward the Jews who are blameless of any guilt and proceed innocently to observe their Torah with all their heart, imbued with the fear of God. They should instead bring their people to love the ancient Children of Israel who remain loyal to their God, as indeed commanded to Christians by their original teachers.
>
> They even said to love one's enemies. How much more so to us! In the name of heaven, we are your brothers! One God has created us all. Why should they abuse us because we are joined to the commandments of God, to which we are tied with the ropes of his love? We do this not to enjoy the pleasures of the (evil) inclination and emptiness of a passing world. *For truly we have become a byword among the nations, and in all this...In God have we gloried all the day, and we will give thanks unto Thy name for ever* (Ps. 44). We pray for the good of the entire world, and especially for the benefit of these lands in which we reside, protecting us and our observance of the Torah.
>
> You, members of the Christian faith, how good and pleasant it might be if you would observe that which was commanded to you by your first teachers; how wonderful is your share if you will assist the Jews in the observance of their Torah. You will truly receive a reward as if you had fulfilled it yourselves—for the one who helps others to observe is greater than one who observes but does not help others to do so—even though you only observe the Seven Commandments. I have written similarly, in my pleasant work Torat Ha-Kenaot, that the Jew who observes the Torah, but doesn't support it, is considered among the cursed; and the Gentile who does not observe the 613 commandments, but supports it, is considered among the blessed.[24]

It's a remarkable letter with remarkable insights. But one wonders what the rabbis of the Four Lands made of it.

Of course, Rabbi Yaakov ben Zvi says nothing of Jesus's lineage. But one can hardly imagine that he thought that one who observed Torah, upheld Torah, and taught Torah to the nations, was a *mamzer*. It just doesn't fit. It is likely that he saw Jesus as the son of Joseph of Nazareth.

JESUS COMES HOME

A generation later, Moses Mendelssohn made similar comments on Jesus in his book, *Jerusalem: or, On Religious Power and Judaism.*

[24] From the translation of Falk, *Jesus the Pharisee*, chapter one.

> Jesus of Nazareth himself observed not only the law of Moses, but also the ordinances of the rabbis; and whatever seems to contradict this in the speeches and acts ascribed to him appears to do so only at first glance. Closely examined, everything is in complete agreement not only with scripture, but also with the tradition.[25]

Again, nothing on Jesus's conception, but we begin to observe a developing Jewish view of Jesus as *tsadik.* These positive Jewish views of Jesus continue throughout the Enlightenment period. He is seen as a great Jewish teacher who had immense influence on the world. The ancient cry of *mamzer* is barely heard.

This all led, in the twentieth century, to the view sometimes called the *Heimholung* (Home-bringing) of Jesus. With the return of Jews to the Holy Land, the declaration of the State of Israel, and the discovery of the Dead Sea Scrolls, there arose a new awareness of Jesus within the context of first-century Israel and of the New Testament as a Jewish book. Jesus came to be seen as an alternative first-century rabbi within the complex religious and political context of the time.

Jesus in modern Israel

The first major Israeli writer on Jesus was Joseph Klausner, professor of Hebrew literature at the Hebrew University in the early twentieth century. Klausner enjoyed an enormous academic reputation. He was also active in the political sphere, standing against Weizmann in the first Israeli presidential election in 1949.

Klausner's books—*Jesus of Nazareth: His Life Times and Teaching* (1921), *From Jesus to Paul* (1942), and *The Messianic Idea in Israel* (1954)—present Jesus as a Pharisaic Jewish rabbi who claimed to be the Messiah. For this claim, says Klausner, he was rejected by the Pharisees and, posing a threat to the Jewish state, he was silenced. In desiring to polarize Judaism and Christianity, Klausner rather distorts both. He makes Judaism a political affair, entirely devoted to the preservation of the national status quo, while the Jesus movement becomes an individualistic moral and spiritual innovation. His views on the resurrection are ambiguous. He thinks, on the one hand, that Joseph of Arimathea removed Jesus's body from the tomb and buried

[25] *Jerusalem, or On Religious Power in Judaism*. Cited in Gottlieb (ed.), 119.

it in an unknown grave. Yet he believes that the disciples saw visions of Jesus risen, yet these were 'spiritual and not material' in nature. He thinks these visions were real enough to say 'The nineteen hundred years' faith of millions is not founded on deception.'[26]

The Israeli interest in Jesus gave rise to the Hebrew University chair of Early Christianity and Judaism of the Second Temple Period. The one appointed to it was David Flusser, an Orthodox Jew with an abiding interest in Jesus and the Nazarene movement. Flusser, as he said, admired and loved Jesus. He tried to put Jesus's teaching on love into practice in his own life. Speaking to the Dominican priest Marcel Dubois, he referred to Jesus as, 'My teacher and your God.' He wrote,

> I personally identify myself with Jesus' Jewish worldview, both moral and political, and I believe that the content of his teachings and the approach he embraced have always had the potential to change our world and prevent the greatest part of evil and suffering.[27]

He even affirmed Jesus's return, in some sense, from death.

> I am convinced that there are reliable reports that the Crucified One 'appeared to Peter, then to the twelve. Then he appeared to more than five hundred brethren at one time.... Then he appeared to James, then to all the apostles.' Last of all, he appeared to Paul on the road to Damascus (1 Cor. 15:3-8).[28]

In all this, Flusser says little about Jesus's conception. But his references to Joseph as Jesus's father, and his statements such as 'Did Luke or his source invent this story to proclaim the virgin birth?'[29] lead us to assume that Flusser too believed that Jesus was the son of Joseph of Nazareth.

Pinhas Lapide, an Israeli statesman and New Testament theologian, went further than anyone in speaking of the resurrection. In his *The Resurrection of Jesus: A Jewish Perspective*, he wrote:

> Thus, according to my opinion, the resurrection belongs to the category of the truly real and effective occurrences, for without a fact of history there is no act of true faith.... In other words: Without the Sinai experience—no Judaism; without the Easter experience—no

[26] Klausner, *Jesus of Nazareth*, 355, 359.
[27] Flusser, *Jesus*, xviii.
[28] Flusser, *Jesus*, 144-145.
[29] Flusser, The Sage from Galilee, 11.

> Christianity. Both were Jewish faith experiences whose radiating power, in a different way, was meant for the world of nations.[30]

Lapide had less to say on the Incarnation. But, in conversation with Hans Kung—before his book on the resurrection—he said:

> With the utmost seriousness, as an Orthodox Jew, I must say that I cannot accept what you call resurrection, *kenosis* [outpouring of deity in incarnation], and *apokatastasis* [cosmic renewal], since this is not suggested by our Jewish experience of God. But neither can I deny it, for who am I as a devout Jew to define a priori God's saving action? To *define* means to assign limits, and this, from a Jewish standpoint, would be blasphemous.[31]

Shlomo Riskin was a student of David Flusser. In a YouTube video, posted on 28 December 2009, he repeats Flusser's dictum that when the Messiah comes to Jerusalem, they will ask him, 'Is this the first time you're coming, or the second time'. Here is part of his video text:

> Shalom to all. My name is Shlomo Riskin. I am the Chief Rabbi of the City of Efrat.....I am an Orthodox Rabbi. And an Orthodox Rabbi who is very profoundly interested in religion in general, in Christianity, and especially in the persona of Jesus in particular.
>
> [He describes his studies with David Flusser in Jerusalem.]
>
> I was truly fascinated by the personality of Jesus, whom certainly to myself I always referred to as 'Rabbi Jesus', because I think he is indeed a 'model Rabbi' in many counts. And he lived the life of a Jewish Rabbi in Israel at a very critical time in our history. I have constantly come back to a study of his personality and his teachings which are very strongly rooted in Talmudic teachings. I have come to the very obvious conclusion that Christians and Jews are the root and the branch because Jesus emerged out of Jewish teachings and Jewish society.
>
> I often think, if someone were to announce that the Messiah is here, who would actually want him? The Jews? Messiah means the Jews would have to move to Israel. I doubt that the Jews throughout the world are ready right now to move to Israel. So I don't think many, many people would be interested in his coming, except religious Christians and religious Jews. And we'll all run out to greet him, and ask him one critical question: 'Is this the first time you're coming, or the second time you're coming.' That's the difference. But in terms of the idea and the ideal of messianism, in terms of perfection and

[30] Lapide, *Resurrection*, 92.

[31] Lapide, 'Jesus: A Bond or a Barrier', 481.

> perfectability of world and society, that is one of the most optimistic and critical ideas which we Jews and Christians share together and give to the world.

The video was met by a backlash of criticism and calls for Riskin's resignation. A week later, he announced that, while his 'Rabbi Jesus' terminology was 'inappropriate', the poorly edited video had mauled his message. Yet he still speaks highly of Jesus and takes part in interfaith praise services with Christians, infuriating segments of the Orthodox Jewish community. The Sephardi Chief Rabbi of Jerusalem says Riskin's interfaith events make his stomach turn.

More recently, Jonathan Sacks, the Chief Rabbi Emeritus of Great Britain and the Commonwealth, developed Rambam's view that Jesus introduced the God of Israel to the world. In the first edition of his *Dignity of Difference*, he wrote,

> God has spoken to mankind in many languages: through Judaism to Jews, Christianity to Christians, Islam to Muslims.

This brought upon him, as upon Riskin, cries of heresy, particularly from the Haredi community. It was duly rephrased to,

> As Jews we believe that God has made a covenant with the singular people, but [this] does not exclude the possibility of other peoples, cultures and faith finding their own relationship with God within the shared frame of the Noahide laws.

This placated some of his critics. But Sacks continued to say that monotheistic non-Jews worship the same God as Jews, and do so acceptably.

Jesus as Messiah ben Joseph

The most recent development in the long Jewish rapprochement with Jesus is the view, now heard in Jewish communities from Jerusalem to San Francisco, that Jesus was Messiah ben Joseph, of whom we spoke in chapter three.

The rabbinic figure of Messiah ben Joseph, remember, arises from the promises to Joseph and his tribes in Genesis 49 and Deuteronomy 33. The rabbis say that he will be a Messiah from Galilee who suffers and dies at the gate of Jerusalem to atone for the sins of Israel.

Of course, such an identification is not hard to make. Jesus fits every part of the Messiah ben Joseph picture point by point: a Galilean *tsadik* of royal blood who spoke of his death as a sacrifice and died just outside Jerusalem's walls. Since many Jews now accept Jesus as the son of Joseph of Nazareth, even the name Messiah ben Joseph fits him well.[32]

However, the flip side of this view is that, if Jesus was Messiah ben Joseph, then he cannot be Messiah ben David who is to come and rule, because, for most Jews, the two figures are seen as quite distinct. They are co-workers, yes, but they are not the same person. Nor, of course, is either of these Messiahs normally seen as anything other than an ordinary mortal, begotten and born in the ordinary way. That, after all, was what the sages taught.

Summary

In all this attention which Jesus is now generating within Judaism, he is viewed much more sympathetically than in the Talmud. Most modern Jews sees him as a fascinating figure, the enigma of Second Temple Judaism. Many admire his teaching. Some accept his miracles. Some speak of some kind of resurrection appearance.[33] But the elephant in the room is his conception. A sharp distinction is drawn between what Jesus did and who Jesus was. Any idea that he could have been some sort of divine man is seen as quite foreign to Judaism.

[32] Ariel Cohen Alloro, a Jerusalemite Orthodox Jew, says Jesus is 'Messiah ben Joseph on the other side', and claims many orthodox rabbis in Jerusalem now accept this too (YouTube, 'Ariel Cohen Alloro - The official return of Yeshua to Israel with a Pidyon Haben & a Retrial'). He asks Israel's top rabbis to re-examine the Sanhedrin's sentence on Jesus almost 2,000 years ago, and to enact a *pidyon ha-ben*—'a redemption of the son', so that Israel may redeem Jesus whom they sold to the Gentiles. He says that, as Judah sold Joseph, so the Judeans sold this [Messiah ben] Joseph. He adds, 'I believe we are 2,000 years in exile on behalf of this 'Joseph' selling.' (YouTube, 'Ariel Cohen Alloro - about the Return of Jesus to Israel and the Retrial')

[33] Mishkin, *Jewish Scholarship on the Resurrection of Jesus* for a detailed discussion.

11

Heavenly Messiah

THE WIDELY-HELD Jewish view is that any claim that the Messiah is a divine man must be rejected. The Messiah, it is said, is a mortal man, conceived in the natural way, for this is what the sages taught.

In the mid-twelfth century, Rambam (Moshe ben Maimon) wrote, in the twelfth of his Thirteen Principles of Faith:

> We believe and affirm that the Messiah will come. One should not think he is detained. *Though he should tarry, await him* (Hab. 2:3). Included within this Principle is that the king of Israel must come from the House of David and the seed of Solomon. Anyone who opposes this dynasty defies the Almighty and the words of his prophets. (Mishneh Torah, Sanhedrin 10)

Two hundred years later, Ramban (Moshe ben Naḥman) was clearer still. At the Barcelona Disputation, he said to James I of Aragon:

> You are a gentile king, and he [the Messiah] is a Jewish king, for the Messiah is but a king of flesh and blood like you.
>
> All of your life, you, our lord king, a Christian son of a Christian father and mother, have heard priests, monks, and preachers speaking of the Nazarene's birth. They have filled your mind and the marrow of your bones with this thing, and it comes to you out of habit. Yet, what you believe—and it is the root of your faith—is not acceptable to the mind. Nature does not work that way, and the prophets never said so. Furthermore, a miracle cannot disseminate itself in that way, as I shall

> explain with valid proofs in its place and in its time. The mind of any Jew or any man will not permit him to believe that the Creator of heaven and earth would enter the womb of a certain Jewish woman, grow there for nine months, and be born as a baby, who afterwards grew up and later was betrayed into the hands of his enemies, who judged him, condemned him to death, and executed him. You then claim, finally, that he became alive and returned to his former state. You voice your opinion in vain and to no purpose, for this is the root of the controversy between us.

Ramban rightly says that this claim—that the Messiah is an incarnate divinity—is the root of the Christian faith and is equally the root of the controversy between Jews and Christians at the Barcelona Disputation. He also says, justly enough, that this claim goes quite against nature. Indeed, he finds it quite irrational. He is utterly opposed to it and insists that such a thing was never spoken by the prophets. That is a claim which deserves investigation.

HEAVENLY MESSIAH IN THE HEBREW SCRIPTURES

Genesis 3: The Seed of the Woman

Right at the outset of the Bible's story of salvation, the one who is to crush the serpent's head is the Seed of the Woman (Gen. 3:15). In Hebrew thought, children descend from their fathers. (Remember, it is not the custom of the Hebrews to give genealogies of women.) So, when the Holy One speaks to the serpent about the woman and 'her seed', then we should see it as pointing to one woman-born but of undisclosed paternity.

One might object that the Angel of YHVH speaks to Hagar about 'your seed', yet the father of her child was Avraham (Gen. 16.10). But he addressed Hagar alone after she was cast out. Yet here he addresses the serpent, in the presence of both Adam and Eve, but speaks only of 'her seed'. Adam does not seem to be included at all. So it looks like the writer of this text expected a child conceived in an extraordinary manner to come and deliver mankind from the power of the serpentine kingdom. That is why the Israelites long saw the passage as pointing to the Messiah.

> Nevertheless there shall be a medicine for the sons of the woman, but for you, serpent, there shall be no medicine. But it shall be that for these

> [the sons of the woman] there shall be a remedy for the heel in the days of the King Messiah. (Targum Yerushalmi on Gen. 3:15)

Psalm 132: The fruit of David's womb

Another passage, too little discussed, is the promise to David in the Psalms: *from the fruit of your womb* (*bitn'kha*) *will I set upon your throne* (132:11). David, of course, did not have a womb. One may reply that the word (*beten*) is used here in its general sense of 'belly' rather than 'womb'. Perhaps. But *the fruit of...womb* is quite different. That phrase is used for the female reproductive organ (Gen. 30:2; Deut. 7:13; 28:4; Isa. 13:18). The sole objection might be Micah's words, *the fruit of my womb/belly for the sin of my soul* (Mic. 6:7). But even there Micah can be seen as speaking of the female organ, that is, the wife's womb. The rabbis tend not to notice this unusual phrase in the psalm. Radak says that it is equivalent to *from your innards* (*mi-mê'ekha*) in 2 Samuel 7:12 without recognizing that the same issue arises there, since that word too usually means the 'womb'.[1] But here, Psalm 132 suggests that one will rule on David's throne who will come from his 'womb', that is, from a female of his line without male conception.

Micah 5: The Bethlehemite moshel

A little later, Micah foretells a *moshel* or ruler, the shepherd of Israel, to be born in Bethlehem, one whose *goings-forth are from long before, from days of everlasting* ['olam] (Mic. 5:2). Some take this to mean that this ruler has a long genealogy. But that is not what it says. It says that the coming one is from days of *'olam*; that is, he existed perpetually before his birth. The Israelites, repeatedly, with one voice, confessed that the passage speaks of the Messiah.

The Targum Yerushalmi on Genesis 35.23, comments on Migdal Eder, 'The Watch-tower of the flock', spoken of in Micah 4:8:

> *He* [Jacob] *spread his tent beyond Migdal Eder*, the place where the King Messiah will reveal himself at the end of days.

The Targum on Micah 4:8 swaps Migdal Eder tower with the Messiah:

> And you, O Messiah of Israel, who has been hidden away because of the sins of the congregation of Zion, to you the kingdom shall come.

[1] Gen. 25:23; Ruth 1:11; Ps. 71:6; Isa. 49:1. But there are exceptions, at Gen. 15:4; 2 Sam. 16:11, where it is used for the offspring of Abraham and David.

Likewise the Targum renders Micah 5:2 as follows:

> And you, O Bethlehem Efrat, you who were too small to be numbered among the thousands of the house of Judah, from you shall come forth before me the Messiah, to exercise dominion over Israel, he whose name was mentioned from before, from the days of creation.

In the time of Herod the Great, the chief priests and teachers of the law saw Micah 5 as the go-to text on the Messiah's birthplace.

> When he [Herod] had called together all the chief priests and scribes of the people, he asked them where the Messiah was to be born. 'In Bethlehem in Judah,' they replied, 'for this is what the prophet has written: *You, Bethlehem in the land of Judah, are by no means least among the rulers of Judah, for out of you will come a ruler who will be the shepherd of my people Israel* (Matt. 2.4–6, citing Mic. 5.2).

The Talmud Bavli, Sanhedrin 98b, witnesses to the same thing:

> Rav said: The son of David [the Messiah] will not come until the [Roman] power enfolds Israel for nine months, as it is written, *Therefore will he give them up, until the time that she which travaileth hath brought forth: then the remnant of his brethren shall return unto the children of Israel* (Mic. 5.3).

So too the Talmud Yerushalmi, Berakhot 2.3:

> He said to him, 'Jew, Jew. Bind your ox, and bind your plough. For today the King Messiah is born.' He said to him, 'Where is he from?' He said to him, 'From the royal city of Bethlehem in Judah' (Mic. 5.2).

And so too Rashi:

> *From you will come forth to me* (Mic. 5.2): Messiah ben David, of whom it is said, *The stone the builders rejected* (Ps. 118.22).

And Radak:

> *You Bethlehem, being least among the leaders of Judah, from you will come forth to me one who will be ruler of Israel* (Mic. 5:2). And this is the King Messiah.

In other words, just about everyone saw the Messiah in Micah's coming ruler or *moshel*.[2] And, according to Micah, this one is from *'olam*.

[2] One may also note Midrash Yelamdenu, which is in §20 of the supplement (*Kuntres Acharon*) to some editions of Yalkut Shimoni. It was republished by Jellinek, *Bet ha-Midrash*, VI.79–90 (81). I cite the text in *Messiah ben Joseph*, chapter 3.

Other heavenly Messiah texts in the Bible

Now, these three texts together address the same question of the Messiah's conception. Any text that hints at fatherless conception, like Genesis 3 or Psalm 132, implies a being of extraordinary nature, for ordinary mortals are begotten by fathers. Likewise, the pre-existent ruler spoken of by Micah must be a heavenly being. And heavenly beings are not conceived by mortal seed. So all three texts point to the coming of a heavenly saviour of extraordinary conception.

We could also add to them Psalm 110 which, as we saw, speaks of an eternal Melchizedek Messiah, existing in Avraham's time and promised eternal dominion and priesthood. We could add Psalm 45, where the psalmist says quite clearly of the *mashiaḥ* king, *Your throne, O God* (elohim), *is for ever and ever.*[3] We could add Daniel 7, where the 'Son of Man' proceeds from beside the heavenly throne to rule the earth. And we could add Zechariah 12, where the promised king of the house of David is like *elohim* and *the angel of YHVH* (12.8), and whose piercings are the piercings of YHVH himself (12.10). Finally, we could perhaps add Isaiah 7:14: *Behold, the 'almah is pregnant and is bearing a son.* It is a complex text, which can be taken as a prophecy of the Messiah's virgin conception, as in Matthew 1:23. But it is also amenable to other interpretations. I discuss it at length in Appendix 3.

So there are several texts in the Hebrew (and Aramaic) Scriptures which point to the coming of a heavenly saviour.

Heavenly Messiah in Second Temple times

The same theme appears in post-biblical literature too. The Similitudes of Enoch tell how Daniel's 'Son of Man' figure was hidden 'from the beginning', and then revealed to the elect.

> The kings and the mighty and all who possess the earth
> shall bless and glorify and extol him who rules over all,
> who was hidden,
> For from the beginning the Son of Man was hidden,
> And the Most High preserved him in the presence of his might
> And revealed him to the elect. (1 Enoch 62:6–7)[4]

[3] See Postell, 'Analysis of Psalm 45', for a messianic interpretation of the psalm.
[4] Numeration as in Charlesworth (1983) and Charles (1919).

Something similar is found in the fifth book of the Sibylline Oracles. These texts are a mix of pagan, Jewish, and Christian prophecies which were preserved by the early church. Yet Josephus knew and cited parts of them as prophetic texts in the first century AD.[5] Modern scholarship tends to see the third, fourth, and fifth books of the oracles as Jewish texts written in Alexandria.[6] This passage, which appears in the fifth book, describes a hero-saviour coming from heaven to earth.

> For a blessed man came from the expanses of heaven
> with a scepter in his hands which God gave him,
> and he gained sway over all things well, and gave back the wealth
> to all the good, which previous men had taken.
> He destroyed every city from its foundations with much fire
> and burned nations of mortals who were formerly evildoers.
> And the city which God desired, this he made
> more brilliant than stars and sun and moon. (*Sib. Or.* 5:414–421)[7]

Something similar appears in the Testament of Levi 18. It speaks of the demise of the Aaronite temple priesthood and the arrival of a new *kohen.*[8] To this one, the divine Father shall speak as Abraham to Isaac, that is, as father to beloved son, delivered to death and redeemed. He shall live forever without successor (v. 8), illumining the world and opening the gates of Paradise.

> [1] When vengeance will have come upon them from the Lord,
> the priesthood will lapse.
> [2] And then will the Lord raise up a new priest.
> And to him all the words of the Lord will be revealed.
> And he shall execute righteous judgement on the earth
> for many days.
> [3] And his star shall arise in heaven like (the star) of a king,
> illuminating the light of knowledge as day is illumined by the sun.
> And he shall be extolled by the whole inhabited world.
> [4] He will shine forth like the sun in the earth;
> he shall take away all darkness from under heaven,

[5] *Ant* 1:4:3 [118] citing *Sib. Or.* 3:101–110.

[6] Collins, 'Sibylline Oracles', 322, 390–91, 403. Collins thinks Book 5 is Jewish except for lines 256–259, which he says have undergone Christian redaction to speak of crucifixion (390). But O'Neill, 'Man from Heaven', argues that Book 5 is Jewish in its entirety. I discuss the passage in *Messiah ben Joseph*, chapter 5.

[7] This 'man from heaven' appears a little earlier in the same text, in Sib. Or. 5:256–259, as a second Joshua. I refer the reader to my *Messiah ben Joseph*, chapter 5.

[8] Text from Kee, 'Testaments', pp. 794–795. The passage in square brackets is the only one Kee regards as Christian interpolation.

and there shall be peace in all the earth.
[5] The heavens shall exult in his days and the earth shall be glad;
the clouds will be filled with joy
and the knowledge of the Lord shall be poured out on the earth,
as the water of the seas.
And the angels of glory of the Lord's presence will be glad in him.
[6] The heavens shall be opened,
and from the temple of glory shall come upon him sanctification,
with the Father's voice, as from Abraham to Isaac.
[7] And the glory of the Most High shall burst forth upon him.
And the spirit of understanding and sanctification (Isa. 11:2)
shall rest upon him [in the water].
[8] For he shall give the majesty of the Lord
to those who are his sons in truth forever.
And none shall succeed him from generation to generation for ever.
[9] And in his priesthood the nations shall be multiplied
in knowledge on the earth,
and they shall be illumined by the grace of the Lord,
but Israel shall be diminished by her ignorance
and darkened by her grief.
In his priesthood sin shall cease
and lawless men rest from evil deeds,
and the righteous shall find rest in him.
[10] And he shall open the gates of paradise;
he shall remove the sword that threatened Adam.
[11] And he will grant to the saints to eat of the tree of life;
the spirit of holiness shall be upon them.
[12] And Beliar shall be bound by him.
And he shall grant to his children
the authority to trample on wicked spirits.
[13] And the Lord will rejoice in his children;
And he will be well pleased by his beloved ones forever.
[14] Then Abraham, Isaac, and Jacob will rejoice, and I shall be glad,
and all the saints shall be clothed in righteousness.

A similar passage appears in column 2 of the Dead Sea Scrolls text 4QAramaic Apocalypse (4Q246). It is dependent on the Son of Man passage from Daniel 7, especially in the phrases *his kingdom is an eternal kingdom* and *his dominion is an everlasting dominion* (Dan. 7:14, 27). But, for this writer, 'Son of Man' means the 'Son of God' and the 'Son of the Most High', and he shall be 'a great god'.

He will be called the Son of God, and they will call him the Son of the Most High...His kingdom will be an eternal kingdom...The earth will

> be in truth and all will make peace. The sword will cease in the earth, and all the cities will pay him homage. He is a great god among the gods... His dominion will be an everlasting dominion.

Nothing is said, in these passages, about the heavenly saviour's conception or birth. We are left to wonder how he is to enter the world. But one Dead Sea text does seem to speak of such a thing. This is the appendix to the Community Rule, the regulations for the priestly community who wrote it. It tells how the Messiah will appear at their table, after God has begotten him.

> [11][This shall be the ass]embly of the men of renown [called] to the meeting of the Council of the Community when God will beget [12]the Messiah, he shall come [at] the head of the whole congregation of Israel with all [13][his brethren, the sons] of Aaron, the Priests [summoned] to the assembly, the men of renown; and they shall sit [14][before him, each man] in the order of his dignity.

So some Israelites expected the Messiah to be a divinely-begotten heavenly man, long before the Christian period.

Heavenly Messiah in the New Testament

New Testament writers, of course, subscribed to the idea of a divinely-begotten, heavenly Messiah. They believed that Jesus was this very one. The evidence hardly needs citing. It appears in the earliest New Testament texts. In the 40s AD, within a decade of the cross, Paul speaks of Jesus's divine pre-existence. He was the son of God sent forth, the promised Seed of the Woman (Gal. 4:4). He was in very nature God but was made in human likeness (Phil. 2:6–7). He is the image of the invisible God through whom all things were created, who was before all things, in whom all things hold together (Col. 1:15–17). Only a decade later, the birth narratives of Matthew and Luke show that they too believed in his divine conception.[9] For John, he is the eternal Logos, the agent of creation, the source of life (John 1:1–3).

[9] Luke's Acts closes before the execution of Paul, and must date from before 62 AD. His gospel must therefore date from some years before, that is, from not later than the late 50s. A similar date should be given for Matthew's gospel, since he wrote it, as Eusebius says, before leaving Jerusalem. Remarkable evidence has come to light in recent decades to confirm the early date of the gospels; see Thiede and d'Ancona, *Eyewitness*; Bauckham, *Jesus and the Eyewitnesses*.

And, for the author of Hebrews, he is the outshining radiance of God's glory, the exact image of the divine being, sustaining all things by his spoken word of power (1: 3). All these passages testify to the fact that many Israelites found such a view to be in accord with the prophets.

HEAVENLY MESSIAH IN RABBINIC LITERATURE

The rabbinic community, of course, hardly subscribed to the New Testament view. Yet they too retain among themselves the ancient belief in the Messiah's heavenly nature.

Pesikta Rabbati is a cycle of Hebrew homiletical midrashim, compiled in the mid-first millennium from older texts. It describes the pre-existent Messiah, hidden under the divine throne. Satan sees him and is dismayed to hear that this one will bring about his downfall. Then the Holy One speaks with the Messiah of his future coming to earth and of the sufferings he will endure there. It is worth quoting at length.

> §36. What is meant by *In your light do we see light?* (Ps. 36:9). What light is it that the congregation of Israel looks for as from a watch-tower? It is the light of the Messiah, as it is said, *And God saw the light that it was good* (Gen. 1:4). This verse proves that the Holy One, blessed be he, contemplated the Messiah and his works before the world was created, and then hid away his Messiah under his throne of glory until the generation in which he will appear.
>
> Satan said before the Holy One, 'Master of the universe, for whom is the light which is put away under your throne of glory?'
>
> He replied, 'For him who will turn you back and put you to utter shame.'
>
> Satan said, 'Master of the universe, show him to me.'
>
> He replied, 'Come and see him.'
>
> And when he saw him, Satan was shaken, and he fell upon his face and said, 'Surely this is Messiah who will cause me and all the princes of the nations to be swallowed up in Gehenna, as it is said, *He will swallow up death for ever; and the Lord God will wipe away tears from all faces*' (Isa. 25:8).
>
> In that hour the princes of the nations,[10] in agitation, will say to him, 'Master of the Universe, who is this through whose power we are to be swallowed up? What is his name? What kind of a being is he?'

[10] That is, the tutelary deities of each nation.

> The Holy One, blessed be he, will reply, 'He is the Messiah and his name is Ephraim Messiah *Tsidqi*, who will raise up himself and raise up his generation, and who will give light to the eyes of Israel and deliver his people; and no nation or people will be able to withstand him, as is said, *The enemy shall not do him violence, nor the son of wickedness afflict him* (Ps. 89:22). And all his enemies and adversaries shall be beaten before him, as it is said, *I will beat to pieces his adversaries before him* (Ps. 89:23). And even seas and rivers will stop flowing, as it is said, *I will set his hand also on the sea, and his right hand on the rivers* (Ps. 89:25).' [11]
>
> The Holy One, blessed be he, made an agreement with him [Messiah Ephraim]. He said, 'Those whose sins are stored up with you will bring you into an iron yoke and make you like this calf whose eyes are dimmed [with pain]. They will force your spirit into a yoke, and because of their sins your *tongue will cleave* to your jaws (Ps. 22:15). Are you willing for this?'
>
> The Messiah will ask the Holy One, blessed be he, 'Will my suffering last many years?'
>
> The Holy One, blessed be he, will reply, 'Upon your life and the life of my head, it is a period of seven years which I have decreed for you. But if your soul is sad at the prospect of your suffering, I shall banish them forthwith.'
>
> He replied in his presence, 'Master of the universe, with gladness of soul and rejoicing of heart I take it upon me, on the condition that not one will perish from Israel. And not only the living will be saved in my days, but also the dead, who died from the time of Adam up to the time of redemption; and that not only these be saved in my days, but also those who died unborn[12]; and that not only these be saved in my days, but all those whom you thought to create and were not created. Such are the things I desire, and for these I am ready to take upon myself (whatever you decree).'

Now this is a remarkable text. Indeed, Pesikta Rabbati's view of the Messiah is remarkable altogether. It says that he existed from the creation of the world and his merit is equal to the whole household of heaven (34.2). Yet there is no question of these passages being Christian. They are certainly Jewish. For Pesikta Rabbati is marked throughout by anti-Christian polemic. Some argue that the passage above is from as early as the tannaitic period, from before AD 200.[13] Personally, I find it hard to see how such a passage could have arisen

[11] The Messiah will re-enact the miracles at the Red Sea and the Jordan.

[12] The term includes abortions and children dead through miscarriage.

[13] M. Friedmann regarded §34–37 as tannaitic (*Pesikta Rabbati*, 24).

among Christian-period Jews at all. Its view of a pre-existent Messiah coming to suffer for the sins of the world would only have given credence to Christian claims. So it looks to me like a much older text included in the later Pesikta Rabbati compendium.

Yet other rabbinic texts speak of the Messiah's heavenly pre-existence or his creation before the world was made.

> Seven things were created before the world was created, and these are they: the Torah, repentance, the Garden of Eden, Gehenna, the Throne of Glory, the Temple, and the name of the Messiah.... The name of the Messiah, as it is written, *His name shall endure for ever, and existed before the sun.* (Ps. 72:17) (B. Pes. 54a)[14]

Others speak of his pre-existence in the Garden of Eden.[15] Still others speak of his earthly pre-existence. He is the long-lived son of Elijah's benefactress, the widow of Tsarfat.[16] He was born in the days of King David and is hidden until the time of the end.[17] He was born in Bethlehem on the day the temple was destroyed.[18] He is in Rome awaiting the time of his revealing.[19]

The *paytan* Eleazar ben Kallir, who lived in Palestine through the rise and fall of Nehemiah ben Hushiel's brief Jewish kingdom of AD 614, looked for a king far greater than any mortal.

> A king who says to the sea: 'Thus far you shall come!'
> He shall be king!
> A king of abomination, who comes from a vile drop [of semen]
> and goes but to the grave,
> Why should he be king?
>
> A king who builds his upper chambers and his chariot throne
> in the heavens,
> He shall be king!

[14] See likewise B. Ned. 39b; Yalk. Shim. 1:20, where the Messiah's name is among the ten things created on the eve of Shabbat before the world was made; yet the 'name' implies his pre-existence, not simply the intention to create him, which is described as 'another view'. See the rabbinic views of the king figure of Ps. 110 and the enthroned figure of Dan. 7:9–14 cited in chapter four.

[15] *Revelation of R. Joshua b. Levi* (*BHM* II.48–51); *Midrash Konen* (*BHM* II.23–29); *Seder Gan Eden* (*BHM* III.132–140; 194–198); *Zohar* Shemot §106–109; Vayaqhel §335.

[16] Sefer Eliyahu Rabbah 98.

[17] Sefer Zerubbabel 33.

[18] Y. Ber. 2.4; cf. Justin, *Dial.* §8, where Trypho agrees the Messiah may be born.

[19] Exod. R. 1.26 (on Exod. 2.10); B. Sanh. 98a.

A king who returns to the dust like an expiring candle,
Why should he be king?

A king fair among ten thousand, who brings forth thousands
and ten thousands of angels,
He shall be king!
A king who fears, dreads, and is terrified at the judgment of his master,
Why should he be king?

Now none of these texts are Christian. They are Jewish. They simply follow the Hebrew scriptures in looking forward to a heavenly man who is appointed king of Israel to rule the nations. It therefore looks like the idea of a pre-existent heavenly Messiah was quite familiar in Israel both before and after Christian times.

Summary

The idea that the promised world-ruler is to be a heavenly man—that is, a man of extraordinary conception—is found in several passages in the Hebrew scriptures. Later, it was familiar to the writers and readers of the Enoch compendium, the Testaments of the Twelve Patriarchs, the Sibylline Oracles, the Damascus Document, and other Dead Sea texts. It is found, of course, in the New Testament. And it continues in rabbinic literature throughout the first millennium AD. As Boyarin says,

> The reason that many Jews came to believe that Jesus was divine was because they were already expecting that the Messiah/Christ would be a god-man. *This expectation was part and parcel of Jewish tradition.*[20]

In this light, it is not the New Testament which departs from the ancient scriptures. It is Rambam, Ramban, and their modern disciples who depart, when they insist on the Messiah's mortal nature.

[20] Boyarin, *Jewish Gospels*, 12.

12

Jesus the Jew?

THE IDEA that Jesus was a Jew is not one we find much in ancient times. We don't find it, for instance, in the Church Fathers. Yet these days everyone says so. It maybe began with Luther's pamphlet, *That Jesus Christ Was Born a Jew* (1523), when Luther initially sought to protect the Jews from the persecution of the Roman church. In the eighteenth century, Moses Mendelssohn agreed. Julius Wellhausen followed him, a century later, saying, 'Jesus was not a Christian, but a Jew.' But it was in the 1970s that the ball really got rolling.

Credit for this usually goes to the book *Jesus the Jew*, published in 1973 by the Hungarian Jew, sometime Catholic priest, and Oxford don, Geza Vermes. Yet Vermes's book had a precursor in the Christmas screening of the BBC sitcom *Till Death Us Do Part* in December 1972.

Till Death Us Do Part was a BBC series written by Johnny Speight. The gentle reader may find it grim viewing with its continual cursing and drunkenness. But, as such things do, it became a satirical classic in its time, and gave rise to imitations, such as *All In The Family* in the USA. The anti-hero of the piece is Alf Garnett, a working-class, Conservative-voting, Church-of-England-attending loudmouth, played by British-Jewish comedian Warren Mitchell. After a boozy Christmas dinner, Alf launches forth on the subject of Jews in London. (Mitchell used to say, 'I'm Jewish so I can make anti-semitic jokes.') His long-suffering wife insists that Alf's father was Jewish, but Alf denies it. Then his son-in-law says Jesus was Jewish. Alf is completely shocked.

Jesus wasn't Jewish, he replies. 'That's blasphemious, that is.'

The irony has been laid on with a trowel: an atheist-Jewish comedian playing a non-Jewish Christian who swears blind that Jesus was not Jewish. But since Alf Garnett talks rubbish, the sub-text is clear: Jesus was a Jew.

Now I don't know whether Vermes took his cue from Speight, or whether Speight got rumours of Vermes's forthcoming book, but, one way or another, the modern Jewish Jesus movement started somewhere between Alf Garnett and Geza Vermes.

Vermes's book was enthusiastically taken up by the media and made him an instant academic celebrity. It started what Professor Dunn calls 'the third wave of the quest for the historical Jesus'.[1] And the wave has rolled deep and wide.

Since then we've had *Christianity is Jewish* (Schaeffer 1975), *Jesus the Jew, The Historical Jesus: The True Story of Jesus* (Bazes 1976), *Jewishness and Jesus* (Juster 1977), *Jesus the Pharisee: A New Look at the Jewishness of Jesus* (Falk 1985), *The Galilean Jewishness of Jesus* (Lee 1988), *Jesus' Jewishness* (Charlesworth 1991), *A Marginal Jew* (Meier 1991), *A Mediterranean Jewish Peasant* (Crossan 1991), *The Religion of Jesus the Jew* (Vermes 1993), *Jesus the Jewish Theologian* (Young 1995), *The Jesus Quest: The Third Search for the Jew of Nazareth* (Witherington 1995), *Jesus of Nazareth, King of the Jews: A Jewish Life* (Fredriksen 1999), *Rabbi Jesus* (Chilton 2000), *Jesus in His Jewish Context* (Vermes 2003), *Jesus was a Jew* (Fruchtenbaum 2010), *The Jewish Jesus* (Garber 2011), and again, *The Jewish Jesus* (Schäfer 2012), *The Jewish Gospels: The Story of the Jewish Christ* (Boyarin 2012), *What Every Christian Needs to Know About the Jewishness of Jesus* (Moffic 2016). And there are more.

The view has entered popular culture too. In October 2004, the French Jewish student body, *l'Union des étudiants juifs de France (UEJF)*, produced traditional Catholic devotional posters of Jesus and his mother with the slogans *Sale juif* (Dirty Jew) and *Sale juive* (Dirty Jewess) stamped on top. They took full-page adverts, paying, no doubt, with their own money, in all the big names of the French press: *L'Équipe, Le Parisien, Le Monde, 20 Minutes, Le Figaro,* and *Le Journal du Dimanche.* Their president, Yonathan Arfi, said,

[1] Dunn, *Jesus Remembered*, 85.

> It's a way to wake people up and make them aware. That's what is important. Today, it is difficult to wake people up without running the risk of shocking them a bit.

If the posters had an actual message, it was perhaps about the growing harassment faced by the Franco-Jewish community, as if to say, 'He whom you honour was one of us, whom you despise.' But they were jousting at the wrong windmill. For it is hardly the Christians in France who target Jews these days.

Of course, Messianic Jews make similar claims about Jesus. One such website says: 'Remember: Jesus was (and is) a Jew…in the *olam habah*, the world to come, we will all give homage to a Jewish Lord and Jewish Saviour!' Well, yes. If Jesus was Jewish.

Jews and Jesus

Many Jews stress the Jewishness of Jesus. They have jokes about it.

> A rabbi asked his friend, a Catholic priest, 'Could you be promoted within the Church?'
> The priest says, thoughtfully, 'Well, I could become a bishop.'
> The rabbi says, 'And after that?'
> The priest replies, 'Maybe I could become a cardinal.'
> 'And then?'
> The priest replies, 'Perhaps someday I could even be the Pope.'
> The rabbi says, 'And then?'
> Incredulous, the priest replies, 'What more could I be? God himself?'
> The rabbi says, with a wink, 'One of our boys made it.'

This Jewish attitude to Jesus is both strange and understandable. It is strange because of the history of Jesus and the Jews that we have covered in the last few chapters. Jewish rejection of Jesus has usually been systematic and sustained.

But it is also understandable. It is understandable, on the one hand, as a defence mechanism. Given the persecution Jews have faced in the Christian world, it makes sense to assert their kinship with Jesus as a shield against their attackers. Some even depict Jewish sufferings as the sufferings of Jesus. Marc Chagall's *White Crucifixion* (1938) shows a crucified Jesus, dressed in a *tallit* loincloth, surrounded by lamenting, flying patriarchs and a matriarch, with a burning *shtetl* and synagogue in the background. Robert Aldrich's *Frisco Kid* (1979) features a Polish rabbi (Gene Wilder), wandering in the Wild West, who is seized by Indians and hanged, to be burnt, on a cross-shaped stake.

But, defence mechanisms aside, Jesus is popular. The recent study by Skiena and Ward proposes that Jesus is the most influential person in history.[2] Skiena and Ward are data analysts with a Google background. Their results are based on the analysis of which people receive the highest number of online searches and discussions, particularly on Wikipedia. Critics note that Skiena and Ward's analyses are based on English-language searches, and that the inclusion of searches in, say, Mandarin, would give a different result. That might just be true if no-one at all is searching for Jesus in Mandarin, which is far from certain. But the English figures show Jesus leading by so very far that it would take massive searches for another figure in many other languages to knock him from the throne.

So who wouldn't be proud to be related to him? In America, polls reveal that people of all faiths view Jesus 'overwhelmingly in a favorable light'. Amazingly, half of America's avowed non-Christians believe that Jesus was born of a virgin and raised from the dead.[3] For Jews, it must be tempting to claim kinship with the greatest man who ever lived. Publicly, at least, many want to claim him as their own.

And so Jewish pride in Jesus co-exists with Jewish rejection of him. He is both theirs and not-theirs. 'Yes, he's my brother. No, I don't believe a word he said.' These days, it's OK for Jews to be proud of Jesus being Jewish. They can even admire Jesus and say, 'I have no doubt that he was a remarkable person.'[4] But they cannot believe the things he said in the gospels about his birth and Messiahship. After all, Jews don't believe in Jesus. If they do, they cease to be Jews.

[2] Skiena and Ward, *Who's Bigger?* Their book is a response to Michael Hart's *The 100* (1978), which concluded that Muhammad was number one. Hart's conclusions are based only on his own estimates. He says that, although many might expect Jesus to be first, "Christianity ...was not founded by a single person but by two people—Jesus and Saint Paul—and the principal credit for its development must therefore be apportioned between these two figures" (17). Paul, he adds, was the one who changed Jesus from a human prophet to a divinity (34). He also reckons, since religious and political leaders are both significant, that Muhammad must be greater than Jesus, for Muhammad was both, but Jesus was not a political leader. He therefore places Muhammad first, Isaac Newton second, and Jesus third, with Paul in sixth place (after Buddha and Confucius).

[3] Prothero, *American Jesus*, Introduction.

[4] Boyarin, *Jewish Gospels*, 159.

WHO IS A JEW ANYWAY?

When we ask who is a Jew, two things must be considered: the historical origin of the word, and the question of who actually decides who is a Jew.

The word 'Jew' comes to English from Greek *ioudaios.* That comes in turn from Hebrew *y'hudi,* a patronymic meaning a descendant of Judah the patriarch, the son of Jacob. Therefore to say, as some do, that Abraham was a Jew is incorrect, for Abraham was not a descendant of Judah. Nor was Moses a Jew, for he was not a descendant of Judah. Nor was Aaron a Jew, nor Joshua, nor Gideon, nor Samson, nor Samuel, nor Isaiah, Jeremiah, or Ezekiel. They were all from other Israelite tribes. And to speak of the Jews conquering the Promised Land is inaccurate, for the *y'hudim* (Jews) were only one of the twelve tribes who entered the land. Even to speak of the Jewish temple is imprecise. It was built by Judahite kings, but it was run and managed by Levites.

The oldest strands of biblical history tell the story of the people of Israel as a whole, all the tribes descended from Jacob. But when, in 925 BC, Solomon's kingdom was torn in two, the northern Ephraimite kingdom claimed for itself the name of the Kingdom of Israel, while the southern kingdom called itself the Kingdom of Judah. In time, all the people of the southern kingdom came to be called *y'hudim,* even though they included many Aaronite *kohanim* and Levites, and not a few Benjamites, Reubenites, and Simeonites.

Later, after the deportation of the Ephraimites to Assyria in the eighth century BC, and the Babylonian exile and return of the Judahites in the seventh century, the people of Judah self-identified as the only true Israelites in the Holy Land. (The Samaritan descendants of the Ephraimites also claimed, with some justification, to be Israelites, but were not reckoned so by the *y'hudim.*) The area around Jerusalem became known to their neighbours as the land of Judah. Its people, a mixture of various Israelite tribes, were known to outsiders as *y'hudim* or, in Greek, *Ioudaioi,* translatable equally as Judahites or Jews.

We see this later tribal ambiguity reflected in the Bible. Mordecai is presented as *a Jew of the tribe of Benjamin* (Est. 2:5). That is, from a Persian viewpoint he was identified as a Jew, from the land of Judah. But within Israelite society he was, more accurately, a Benjamite. Presumably, if a Persian had asked about his ethnicity, he would have said he was Jewish, but if a Judean had posed the same question, he would have self-identified as a *ben-y'mini* or Benjamite.

The period of the Babylonian Exile is something of a watershed in the use of the word 'Jew'. It is reflected in many of our English Bible translations. When they speak of the kingdom period, before the Exile, they translate *y'hudim* as 'the people of the tribe of Judah'. But in the post-exilic books—Ezra, Nehemiah, Esther—they translate the same word as 'Jews'. This change well reflects the changing political reality, as Israel moved from a united monarchy of twelve tribes, through two rival kingdoms of Ephraim and Judah, to a Judahite state centred on Jerusalem, with estranged Israelite groups in Galilee and Samaria.

By Roman times, Palestinian Jews described a native of the region around Jerusalem as a *Ioudaios* and someone from the north of the country as Samaritan or Galilean. But when speaking of the entire land, they would still refer to Israel. But Romans were less discriminating. For them, a *Ioudaios* was someone from Judah, but also from Galilee or Samaria, or from the Hebrew diaspora, from India to Spain, no matter what their Hebrew tribal origin.[5]

Yet, among the Israelites, the ancient tribal distinctions remained. Josephus boasted of his descent from the Aaronite *kohanim.* Paul boasted of his descent from Benjamin. And even old Anna in the temple knew, and so did everyone else, that she was from the northern tribe of Asher (Luke 2:36). People from these other Israelite tribes did not refer to themselves as Jews. Yes, they knew that was how others—Greeks, Romans, and Syrians—spoke of them. But they identified themselves by tribal descent.

All this provides the answer to the puzzle of John's gospel's famous antipathy to the 'Jews' (*ioudaioi*). John was not anti-semitic. He was semitic himself. Nor was he anti-Israelite, for he was, as we have seen, an Israelite of Aaronite descent. But evidently he was anti-*ioudaioi*, which forces us to ask just what he meant by the term. The answer is surely that John, an Zadokite *kohen* from Galilee, used *ioudaioi* as shorthand for the Jerusalem establishment in its opposition to his beloved teacher. In using this term, he refers mainly to the Pharisees, who were mostly Judahite. For John, like Luke, presents the Pharisees rather than the Zadokites-Sadducees as Jesus's mortal enemies. He

[5] See Lowe, ''Ιουδαῖοι of the Apocrypha' and 'Who were the Ἰουδαῖοι?'

does not deny the involvement of the *kohen gadol* Caiaphas and his entourage in the plot to kill Jesus. But, as a Galilean and a Zadokite, he prefers to lump all these opponents together as *Ioudaioi* or 'Jews', both to focus on the Pharisees and because Judea was their territory.

JUDAISM: ETHNICITY OR RELIGION?

What complicates matters further is whether Judaism is an ethnicity or a religion, for it is, to a large extent, both.

In ancient times, religions were ethnic. Every tribe or people had its own pantheon of chief gods and their minions. The Ammonites had Moloch; the Edomites, Qos; the Moabites, Chemosh; the Hittites, Teshub; and so on. Some peoples, like Ashur or Athena, took their name directly from their god. Israel were part of this schema: they were the people of Yehovah.[6] Gods were linked to nations.

What changed this was the advent of Christianity.[7] In proclaiming one God for all nations, the apostles severed the link between nations and their gods. From that time on, ethnicity and religion gradually became two different things. One could be a Roman or Phrygian or Syrian or Ethiopian or Israelite Christian. Or one could come from these nations and and not be Christian.

For centuries, Judaism continued mostly as an ethnic label. Indeed, Boyarin thinks it didn't properly become a religious label until the eighteenth century—around the same time when Jews first started identifying Jesus as Jewish. But certainly, before that time, the label 'Jew' was principally ethnic rather than religious.

After the Roman destruction of Jerusalem in AD 70, the ethnic Israelites comprised large numbers of Nazarenes, Pharisees, and others. The Nazarenes worshipped Jesus and treasured the texts that would become the New Testament. The Rabbis—Ben Zakkai, Gamliel II, Judah ha-Nasi and their community at Yavneh—upheld the views and practices of the temple-period Pharisees. They preserved the Pharisees' oral teachings and ultimately codified them in the Mishnah, in the late second century. Their successors, in the fourth and fifth centuries,

[6] For 'Yehovah' as the pronunciation of the Tetragrammaton, see the Glossary.

[7] Some might say Buddhism began the same process some centuries before. But Buddhism is a philosophy that requires no allegiance to a particular deity; its adherents could worship ancestral deities while practicing the new philosophy.

developed these teachings in the Talmuds of Jerusalem and Babylon.

So these texts—Mishnah and Talmud—are, as it were, the distilled essence of Pharisaism. They form the core of Rabbinic Judaism. And they are, to some extent, a response to the New Testament. For whereas the New Testament hails Jesus as the Messiah who has come, the Talmud's message is that the Messiah has not come, and Israel must wait for him. And, since the Talmuds of Jerusalem and Babylon were codified in the fourth and fifth centuries, it means that what we now call Judaism is, strictly speaking, a later religion than Christianity.

Judaism, then, as a religious system, was codified in the Talmud. But this did not happen smoothly. Many Jews objected to the growing dominance of Pharisaic or Rabbanite Judaism and its 'oral law'. This issue had divided Israel since the first century BC. The Pharisees, following Hillel, said that their own oral traditions overruled the law of Moses. Everyone else—whether Zadokites, Essenes, Zealots, or Nazarenes—objected. So while the Pharisees were codifying their Mishnah and Talmud, non-oral-law Jews were living independently of the Rabbinic movement. The disputes remained relatively muted in the first half of the first millennium. Jews were busy just trying to survive, and they mostly lived together in community. But, in 641, there were violent conflicts between them in Egypt, resolved only by the intervention of the first Muslim governor of Egyptian, Amr ibn al-Aas. Then, in the eighth century, as the Babylonian Rabbanites became stronger, division over the oral law became acute. Ultimately, the oral-law Rabbanites took control of the Babylonian Jewish community, while the Karaites or 'Scripturalists'—as the non-oral-law party came to be known—fled to Palestine.

At this point, to increase the authority of their texts, the Rabbanites developed a strange belief. In the tenth century, Saadia Gaon began to teach that the Talmud, the 'oral law', did not actually derive from the Roman-period Pharisees at all, but was given to Moses at Sinai. That is, God taught Moses the text of the Talmud—millions of words of 'Rabbi X said in the name of Rabbi Y, but Rabbi Z differs'—and this was passed down orally for 2,000 years, from Sinai to Babylon, and was written down there in the mid-first millennium AD.

In other words, ethnic Israelites never subscribed to one faith system. There was not one Judaism, but many. In Roman times, there were Pharisees, Zadokites, Essenes, Galileans, Zealots, Nazarenes,

Ebionites, Samaritans, all with varying traditions and beliefs. And if the Rabbanites split with the Nazarenes, they split also with the others.

The Karaites remained a strong community, particularly in Russia, until the early twentieth century. But the growth of Rabbinic Judaism in recent centuries now permits a revisionist perspective that sees the Rabbanites as 'Orthodox' Jews. But that is a terminology which groups like the Karaites do not always accept.

As for the split between the Nazarenes and the rabbinic community, that had already been initiated from Jewish side by the 'Blessing on the Minim'. But in the early fifth century, Jerome took up the very language of the 'Blessing on the Minim' to exclude the Nazarenes from the Gentile church. He counselled Augustine as follows:

> In our own day there exists a sect among the Jews throughout all the synagogues of the east, which is called the sect of the Minei [*minim*], and is even now condemned by the Pharisees. The adherents to this sect are known commonly as Nazarenes; they believe in Christ the Son of God, born of the Virgin Mary; and they say that he who suffered under Pontius Pilate and rose again is the same as the one in whom we believe. But while they desire to be both Jews and Christians, they are neither the one nor the other.[8]

Jerome is excluding Jewish Christians who believe the Nicene Creed from the Christian community, because they do not fit his categories or submit to his teaching. Good old Jerome, the Doctor of the Church. Doing the Pharisees' work for them again.

PATRILINEAL AND MATRILINEAL

There is another important issue to consider. It is this. Is one a Jew because one's father is Jewish or because one's mother is Jewish?

In Orthodox Judaism the maternal line is all-important. If your mother is Jewish, you are Jewish. If she's not, you're not.

This was not so in ancient times. Back then, the paternal line was everything. This was so from the beginning of the Israelite nation. Judah married a Canaanite, known in the Bible only as Bat-Shua (Gen. 38:2). From her, descended the stirp of Shelah, as told in 1 Chronicles

[8] Jerome, letter 112 §13 (ad 404); tr. J.G. Cunningham in Schaff (ed.), *Nicene and Post-Nicene Fathers.*

4:21–23. Later, Judah begot Perez and Zerah by Tamar who, for all we can deduce from the Bible, was a Canaanite too, though the Testament of Judah presents her as Mesopotamian, perhaps an Aramean of Avraham's distant clan (T. Jud. 10:1). Joseph married an Egyptian, Asenath, the daughter of his former master, Potiphar.[9] Yet the sons of both patriarchs were accepted as Israelites.

Perhaps the patriarchs didn't have much choice. Females of Avraham's seed were thin on the ground. But hundreds of years later, the Israelites were still marrying foreign women and bringing their children into the Israelite fold. Moses first took a Cushite wife. Her name, according to Josephus, was Tharbis, a princess of Saba (Meroë) in Sudan, who betrayed her city to Moses, commander of Pharaoh's army, in return for his promise to marry her.[10] (When Miriam objected to this dark-skinned woman among the Israelites, she was turned leprous white.) Later, Moses married a Kenite-Midianite, Zipporah, from the Sinai region, whose children were duly reckoned as Israelites (Exod. 2:21–22; 1 Chr. 23:15-17).

Then there's David's line. Salmon took to wife the Canaanite Rahab from Jericho (Matt. 1:5). Their son Boaz was accepted as an Israelite. Boaz, in turn, married Ruth the Moabitess, and their son, Obed, was also accepted as Judahite. If it had been otherwise, Salmon's offspring would have been Canaanites and Obed's would have been Moabites, and David would never have been king of Israel. Reckoned matrilineally, David would have been twice disqualified from being Jewish.

David, in turn, took a non-Israelite wife, Maacah the princess of the Aramean kingdom of Geshur (2 Sam. 3:3). Yet her son, Absalom, was recognized as an Israelite. And Solomon loved many foreign women—not only Pharaoh's daughter, but Moabites, Ammonites, Edomites, Sidonians, and Hittites (1 Kgs 11:1). His heir, Rehoboam, was the offspring of an Ammonite woman, Naamah (1 Kgs 14:21). In short, the entire clan of David was reckoned only patrilineally. Matrilineally reckoned, David's clan would have been multiply excluded from Judah and Israel. Other Judahite clans had foreign matriarchs too. The Ezrahites descended from an Egyptian princess (1 Chr. 4:17–18).

[9] However, some post-biblical traditions wish to sanitize Asenath by making her the daughter of Joseph's sister, Dinah, following her rape by Shechem (Pirke de-Rabbi Eliezer §35, 37; Midrash Aggadah [Buber] Gen. 41:45).

[10] Num. 12:1–15; Josephus, *Ant.* 2:10:2.

But all this began to change after the Babylonian Exile. Ezra the *kohen*, to preserve the purity of the Judean confederation, obliged the returnees to divorce foreign wives and put away foreign children (Ezra 9–10). Only Israelite wives and children were permitted. In ruling thus, Ezra effectively established the principle that one is Jewish only if one has a Jewish mother as well as a Jewish father.

This situation prevailed for five hundred years, while matrilineal descent became more and more important. Philo judged that the child of a Jew and a non-Jew, whether father or mother, was a *nothos,* that is, a bastard or low-born.[11] In time, matrilineal descent became so important that early Nazarene leaders, like James the Just, were perhaps reckoned as *kohanim* on matrilineal grounds alone.

The final step was the official change to matrilineal descent alone. This took place after the destruction of Jerusalem in AD 70. The logic was simple: the Israelites were scattered among the nations; the chance of a non-Jewish father could not be excluded, yet maternity is always beyond dispute. Since a certainty overrules a doubt, the certain fact of Jewish motherhood became the only factor in determining Jewishness. The Mishnah duly ruled that the son of a non-Jewish woman was not Jewish, and the ruling was elaborated by both Talmuds.[12]

This ruling was accepted by all forms of Rabbanite Judaism until 1983, when Reform Judaism again recognized patrilineal descent, despite great opposition from Orthodox and Conservative Judaism.

However, matrilineal descent was never accepted by Karaite Jews. For them, patrilineal descent has always been decisive.

So nowadays, the question of whether or not one is Jewish rather depends on who you ask.

In Orthodox Judaism, the mother is the determining factor. If your mother is Jewish, you are Jewish. If she's not, you're not. Conservative Judaism takes the same line.

Reform Jews accept a person as Jewish if either parent is Jewish. Since many Reform men now take non-Jewish wives, their children are not accepted as Jewish by Orthodox and Conservative Jews.

The State of Israel takes a similar line. The law of return grants

[11] *Life of Moses* 1:27 (147): Jewish father–Egyptian mother; 2:36 (193): Egyptian father–Jewish mother; *On the Virtues* 40 (224): the sons of Bilhah and Zilpah. By *ioudaios*, Philo includes as Jews, of course, the Israelite tribes affiliated to Judah.

[12] Yeb. 2:5; Kid. 3:12; B. Yeb. 17a; Kid. 68b; Y. Yeb. 2:6.

Israeli citizenship if any of one's four grandparents is demonstrably Jewish. This is based, not on the Reform decision of 1983, but, ironically, on the Nazi definition of Jewishness, which was based on a single Jewish grandparent. The law of return was framed to accept all who escaped that terrible persecution.

Yet all forms of Judaism recognize that the *k'hunah* or 'priesthood' is transmitted only patrilineally. One who self-identifies as a *kohen* must be able to advance a tradition of genetic inheritance from father to son, right back to biblical times. If there is a suspected non-Jewish father anywhere in the line, then the individual is disqualified from *k'hunah.* There is no halakhically-sanctioned process to remedy the introgression of males who are not patrilineal descendants of Zadok.

JESUS ON JESUS

So was Jesus a Jew? What I find surprising about the modern consensus on 'Jesus the Jew' is how it takes no account of what Jesus said about himself. After all, if you want to know about someone's ethnicity, you should ask the person concerned. Yet everyone insists on not doing this with Jesus. For it seems to me that Jesus deliberately cast doubt on his Jewishness. We have already spoken about this. But let's revisit it.

Let's begin with his strange comment to the Pharisees that the Torah is *their* Torah or 'law'. First, citing the law of the two witnesses in Deuteronomy 19:15, he says, 'It is written in your law' (John 8:17). Then, later, he cites Psalm 82, saying, 'Is it not written in your law?' (John 10:34).

The latter comment can maybe be explained more easily. The Pharisees accepted the Psalms as Torah, but others, like the Zadokites-Sadducees and the Samaritans, did not. Could it be that Jesus shared this lower view of the Psalms? The Samaritan view might have been prevalent in Galilee. And his mother, after all, was Zadokite. Still, in Luke 24:44, he accepts the Psalms as prophecy. So it's not all clear. That leads to the next passage.

What can we say about his comment on Deuteronomy 19:15? Every Israelite accepted this text as Torah. Nor is it a case of Galilean Jesus preferring the Samaritan text. For the Samaritan Torah is identical at this point to the Judahite Sanhedrin text preserved by the Masoretes. It really looks like Jesus is saying that the Torah of Moses is not his Torah. We can puzzle over what this means. Perhaps he means that this is not the Torah or 'teaching' anyone gave to him: rather, he gave it to them. However, Israelites are subject to Torah. So his comment suggests that he is not an Israelite. Such a conclusion, though shocking, is fully confirmed by what he says a little later in the same chapter.

He tells them, *Your father Abraham rejoiced to see my day* (John 8:56). The regular Hebrew expression was (and is) *Avraham avinu* (Avraham *our* father). For Jesus to say *Avraham avikhem* (Avraham *your* father) was to say that he is not one of them and Avraham is not his father. If he says he is not a son of Avraham, then it hardly seems fair to insist that he is Jewish or even Israelite.

Then, in case anyone missed his meaning, he says again, two verses later, *Before Avraham was, I am* (John 8:58). If he existed before Avraham was born, then he cannot be Avraham's son, nor Judah's, nor any of the other patriarchs'.

And, as we saw, Jesus, unlike the crowds who surround him, never calls himself the son of David. When he says, 'Whose son is the Messiah?… If David calls him "lord", how can he be his son?' (Matt. 22:42, 45) he is saying that he is not a descendant of David and that Joseph of Nazareth was not his father.

Yes, the Samaritan woman calls him a Jew, and he does not object (John 4:9). But, a little later, the Pharisees call him a Samaritan, and he does not object to that either (8:48). He was probably quite used to the 'Samaritan' label, since the Pharisees saw a Galilean as only slighter better than a Samaritan. In fact, unlike the Pharisees, Jesus willingly mixed with Samaritans and we are told that some of them recognized him as Messiah (4:40–42). In fact, his Good Samaritan—who descends from high Jerusalem to low Jericho to save one wounded and ignored by the religious leaders—may, I suspect, be Jesus's own picture of himself as a despised Samaritan.

So Jesus didn't protest against labels, neither 'Jew' nor 'Samaritan' nor 'son of David'. But, from his own mouth, he owned none of them. He repeatedly made statements claiming that he did not descend from Avraham, Judah, or David. In other words, he didn't self-identify as Jewish or even Israelite.

Now I know that such comments may give rise to strong reactions. So I beg you to bear with me as we unpack this a little further.

Jesus could, presumably, have said, 'Before Adam was, I am.' That would not have meant he was not human. Clearly, he was. But it would have meant that he did not see humanness as his true identity. In the same way, his comments in John 8 do not mean that he was not an Israelite—nor perhaps Jewish in some way—but they do suggest that he did not see these things as his true identity.

Jesus the Jew?

Let's return to his Jewishness. If Jesus was a Jew, he had to be a Jew in one of two ways: either matrilineally or patrilineally.

Was his mother Jewish? We saw, in chapter eight, that Mariam was descended patrilineally from Judah and matrilineally from Aaron. People from the clan of Aaron are not Judahites. Thus, by matrilineal descent, Jesus was not a Judahite, but an Aaronite *kohen.*

Of course, Jesus did descend from Judah and David by his mother's paternal line. This is exactly what the gospel genealogies of Matthew and Luke, and the comments of Paul and the author of Hebrews refer to (Rom. 1:3; Heb. 7:14). And, of course, Matthew's opening words assert that Jesus descends both from Abraham and David (1:1). But the mother's paternal line was never considered as determining ancestry in ancient times, neither in Israel not anywhere else.

If Jesus was not matrilineally Jewish, was he patrilineally Jewish? The answer depends on the options of his paternity outlined earlier.

If, as Flusser, Riskin and others imply, Jesus was the legitimately-begotten son of Joseph of Nazareth, then he was indeed patrilineally Jewish. As Joseph's son, he could have been the legitimate heir to David's throne, a circumcised, kosher-keeping, synagogue-attending, Torah-observant rabbi. As Joseph's son, he could have been a worker of miracles, a prophet, and even a Messiah. Indeed, if God willed, he could—as Shimon ben Lakish, Rashi, Klausner, Flusser, and Lapide say—in some way have reappeared after death.

The problem with this view of Jesus's paternity is that none of the ancient sources—Jewish, Christian, or even Islamic—endorse it. They agree that Jesus himself, and his disciples, and his enemies, all said that he was not the son of Joseph.

The Pharisaic claim is that he was a child of adultery. If he were the adulterous offspring of a Jew, as in the version of *Sefer Toldot Yeshu* cited in chapter ten, then he would be patrilineally Jewish, but nothing would be known of his paternal ancestry. Or if he were the adulterous son of a non-Jew, then he was not patrilineally Jewish, though he would remain matrilineally Aaronite.

Or there is the third option. Surely what Jesus intends, in denying his descent from Abraham and David, is to speak of his paternity. He knew his mother's genealogy well enough. He knew that she descended from David on her father's side and from Aaron on her mother's. But the point that he is making, especially in John 8, is one of paternity. He is claiming that he is the divine son of the Most High, incarnated in the womb of virgin Mariam by the Holy Spirit. He is not patrilineally Jewish. His paternity is from another place.

So let's sum up it all up, catechetically, as it were, in a few points.

1. Jesus's self-consciousness was not a Jewish self-consciousness. One who says he existed before Avraham cannot believe he is Avraham's son. Like it or not, he had a divine self-consciousness.
2. Jesus was not culturally Jewish, but Galilean. His native tongue was Aramaic. He lived by choice in Galilee. He kept the Israelite feasts according to the Galilean, not the Judahite, calendar. He did not celebrate the exclusively Judahite feasts like Purim (John 5:1). His disciples were Galilean, except for Judas. To say he was Jewish makes him seem like a Hillel-type figure. But he was not. He didn't even dress like a Judean (Matt. 23:5; Luke 20:46).
3. Jesus's genetic descent was not halakhically Judahite. His mother's mother was Zadokite. Thus he was matrilineally Zadokite, not Judahite. Yes, his mother's father was Jewish. This is what New Testament writers mean when speaking of his Davidic and Judahite descent. But that does not make him halakhically Judahite, for the mother's father does not figure in that reckoning. We can call Jesus part-Jewish on the basis of his mother's father. But those who affirm matrilineal descent and assert his Jewishness are being inconsistent.
4. Jesus inherited the throne of David from his adoptive father, Joseph of Nazareth. By that route he was rightly 'King of the Jews'. It is also likely that, through Joseph and his mother's father, there were Judahite practices in his family. And he certainly spoke Hebrew.
5. As for the related issue of John's anti-Semitism, John was not anti-

semitic. He was an Israelite. But, as a Galilean Zadokite, he was not pro-Judahite. We must recognize the sharp ethnic and tribal tensions that existed in first-century Israel.

6. Some may reply that to say Jesus was Zadokite, not Jewish, is too fine a distinction. I reply that to confuse the two is simply inaccurate. It was an important distinction in first-century Israel.

Boyarin says that these days 'almost everyone, Christian and non-Christian, is happy enough to refer to Jesus, the human, as a Jew.'[13] (Boyarin, in fact, wants to 'baptize' the whole New Testament into Judaism, a bigger matter than we can broach here.[14]) I'm not sure I agree. Bearing in mind that Jesus says his true identity predates Israel and Judah, and even humankind, yet he was born of an Israelite mother, I would be happier to call him by the broader term 'Israelite'. An Aramaic-speaking Galilean, who does not observe Judean feasts, whose father is God, and whose mother is an Aaronite princess, is certainly an Israelite. But I would not be too quick to call him Jewish.

PARADIGMS FULFILLED

We spoke in chapter three about the promises of a deliverer to the tribes of Judah, Joseph, and Levi. Since Mariam descended both from Levi and Judah, her son received the blood-line of both tribes. Therefore he is the fulfilment of the prophecies to both tribes.

But what of the promise to Joseph? Jesus certainly fulfilled it typologically. He was the beloved of his father, betrayed by his brothers to death and buried, but who rose again to rule. As Irenaeus said:

> By these Christ was typified, and acknowledged, and brought into the world; for he was prefigured in Joseph: then from Levi and Judah he was descended according to the flesh, as King and Priest. (Frag. 17)

But did Jesus fulfil the paradigm of the Messiah from Joseph genetically as well as typologically?

[13] Boyarin, *Jewish Gospels*, 5–6.

[14] Boyarin, *Jewish Gospels*, 22–24. Many contributors to the New Testament cannot simply be described as Jewish. John the Evangelist was Aaronite. Paul was culturally Judean, but of Benjamite descent. As for Luke, the biggest single contributor to the New Testament, I take Col. 4:11–14 to mean that he was not Jewish. However, as noted earlier, some think otherwise (Strelan, *Luke the Priest*).

His descent from Joseph is as follows. Omri king of Ephraim, from the house of Joseph, begat Ahab. Ahab begat Athaliah who married Jehoram of the house of David. Through their son, Ahaziah, the seed of Omri entered the Solomonic lineage of David. This continued through ten generations to Josiah. Then, as we saw in chapter seven, it passed through Josiah's daughter Tamar to Shealtiel and Pedaiah, whom she bore to Neri. Then Pedaiah (in the name of Shealtiel) begat Zerubbabel who begat Rhesa. From Rhesa, the seed of Omri descended fifteen generations to Levi, and thence to Panther, Joakim, and Mariam.

Meanwhile, Ephraimite royal status passed by the same route to Zerubbabel, then to Abiud and Rhesa, and converged in Joseph, begotten by Jacob, according to the law of levir, for his brother Heli.

The only doubt that may be raised is whether Omri was a son of Joseph, for nothing is said of his parentage. But it is highly likely that, as a ruler of the Ephraimite kingdom, Omri sprang from Joseph. The Ephraimites would never have acquiesced in his rule otherwise.

It follows further that, as a descendant of Joseph, Jesus received genetic material from Joseph's Egyptian wife, Asenath. He also inherited genetic material, via Tamar, from the Moabitess Ruth, great-grandmother of David, from the Ammonite Naamah, mother of Rehoboam, and from the Phoenician Jezebel, grandmother of Ahaziah. After the Exile, he received genetic material from the Persian Rhoda, the wife of Zerubbabel, the mother of Rhesa. Thus he traced his descent not only from Israelite women, but also from a Hamite woman, Asenath, a Japhethite woman, Rhoda, and non-Israelite Shemite women, Ruth, Naamah, and Jezebel.

Thus Jesus's genetic descent fulfilled the promises made to Judah, Joseph, and Levi, and qualified him to be the saviour of the Gentiles.

13

His Name Shall Be Called Wonderful

BEFORE Jesus was born, Mariam, who would bear him, and Joseph, who would name him, each received instruction from on high that his name should be Yeshua (Matt. 1:21; Luke 1:31). In the Hebrew language, in which Matthew wrote his gospel, this involves a play upon words: *You are to give him the name Jesus* (yeshua‘), *for he will save* (yoshi‘a) *his people from their sins* (Matt. 1:21).

This same word-play conceals a statement about his divine nature. Yeshua is a later form of the name Joshua, which means ‘Yehovah saves’.[1] But the angel says this child will save his people from their sins. And so, if it is Yehovah who saves, then this child is he.

Later, Paul says that this name is *the name that is above every name so that at the name of Jesus every knee should bow* (Phil. 2:9–10). And the writer to the Hebrews says that Jesus is *as much greater than the angels as the name he has inherited is greater than theirs* (Heb. 1:4). Is all this simply rhetoric, or is there something intrinsically powerful to this name? Let's start at the beginning.

YEHOSHUA TO YESHUA TO IESOUS TO JESUS

The name Y^{e}hoshua (in English, Joshua) is first given to the great Ephraimite commander Y^{e}hoshua ben Nun, who led Israel out of the

[1] For ‘Yehovah’ as the pronunciation of the Tetragrammaton, see the Glossary.

desert and into possession of the Promised Land. Joshua's name was originally Hoshea (Ho-*shey*-a'), which means 'salvation' or 'deliverance'.

הוֹשֵׁעַ Ho**shē**a'

The apostrophe at the end of the name signifies a characteristically middle-eastern sound—the consonant *ayin*, a voiced pharyngeal fricative. (It can be heard in the *gh* of Afghan, when spoken by a native of that country.) Those unfamiliar with eastern languages may find it tricky, especially in the middle of a word. But, in this position, at the end of a word, it just means that the final vowel sinks into a throaty guttural.

Moses changed Hoshea's name by adding one Hebrew letter *y* (*yodh*). In this way, the beginning of Hoshea became Y^{e}ho, a short form of the name Y^{e}hovah. A vowel was altered too—*ē* to *u*—changing the meaning from a noun, 'salvation', to a verb, 'saves'. (Neither of these vowels—*ē* or *u*—was written, for in early biblical Hebrew many vowels are unwritten.) And so Hoshea became Joshua, that is, Y^{e}ho**shu**a', meaning 'Yehovah saves' (Num. 13:16).[2]

יְהוֹשֻׁעַ Y^{e}ho**shu**a'

This prefix is significant. Joshua-Y^{e}hoshua becomes the first person in the Bible to bear the holy name Y^{e}hovah within his own name. Yes, Moses's own mother, Yo-khe<u>b</u>ed, mentioned in Exodus 6:20, bore a very short form of the holy name. But she doesn't actually receive the letters of the name in order, but just an abbreviation—Yo. But Joshua gets the first three letters of the Name, exactly as they occur in order, reading the Hebrew, of course, from right to left.

יְהוָֹה Y^{e}ho**vah**
יְהוֹשֻׁעַ Y^{e}ho**shu**a'

In other words, Joshua-Y^{e}hoshua receives in his name a portion of divine power unlike anyone ever before him.

[2] The best explanation for the formation of Yehoshua is a portmanteau of Yehovah and the *hiphil* imperfect of *yasha'* (he saves)—*Yeho[vah]+[yo]shia*—the penultimate vowel morphing from *-shia* to *-shua*, as also in Elishua (2 Sam. 5:15; 1 Chr. 14:5) and Abishua (1 Chr. 6:35; 8:4; Ezra 7:5). But Gesenius thinks it comes from *Yeho+yeshu'ah* (salvation).

Now the name Y^e^hovah is a portmanteau of the future, present, and past forms of the Hebrew verb 'to exist'—*yihyéh-hóveh-hayáh.* It means 'Will-be-is-was'. It is a declaration of eternal uncaused being. But the name Yehoshua goes further still. It declares that the eternally self-sufficient one is also the all-sufficient saviour. For anyone in need, it truly is a name above all names.

FROM YEHOSHUA TO YESHUA

Later, other Israelites, like Joshua of Beth Shemesh (1 Sam. 6:14), bore the same name. But later it began to change. The *h* softened and the two vowels of Y^e^ho elided into a long *e*-vowel (ē, as in 'hey').

The written form followed suit: the *h* (*heh*) disappeared and the *o* (*vav*) moved up to become the *u*-vowel. (The Hebrew semi-vowel *vav* can represent *o* or *u* or *v*.) Thus Yehoshua became Yēshua.

יהושע **Y^e^hoshua'**
ישוע **Yēshua'**

It first appeared in David's time (1 Chr. 24:11), then in Hezekiah's (2 Chr. 31:15). Then it became quite common. Nehemiah lists several Israelite patriarchs called Yeshua among the returnees from Babylon (7:7, 11, 39, 43). Then he refers to historical Joshua ben Nun as Yeshua (8:17). Then both he and Ezra use the same name for their contemporary, the *kohen gadol* Joshua-Yeshua ben Jehozadak (Neh. 12:1, 7, 10, 26; Ezra 5:2; 10:18). Meanwhile Haggai and Zechariah still call the same man Y^e^hoshua (Zech. 3:6–10; 6:9–14).[3] So both forms of the name—Yeshua and Y^e^hoshua—were interchangeable.

In the third century BC, the Septuagint translators of the Bible had to render 'Yeshua' into Greek. Their Greek transcription kept the long *e*-vowel of Yēshua. But, since the Greek alphabet had no letter *sh*, the *sh* became *s*. Then the final guttural *ayin*—another sound unknown in Greek—was removed along with its *a*-vowel. Then the name received the *s*-ending which terminates every Greek masculine name. Thus Hebrew-Aramaic Yēshua' became Greek Yēsous or Iēsous (Ιησους). This form of the name became the standard written form of the name

[3] The difference between the two forms can be seen only in the Hebrew text. English Bibles simply call him Joshua.

among Greek-speaking Israelites, like Ben Sira (and his grandson), Philo, Josephus, and the New Testament writers.[4] In time, the Greek form was Latinized as IESUS.[5] This then passed into English as Jesus.

Meanwhile, in Hebrew and Aramaic, Yeshua became commoner than Yehoshua. Joshua ben Nun is called Yeshua in the Dead Sea text, 4QTestimonia (4Q175), which dates from about 100 BC. By Roman times, the short form of the name, Yeshua, had largely displaced the longer form, Yehoshua, in funerary inscriptions. Yet this short form, Yeshua, still carried the same meaning as its original: 'Yehovah saves'.

The Name Foreknown

Some Israelites expected the name of the Messiah to be Yehoshua or Yeshua. We first saw this in chapter two, in the promise to Joseph of a Messiah who would be a second Joshua. Later texts echo the same idea. The Dead Sea text, 4QTestimonia (4Q175), alludes to four messianic deliverers: a prophet like Moses, a star come out of Jacob (David), a priest Messiah; and a Joshua figure.[6]

We see it also in prophetic literature of the second and third centuries BC. In these texts, preserved in Greek, we meet the phrase, *sotería kuríou*, meaning 'the salvation of the Lord'. It is a direct translation of Hebrew *y'shuat YHVH* and is dynamically equivalent to the name Yehoshua, 'Yehovah saves'. Philo says as much:

> Moses changes the name of Hoshea to Joshua…which means salvation of the Lord (*sotería kuríou*).[7]

So when second or first century BC Greek texts speak of 'the salvation of the Lord' (*sotería kuríou*), they seem to be suggesting that the Messiah's name will be Yehoshua.

So, for instance, the book of Ben Sira, from the second century BC, says:

[4] In the foreword to Ben Sira's book, the grandson calls the grandfather Iesous ben Sirach.

[5] Greek (like French) has two u-vowels—*u* and *ou*. The latter was equal to Hebrew vocalic *vav*. Latin has only one *u*-vowel and so the unnecessary *o* dropped out.

[6] The text is discussed in chapter 3 and, more fully, in my *Messiah ben Joseph*, chapter 6.

[7] Philo, *On the Change of Names* 121.

> Happy are those who will live in those days and who will be permitted to see the salvation of the Lord (*soteria kuriou*). (48:11)[8]

The Testament of Dan is clear that this refers to a person:

> There shall arise unto you from the tribe of Judah and of Levi the salvation of the Lord (*soteria kuriou*). He shall contend against Beliar and subdue him, and turn the hearts of the disobedient to the Lord, and give eternal peace to all who call upon him. (T. Dan 5:10)

And the Psalms of Solomon, from the mid-first century BC, say,

> The salvation of the Lord (*soteria kuriou*) be over Israel his servant for ever. (12:6)

Such texts seem to be pointing to the belief that the Messiah's name will be Yeshua-Yehoshua. And the same thing can be detected in other texts from the period before and after the turn of the millennium.[9]

This belief that the Messiah was to be called Yeshua is seen in the prevalence of the name in early first-century Judea. In 2002, an ossuary came to light bearing the Aramaic inscription 'Ya'aqov bar Yoseph, the brother of Yeshua'. Many eminent authorities said it was from the first century, and that it was likely to be the ossuary of James (Jacob) the Just, the brother of Jesus. They pointed out that a brother's name would not appear on an ossuary unless the brother were a person of exceptional significance, and that the occurrence of these three names was unlikely to be coincidental. But others said it was fake, insisting, rightly enough, that the names Jacob, Joseph and Jesus—along with Judah—were by far the commonest male names in Jerusalem and Judea at the time. After ten years of court hearings the artefact was judged to be authentic.[10] But the point remains about the popularity of these names. For it is actually very suprising.

One can understand why the name Jacob would be popular. He was the father of all the Israelites. But the popularity of Joseph and Jesus is much less easy to understand. For Joseph was the father of the Ephraimites and Manassites, and Joshua was an Ephraimite general.

[8] The fragmentary Hebrew text in the Bodleian library (MS.Heb.e.62; B XVII Verso) ends with *yodh* or *vav-heh*, indicating the words *y'shuat yhvh*.

[9] See particularly my comments on 4 Ezra 7:28 in *Messiah ben Joseph*, chapter 5.

[10] In 2013 it was judged to be authentic in a high-profile Israeli court case. See www.biblicalarchaeology.org/daily/biblical-artifacts/inscriptions/israel-antiquities-authority-returns-jesus-brother-bone-box-to-owner/

After the break-up of Solomon's kingdom in 930 BC, the Ephraimites were Judah's bitter enemies. And even after the Ephraimite kingdom was carried into exile in 722 BC, the Judeans remained at unceasing enmity with the remnant of Joseph, the Samaritans. So one can see why first-century Judeans might call their sons Abraham, Moses, Aaron, David or Solomon. Yet these names, popular enough among medieval Jews, are absent from the populace of Jesus's day. Instead, they prefer the names Joseph and Joshua, the fathers of the hated Samaritans.[11] And this was not only among the ordinary people, but particularly among the rulers. In the century before Jesus was born, we find no less than seven high-priests bearing the name Yeshua. This rather suggests that some Israelites believed that the coming Messiah was to be called Yeshua, and they named their sons in this hope.

Finally, we return to the liturgy for the *shofar*-blowing of Rosh Hashanah which we spoke of in chapter one.

> May it be pleasing in your sight that the blowing of *tekia-shebarim-tekia* that we blow before you be embroidered in the curtain by the hands of the overseer just as you received it by the hands of Elijah, peace be upon him, and Yeshua, Prince of the Presence and Prince Metatron, and fill us with mercy. Blessed are you the Merciful One.

Professor Leibes thinks the prayer refers to Jesus of Nazareth, and that it entered the liturgy from early Hebrew Nazarenes, rather than later Christian interpolators.[12] But it is also quite possible that it predates Christian times and comes from the ancient belief, based on Deuteronomy 33:17, that the Messiah was to be a second Joshua and would bear that name.

Yeshua to Yeshu

When we turn to rabbinic writing, we find that Jesus is mostly called Yeshu rather than Yeshua. In other words, the *a*-vowel and the letter *ayin* have been cut off the end of the name. At the same time, the stress moves from the second syllable to the first.

[11] Ilan, *Lexicon*. In terms of popularity, Simon is first, Joseph second, Judah third, Eleazar fourth, Yohanan (John) fifth, Yeshua sixth. Bauckham, *Eyewitnesses*, chapter four, and Hachlili, 'Hebrew Names', have the same names, but rejig the order a little.

[12] Leibes, מלאכי קול השופר.

ישוע Yē**shu**a‘

ישו **Y**ē**shu**

This probably happened early. It appears in the Toldot Yeshu and in the tannaitic account of Jesus's execution in Sanhedrin 43a: ‘On Shabbat on the eve of the Passover Yeshu was hanged’ (Sanh. 43a).

Since then, Yeshu has been the preferred form in Jewish usage. It's fair to say it has often been used polemically. The Toldot Yeshu (see chapter ten) makes this quite clear. It tells how Miriam gave birth to a son and named him Yehoshua after her brother, but when it was found he was a *mamzer* the rabbis changed his name to Yeshu.

Yet, throughout the whole period, there was a continual awareness that the real name was Yeshua. Among the manuscripts of Sanhedrin 43a, the Temani manuscript preserves Yeshua.[13] Likewise, the Vienna manuscript retains the name of Yeshua ben Pantera in the story of Rabbi Eliezer and Yaaqov of K'far Sekhanya (cited in chapter ten).[14] Later still, Maimonides refers to ‘Yeshua’, both in the passage from Mishneh Torah (cited in chapter ten) and in his letter to Yemen, but later editors changed it to ‘Yeshu’.

So we may ask, ‘How did this short form, Yeshu, arise?’ And ‘Why did the rabbis prefer it?’ And ‘Why does it remain to this day?’

How did ‘Yeshu’ arise?

There are several views on how ‘Yeshu’ arose. Some say it was another contraction. As Yehoshua became Yeshua, so Yeshua became Yeshu. This is sometimes linked to Galilean dialect. For instance, the *tanna* Rabbi Yose the Galilean was presumably called Yosef, but his name is always given without the final letter. So perhaps Galileans did not pronounce final letters and so the end of the name was swallowed.[15] As Flusser said,

> The Hebrew name for Jesus, Yeshu, is evidence for the Galilean pronunciation of the period, and is in no way abusive. Jesus was a Galilean, and therefore the *a* at the end of his name, Yeshua, was not

[13] Rokeaḥ, ‘Ben Stara’, 11, who says the original form of the text had *Yeshua.*

[14] The Vienna ms of Tosefta Ḥullin 2:22–24.

[15] Krauss, *Leben Jesu*, 250; Neubauer, ‘Jewish Controversy’, 24.

pronounced. His full name was thus Yeshua. In the Talmudic sources, which are from a later period, there is reference to a Rabbi Yeshu, who is not to be confused with Jesus.[16]

The *a* at the end of Yeshua is joined to the guttural *ayin*. And apparently some Galileans did mispronounce gutturals. The Judeans found it hilarious.

> A Galilean cried, 'Who wants *amar*? [a bargain]' They replied, 'Do you mean *ḥamor* [donkey] to ride on or *ḥamar* [wine] to drink or *amar* [wool] to wear or *imar* [lamb] for slaughtering. (B. Erub. 53b)

Yet Kutscher, the authority on Galilean Aramaic, says most Galileans, if not all, were perfectly able to pronounce gutturals.[17]

Nor should Flusser's reference to another Rabbi Yeshu be simply accepted. Yeshu simply is not a Hebrew name. It does not correspond to any known Hebrew root and no other individuals are known ever to have borne this name. There are other people called Yeshua and Yehoshua in the Talmud, but every occurrence of Yeshu should be taken as referring to Jesus, despite some issues with dates.

Another view is that 'Yeshu' was a deliberate mutilation of the name 'Yeshua'. This was the view of Lauterbach:

> The name *Yeshu* by which Jesus is here mentioned is probably merely a shortened form of the name *Yeshua*. But since such an abbreviated form of the name is not used in any other case of a person named *Yeshua* or *Yehoshua*, but persistently and consistently used when the name refers to Jesus, it may be assumed that this shortening of the name was probably an intentional mutilation by cutting off part of it. The rabbis mention other instances of the names of persons being shortened because of their misconduct.[18]

This, I think, is a fair assessment, given the way the name is used in Judaism.

But perhaps the best explanation combines Galilean accent and mockery. Galileans did indeed omit the last syllable of names. But the Judean hierarchy, keen to ridicule Jesus and diminish his influence, quickly turned this into what Kjær-Hansen calls 'a vocal sneer',

[16] Flusser, *Jewish Sources*, 15; similarly, *Jesus*, 6.

[17] Kutscher, *Galilean Aramaic* (67–70; 80; 89–96) says that in most places in Galilee and the rest of Palestine Jews were indeed able to pronounce the gutturals, but in a few places, such as Haifa, Beisan and Tibon, they were generally not pronounced.

[18] Lauterbach, 'Jesus in the Talmud', 482.

mocking the Galilean accent, which they saw as ignorant and uncouth. This had the triple advantage of mocking Jesus, his disciples, and the Galilee. Using it distanced the speaker from all three. So maybe 'Yeshu' was indeed a Galilean nickname for 'Yeshua', just as Jim is short for James. And by picking up the nickname this way, the Judeans signalled that Jesus was a person of no consequence, fit to be spoken of in familiar and unceremonious terms.

So I think Flusser is mistaken in saying that the name Yeshu 'is in no way abusive'. Among the Judean authorities it was always meant to be demeaning, as the Sefer Toldot Yeshu spells out. But perhaps it arose naturally from the Galilean speech of the disciples. Who knows, perhaps his mother called him Yeshu.

WHY DO THE RABBIS STILL PREFER 'YESHU'?

So the rabbis were always aware that the real name of Jesus was Yeshua, but they preferred to call him Yeshu. In time, this name came to embody Jewish contempt for Jesus. Eisenmenger's *Entdecktes Judenthum* (*Judaism Uncovered*) is polemical. But it was based on his dealings with Jews of his own time. His summary of why Jews use 'Yeshu' rather than 'Yeshua' looks to me like a fair summary of the facts.

> First, Jews do not recognize that Jesus is Messiah. Therefore they do not say 'Yeshua' (an honourable Hebrew name) but 'Yeshu'.
>
> Second, Jesus was cut off, therefore the end is cut off his name.
>
> Third, Jesus was not able to save himself. That is wht the *ayin* is left out his name, removing any reference to the verb *yasha'*, 'save'.
>
> Fourth, Jews are told to *Make no mention of the name of other gods* (Exod. 23:13). The Christians made him a god, therefore Jews cannot speak his name. In fact, Jews are not only permitted to mock false gods; they are commanded to change and defame their names.
>
> Fifth, the three letters of Yeshu are made into an acronym for a three-word curse that his name and memory be blotted out. When this curse is implied, the name is often written with the Hebrew sign for an acronym, the double apostrophe *gershayim,* inserted before the last letter: ישׁ״ו.

To this day, Yeshu remains the standard form of the name of Jesus in modern Israeli school textbooks. In these texts it is written without *gershayim*, and so presumably no curse is intended. Nonetheless, the curtailed form of the name is standard throughout modern Israel.

Kjær-Hansen contrasts the work of Eliezer ben Yehuda, the reviver of modern Hebrew, with that of later prominent Israeli writers on Jesus. Ben Yehuda routinely referred to Jesus as Yeshua, signifying perhaps the need for a Jewish reappraisal of Jesus. But Joseph Klausner, the foremost 20th-century Jewish writer on the New Testament, invariably called him Yeshu. David Flusser also preferred Yeshu. Perhaps if Klausner and Flusser had followed Ben Yehuda, then the accepted name in modern Israeli discussion would now be the more honourable Yeshua, rather than Yeshu.

AS HIS NAME IS, SO IS HE

But there is more to the name of Jesus. To find it, we must touch on numerology. Now, some find numerology subjective, lacking in rigour. But it has always been part and parcel of Israelite interpretation. It was also much studied by Renaissance humanists, like the great Johannes Reuchlin. So it has its place.

Before the Arabic invention of numerals, numbers were represented by letters of the alphabet. In Latin, of course, I was one, V was five, X was ten, L was fifty, and so on. But the same thing existed in Hebrew and Greek. The numerical values of the Greek alphabet are as follows:[19]

Α	alpha	1	Ι	iota	10	Ρ	rho	100
Β	beta	2	Κ	kappa	20	Σ	sigma	200
Γ	gamma	3	Λ	lambda	30	Τ	tau	300
Δ	delta	4	Μ	mu	40	Υ	upsilon	400
Ε	epsilon	5	Ν	nu	50	Φ	phi	500
Ϝ	digamma	6	Ξ	xi	60	Χ	chi	600
Ζ	zeta	7	Ο	omicron	70	Ψ	psi	700
Η	eta	8	Π	pi	80	Ω	omega	800
Θ	theta	9	Ϙ	qoppa	90	ϡ	sampi	900

[19] Although the letters *digamma, qoppa,* and *sampi* were obsolete by the mid-first millenium BC, they were retained for numerical purposes in later Greek.

There ancients made much of of deriving meanings from the numerical values of letters. In Hebrew, it is called *gematria* and in Greek *isopsephy*.

The best known example of Judeo-Greek isopsephy is in the book of Revelation: *Let him that has understanding calculate the number of the beast, for it is the number of man. And his number is six hundred and sixty six* (Rev. 13:18).

The reason why 666 is man's number is, of course, because it falls thrice short of seven. In the thought of the ancient east, seven is the number of completion or perfection. On the seventh day, God ceased from his work of creation and so the days of the week are completed by the seventh-day Shabbat. There are seven heavens. In the seven heavens are seven fixed spheres. Music, the language of heaven, has seven notes. The Book of Revelation, with its heavenly visions, abounds in sevens. It has 54 explicit sevens, all signifying completion. Seven spirits of God to signify divine omnipresence. Seven seals, seven trumpets, seven bowls, signify complete judgement. The beast's seven horns and seven crowns represent his complete rule for a time. There are also many hidden sevens.

Seven, then, is the number of perfection, especially in Revelation. So it follows that, in Revelation, six is the number that falls short of perfection. And so the one called 666 is a trismegistus of imperfection. The number surely signifies the Emperor Nero, whose name and title, Neron Caesar, when rendered in Hebrew—נרון קסר—do indeed equal 666.[20] Yet Revelation also presents the beast as a figure yet to arise, perhaps reflecting the contemporary belief that Nero would return in the future.

But, of course, if seven represents perfection, then eight represents that which is beyond perfection. As the eighth day begins a new week, as the eighth note begins a new octave, so the number eight represents a new dimension. And what John does not say, but certainly implies, is that, just as the beast's number is 666, so Jesus's number is 888.

English	J	E	S	O	U	S	
Greek	I	H	Σ	O	Y	Σ	
Number	10	8	200	70	400	200	= **888**

[20] That the reference is to Nero is confirmed by some later mss., which have the number 616, equivalent to the Latin form, Nero Caesar, without the 'n' of Greek Neron.

John didn't need to spell it out, for the Greeks were well aware of the numerology of names. A graffito on the wall of Pompeii says, 'I love her whose number is 545.'[21] John's readers in Asia Minor would have understood well enough what he meant. Just as the beast is imperfect, Jesus is *plus quam perfectum.* Just as Jesus rose on the day after Shabbat, the eighth day, so he initiates a new order of being altogether. All this is implicit in the number of his name—888—thrice pluperfect.

Summary

It is a basic idea of the Bible that there is power in names. Every Hebrew knew that, from the *kohen gadol*, blessing Israel in the divine Name, to the roving magician, mumbling spells in the name of Yao.

And there is particular power in the personal names of God revealed to mankind. The first name revealed was Yehovah, the declaration of God's eternal sovereign essence. With this name came great promises.

> In every place where I cause my name to be called upon, I will come to you and bless you (Exod. 20:24).

> They will put my name upon the Israelites and I will bless them (Num. 6:27).

> I will call upon the name of Yehovah, so shall I be saved from my enemies (Ps. 18:3).

> The name of Yehovah is a strong tower; the righteous run into it and are saved (Prov. 18:10).

> Everyone who calls upon the name of Yehovah shall be saved (Joel 2:32).

But, later, another name was given which joined the name of Yehovah to a promise of salvation, the name Yehoshua. Because of this promise, it was a greater name. And it was revealed that this was to be the name of the Messiah promised to Joseph.

In time, Yehoshua was shortened to Yeshua. It was done without malice, and the new name retained the power of the old. And when the promised one appeared, this new name was announced as the greatest name of all.

[21] Φιλω ης αριθμος φμε.

> You are to give him the name Jesus because he will save his people from their sins (Matt. 1:21).
>
> Nor is there salvation in any other, for there is no other name under heaven given among men by which we must be saved (Acts 4:12).
>
> He has been given the name that is above every name so that at the name of Jesus every knee should bow (Phil. 2:9–10).
>
> Jesus is as much greater than the angels as the name he has inherited is greater than theirs (Heb. 1:4).

This name is superlative. It is 888, the number beyond perfection.[22] Over the centuries, many have found it to be a fortress and a fount of blessing.

Two names were given to mankind for salvation. A great name and a greater name. But some forbade the speaking of the great name under the threat of a curse, and then forgot it altogether. As it is said,

> Why does Israel pray in this world and is not answered? Because they have forgotten the *shem meforash.* (Mid. Teh. on Ps. 91:8)

But worse was to come. Having forgotten the great name, they twisted the greater name into a thing of mockery. What help was left for them?

Eliezer ben Yehuda's motive for reviving the Hebrew language was to fulfil Zephaniah 3:9: *For then I will restore to the peoples a pure speech that they may all call on the name of Yehovah to serve him side by side.* Yet the name of Yehovah is continually obscured—as *adonai* or *HaShem*—or twisted into Yahweh or Yahuwah. And the name Yeshua is still routinely shortened to Yeshu.

To speak of Yeshua instead of Yeshu, as Ben Yehuda himself did, would be an important step in the modern Jewish reconciliation with Jesus.

[22] More can be said on the numerology of the name of Jesus. I refer the reader to the longer version of this chapter, 'The Name of Jesus', on my site brightmorningstar.org.

14

Conclusion

JESUS, as we saw, is by far the most influential person ever to have lived. Yet we have seen that he appeared in various personae throughout the history of Israel. He appeared to Avram and David as Melchizedek, and to others as the Angel of YHVH or the Commander of the host of YHVH.

This has implications for our understanding of biblical inspiration. It is a common view nowadays that, in some biblical prophecies—say in Psalm 2 or Psalm 110 or Isaiah 53—the prophets actually spoke of events in their own time and, quite unconsciously, also spoke of the Messiah. The more cynical may think they just 'lucked out' in getting it right. Others would say the Holy Spirit led them to say things they did not fully understand. And that may sometimes have been true. But, given what we have seen, there were times when the Logos appeared to the prophets face to face and told them of his coming incarnation, sufferings, and triumph. The Holy Spirit, of course, directed their writing. But the revelation came directly from the Logos, the heavenly man.

It also has implications for the development of the messianic idea in Israel. Many argue that this was a late idea, arising long after the Babylonian exile. For instance,

> In scriptural usage, "anointed one" (*mashiaḥ*), does not refer to an eschatological figure whose coming would inaugurate a new era of salvation, but rather to contemporary kings and priests. By the first century BCE, however, *mashiaḥ* and its Greek equivalent *christos*

> carried connotations that were distinctly eschatological in nature, connotations that continued to influence both Judaism and Christianity in succeeding centuries.[1]

But if this book is correct, then such views need revised. For, as we saw in chapter four, unless we allow two eternal priests in Psalm 110, the only option is that the Logos-Melchizedek revealed himself to David as the coming eternal *kohen* and king of the world. If that is so, the idea of an eschatological saviour is not a later idea read into Psalm 110, but rather is something clearly taught by that psalm. If the psalm dates from Israel's kingdom period—as its heading maintains and its language shows—then the messianic idea cannot be any later. One may reply that, even if the concept is early, the use of the term *mashiaḥ* is still late. But that will depend entirely on how we read Psalm 2:2.

We looked at the genetics of the incarnation. How the messianic royal title and the messianic DNA descended from ancient times to the Messiah. We also spoke of the ancient expectation that the Messiah would be a heavenly man, conceived in an extraordinary manner.

Since his mother's mother was Zadokite, the routine assertion of his Jewishness is an overstatement. You might object that I am splitting hairs. Surely Zadokites are Jews. But, in the first century, they were not. If you had asked the high priest in the temple, *Ha-attah yehudi?* (Are you Jewish?), he would have replied, *Lo, mi b'nei Aharon ani.* (No, I am of the sons of Aharon.) And, more specifically, if you had asked Jesus's mother's mother, *Ha-at yehudit?* (Are you Jewish?), she would have replied, *Lo, mi b'not Aharon ani.* (No, I am of the daughters of Aaron.) It follows then that, by matrilineal descent, Jesus was not Judahite but Zadokite-Aaronite. Those who subscribe to matrilineal descent as determining Jewishness should not call him Jewish.

But his paternity was always a big issue too. There were always three views.

The minority view was that he was the son of Joseph of Nazareth. If that were so, then he was indeed patrilineally Jewish, of royal descent, and as such he could have been the Messiah. This view is not new. It always had a following. But it has become popular recently as the 'compromise candidate', allowing one to admire Jesus without subscribing to his divine nature.

[1] P.D. Hanson, 'Messiahs and Messianic Figures'.

Turning to the majority views, the Talmud says Jesus was a child of adultery, fathered either by a Roman soldier or by a lawless Jew. If the former were so, then he was not patrilineally Jewish. If the latter were so, then he was Jewish, but born under a curse and excluded from Israel.

The other majority view is that of the New Testament. It says that both Jesus and his disciples claimed that he was the divine Logos, begotten by the Holy Spirit. In that case, he was not patrilineally Jewish.

So can we work toward a conclusion here? I would leave aside the view that Jesus was the son of Joseph, for it has little support in the ancient sources. In the New Testament, Jesus, his disciples, and the Pharisees all deny that he was Joseph's son. And the texts written by these very same Pharisees and their disciples mostly say the same thing. To assert that Jesus was Joseph's son ignores the best evidence.

The view of the *Toldot Yeshu* and of rabbinic literature in general is that Jesus was an impudent bastard and his mother was no innocent virgin. He worked miracles by unlawful use of the Name and led Israel astray. He was tried by the Sanhedrin for falsely claiming to be the Messiah. But even after forty days no-one had anything good to say of him, and so he was justly executed. He was last seen by Onkelos the necromancer, forever boiling in excrement in Gehenna (B. Git. 57a). Now his name is accursed.

The view of the New Testament is that Jesus is the virgin-born incarnation of the divine Logos, the visible God, the outshining of the Father as the rays shine out the sun. He appeared to the prophets as the Angel of YHVH and told them of his coming in flesh. The Sanhedrin executed him unjustly. But he rose again. Now he sits at the right hand of the Father and he will come again in glory to judge the living and the dead. His name is above every name and all who call upon it are blessed.

These are the two main views on the paternity of the most influential man who ever lived. When one looks at them, one can't help but remark how very different they are. They are polar opposites. And, to state the obvious, they cannot both be right. One of them must be wrong.

Let's look at the implications of the Talmudic view. If Jesus was not the Messiah, then the Messiah has not yet come. Among the scores of Jewish messianic claimants of the last 2,000 years, none has ever done the work of the Messiah.[2] And so, if Jesus was not the Messiah, then the Messiah is still to come.

But consider. If another Messiah comes, will he not be too late? Did not Daniel say the Messiah must come within 490 years of the Persian command to rebuild Jerusalem? (Dan. 9:24–27) Even taking the latest possible date for that command, the Messiah should have come in Roman times. The Talmud confesses this when it says, 'All the [possible] times of his coming are past' (B. Sanh. 97b).

Consider further. If another Messiah comes now, what will he do? Will he teach Torah to the nations? Too late. Are not the Law, Prophets, and Writings found from Svalbard to Santiago? Are not Hallelujahs sung from San Francisco to Shanghai? Are not the idol-worshippers in retreat? Who did this? Was it Hillel and his sons? Or was it Jesus and his apostles, as even Rambam said? What if many choose to live in ignorance of Torah? What then? Does it mean the task is not complete? Does it not mean rather that the time for the judgement of all flesh is at hand?

If another Messiah comes now, what will he do? Will he heal the sick and raise the dead? Will he rise from death by the power of the divine Name? Has not Jesus done all these things already, as even the *Toldot Yeshu*, the Talmud, and Rashi teach?

If another belated Messiah comes, how will he demonstrate his descent from David? Were not Israel's genealogies destroyed by Herod and the Romans? Will another claimant to David's throne be believed simply on the basis of his private genealogy? Was not Jesus the last figure in history whose Davidic lineage was verifiable? Does not the Talmud itself acknowledge his royal descent? How can there ever be another Messiah with a verifiable claim to David's throne?

Consider too how the Pharisees and their successors spent 2,000 years cursing the name of Yeshu into oblivion. If he was what they say he was, or if their words ever had power, he would by now be long forgotten. Yet his renown grows every day. Is it not clear that their curse was a vain curse which does not come to rest (Prov. 26:2)?

If another Messiah comes, won't he cut a fine figure, riding a donkey, in the twenty-first century, through the gates of Jerusalem, to fulfil the prophecy of Zechariah 9:9?

[2] For a readable overview of these Messiahs, see Rabow, *50 Jewish Messiahs*.

And what will he say to the Holy One, blessed be he? Perhaps he will say, "Rav shel Olam, you told me—Didn't you tell me?—you told me *I* was to be a light to the nations and *I* was to bring in everlasting justice. Now, see, this impudent fellow has done all my work—all of it—and what is left for me? *Ma ani ez?* (What am I, a goat?)"

Of course, some might object that the Messiah was to bring peace, yet war continues. That's a valid point. But who said the story was finished?

Me, I take the New Testament view. I can see no other explanation for the world-transforming influence of Jesus of Nazareth except that he was the divine Logos born in human flesh. This was the one who ruled as Melchizedek in Shalem, the one who appeared to Moses, David, Isaiah, and the prophets. And when he comes to Jerusalem, it won't be his first or second or third time there. He was there all along. He had a house on Mount Moriah.

This incarnate Logos inherited David's throne through his adoptive father, Joseph of Nazareth. Joseph had a double claim to the throne, inheriting it through the genealogical line given by Matthew and being a blood descendant of David through the line given by Luke. This incarnate Logos inherited David's flesh through Mariam's father, Joakim. But that did not make him Judahite, for the mother's father does not make one halakhically Jewish. His mother's mother was Zadokite, and so he was matrilineally Zadokite. And he was conceived by the Holy Spirit. Thus he was not Judahite either patrilineally or matrilineally. He was the son of God, Jesus the Israelite, the Quarter-Jew.

This may not be quite the Messiah you want, just as he was not quite the Messiah the Sanhedrin wanted. But if we are looking for one to provide for our need, to lead and defend us through a fortuitous world's wilderness, to pardon our acts of failure and our failures to act, to bind our wounds, console our regrets, comfort our sorrows, assuage the grief of mutability, the persistent mortal sense of loss, and to walk with us through the shadow of death's valley; if we want a saviour to deliver us from evil, a friend who will not forsake us, and a King Messiah to rule us in justice and peace, then he's the best we've got.

Appendix 1. The Genesis Genealogies and the Second Cainan

There is some divergence between the Genesis chrono-genealogies of the Hebrew Masoretic text (MT), the Greek Septuagint (LXX), and the Samaritan Pentateuch (SP). The main issues are:

(1) in LXX each patriarch begets his first son later in life, thus extending the time period from Adam to Avram.

(2) there is a second Kenan/Cainan in LXX of Gen. 11:14–15.

Here is a comparison of Gen. 5:3–32 (cf. 8:13–14; 9:28 for Noah) giving the age of each patriarch at the birth of his first son, the years he survived after the birth of that son, and his age at death.

	Masoretic Text			**Septuagint**			**Samaritan Pentateuch**		
	Son born	After	Death	Son born	After	Death	Son born	After	Death
Adam	130	800	930	230	700	930	130	800	930
Seth	105	807	912	205	707	912	105	807	912
Enosh	90	815	905	190	715	905	90	815	905
Cainan	70	840	910	170	740	910	70	840	910
Mahalalel	65	830	895	165	730	895	65	830	895
Jared	162	800	962	162	800	962	62	785	847
Enoch	65	300	365	165	200	365	65	300	365
Methuselah	187	782	969	167	802	969	67	653	720
Lamech	182	595	777	188	565	753	53	600	653
Noah	502	448	950	502	448	950	502	448	950

From Adam to Mahalalel, LXX adds 100 years to the MT age when each patriarch had his first son, but the age at death remains the same; it does the same with Enoch. Meanwhile, SP follows MT.

With Jared, Methuselah, and Lamech, who have their first son at a later age, LXX introduces no or little change, but SP makes a major change, as if trying to correct an imagined error in LXX. The cumulative effect in LXX is to extend the whole timescale of the ante-diluvian era as each successive patriarch is born later.

Gen. 11:10–32 differs from the Gen. 5 chrono-genealogies in not giving each patriarch's age at death. LXX preserved this 'checksum' figure unchanged in Gen. 5, except for Lamech. But its absence in Gen. 11 allows LXX not only to extend the period before the birth of each patriarch's son, but also to add years to the life of every patriarch from Arphaxad to Nahor.

	Masoretic Text			**Septuagint**			**Samaritan Pentateuch**		
	Son born	After	Death	Son born	After	Death	Son born	After	Death
Shem	100	500	*(600)*	100	500	*(600)*	100	500	600
Arphaxad	35	403	*(438)*	135	430	*(565)*	135	303	438
Cainan				130	330	*(460)*			
Shelah	30	403	*(433)*	130	330	*(460)*	130	303	433
Eber	34	430	*(464)*	134	370	*(504)*	134	270	404
Peleg	30	209	*(239)*	130	209	*(339)*	130	109	239
Reu	32	207	*(239)*	132	207	*(339)*	132	107	239
Serug	30	200	*(230)*	130	200	*(370)*	130	100	230
Nahor	29	119	*(148)*	79	129	*(208)*	79	69	148

The cumulative effect of all these changes in LXX is to extend the ante-diluvian genealogies by 606 years, and the post-diluvian genealogies by 780 years, adding a total of 1,386 years to the MT text.

Why LXX extends the chronology in this way is unknown. As Wenham says, 'There is no consensus on this issue except that the LXX looks secondary.'[1] Perhaps the LXX translators were influenced by Manetho's history of Egypt, which dated the founding of Egypt to long before the MT date of the Flood. There is also deep arithmetical patterning with exceptional attention to detail. The added years in each of the LXX tables equals 1,000.[2]

The Second Cainan. LXX also includes another patriarch, a second Cainan, in Gen. 11:14–15, between Arphaxad and Shelah. Until the mid-twentieth century, this was widely thought to result from an error which had crept into Luke's genealogy and had been back-copied into the LXX text. However, the discovery in the Judean desert of 15 Hebrew texts of the Book of Jubilees, all featuring the second Cainan, changed that view entirely. Hitherto, Jubilees had been a little-known work, preserved only in 15th-century Ethiopic texts. But these newly-

[1] Wenham, *Genesis 1–15*, 130.
[2] Jacobus, 'Curse of Cainan' 223.

discovered texts, dating from as early as 100 BC, showed the second Cainan was not a Lukan or Septuagint error, nor was he exclusive to the Greek textual tradition. Rather, he was in the Hebrew genealogies of Genesis at least 150 years before Luke wrote. And this, being a Hebrew tradition, was not dependent on the Septuagint. Suddenly, the evidence pointed the other way. The second Cainan was part of the original Genesis genealogies. He was not added; he was removed.

The question then is why he was removed. Since all three references to him—two in Genesis and one in 1 Chronicles—disappeared, it seems that his disappearance was no accident. Hebrew scribes didn't make errors of this magnitude. There was a department in the temple which existed to verify newly-written biblical scrolls, column by column, against master copies in the temple.[3] Without this verification, no scroll could be used in public reading. Cainan's disappearance must have been the result of a deliberate choice to expunge him from the Hebrew text.

The question then becomes, 'Who would have methodically excised Cainan from the Bible? And when? And why?'

This second Cainan is the thirteenth from Adam. And just as Enoch, the blessed seventh from Adam, was the receiver of divine revelation, so Cainan, the cursed thirteenth, was, according to Jubilees 8:1–5, the receiver of forbidden knowledge. His crime was to read and record the ancient teachings of the Watchers, the fallen Nephilim of Gen. 6:4, on the forbidden secrets of astronomy and astrology, and to conceal them from Noah his great-grandfather.

It therefore seems likely that Cainan's removal from Gen. 11 was linked to his transgression into esoteric and forbidden knowledge. Genealogical numerology may also have been a factor. This deletion probably took place after the time of the Septuagint translation, in the third century BC, but before the time of Josephus, at the end of the first century, who knew only the altered genealogy (*Ant.* 1.146).[4]

[3] B. Ket. 106a; Y. Shek. 4.2; Y. Sanh. 2.6. Rashi says the *kohanim* who served as proof-readers were paid from temple funds lest dependence on those who brought copies for verification sway their judgment (Rashi on B. *Ket.* 106a).

[4] For a much fuller discussion, see Jacobus, 'Curse of Cainan'.

Appendix 2: Jerome, Epistle 73 to Evangelus

Jerome's view on Melchizedek, in his Vulgate translation of Psalm 110 (Vulgate Psalm 109) and in this letter, has influenced Christian views on the psalm and on Melchizedek for 1600 years. I therefore think it is necessary to translate the letter in full, since it does not exist in English translation anywhere else. I have followed the Latin text of Migne, *Patrologia Latina*, XXII: 676–681.

1. You have sent me a letter, without title or name of author. I do not know whether you have erased it yourself, or whether the author did not want to make himself known, from fear of engaging himself badly in some sharp dispute. I read this work and I noted that the author discusses the famous question relating to the priest Melchizedek, and that he advances several reasons to show that the one who blessed Abraham was more than a man and possessed the nature of God himself. Finally, he is so bold as to say that it was the Holy Spirit who, in human form, went to meet this great patriarch. As to the bread and the wine which his so-called Holy Spirit offered Abraham, and the present that this patriarch gave him of the tenth of all the spoils that he took from his enemies, this author says nothing.

You ask my opinion on the author of this book, and on the issue it addresses. I confess to you in good faith that I wish I could have dispensed with explaining myself on this subject and engaging in such a thorny issue; for whatever course I take, I will attract a roll of censors and enemies. But I could not resist the entreaties you make to me at the end of your letter, in which you conjure me in the most lively and urgent manner in the world not to despise a sinner. So I consulted the works of the ancients, to find out what they said on this matter, and to send you in the form of a response a summary of their explanations.

2. I first found that Origen speaks of Melchisedek at some length in his first homily on Genesis, and that he finally ends up saying that this high priest was an angel; which he proves by more or less the same reasons which your author used to show that he was the Holy Spirit. I then took Didyme, a supporter of Origen, and noticed that he was of the opinion of his master. Finally, I consulted Hippolytus, the holy Irenaeus, Eusebius of Caesarea, Eusebius of Emesa, Apollinaris, and our Eustathius, who, the first of all bishops, raised the standard against Arius, and I observed that after several detours and different reasoning, they all agree in saying Melchizedek was a Canaanite and king of the city of Jerusalem, which first was called Salem, then Jebus, and finally Jerusalem.

It is not surprising, they say, that the Scriptures represent to us Melchizedek as a *priest of the most high God*, although he was not of the family of Aaron, and he neither received circumcision nor performed the other ceremonies of the law, since we see that Abel, Enoch and Noah were pleasing to the Lord and offered him sacrifices; and that we read in the Book of Job that this holy man performed the functions of the priesthood, offering gifts to God and immolating to him daily victims and burnt offerings for the preservation of his children. They even claim that Job was not of the family of Levi but of the race of Esau, although the Hebrews are not of this feeling.

3. Now, they add, that we see a figure of the Saviour in Noah, who, during his drunkenness, and by the shameful situation to which it had reduced him, drew the mockery of Ham, the second of his sons, who prefigures the Jews; and in Samson, who loved Delilah in spite of her prostitution and poverty, and who, to represent the Passion of Jesus Christ to us, killed more enemies by dying than he had during his life; in the saints, the patriarchs and the prophets, who almost all have retraced to us in their lives some image of the Saviour, so we find in Melchizedek, who was Canaanite and not a Jew, a figure of the priesthood of the Son of God, of whom he is spoken in the Hundred and Ninth Psalm [according to the Greek numeration]: *You are an Eternal Priest after the order of Melchizedek* [Ps. 110:4].

They explain in several ways what this 'order' is, and they make it consist in that Melchisedek is the only one who was both king and priest together; that he exercised the functions of the priesthood before the establishment of circumcision, which shows that the priesthood passed from the Gentiles to the Jews, and not from the Jews to the Gentiles; that he was not anointed with priestly oil, according to the Law of Moses, but with *the oil of joy* [Ps. 45:7] and by the anointing of pure faith; that he did not sacrifice carnal and bloody victims, nor shed the blood of a slaughtered beast; but bread and wine, a simple and pure sacrifice to proclaim the sacrament of Christ. They also allege several other reasons which the brevity of a letter does not allow me to explain.

4. They also say that in the Epistle to the Hebrews, received by the Greeks and some Latins, it is marked that Melchizedek, which means 'righteous king', was king of Salem, that is to say 'king of peace', and that he was 'without father, mother and genealogy'. It is not that he had neither father nor mother—just as Christ has a father and a mother according to one nature or the other—but it is because the holy scripture, without having said anything about him, and without making any mention of it subsequently, represents him coming to meet Abraham after the defeat of his enemies.

The apostle also affirms that the priesthood of Aaron, that is, of the Jewish people, had a beginning and an end; but Melchisedek, that is, of Christ and of the Church, is eternal, that it has neither beginning nor end, that no one has instituted it, and that *the priesthood having been transferred, the law must necessarily also be changed* [Heb. 7:12], and that not out of Hagar and Mount Sinai, but of Sarah the free and from the fortress of *Zion shall go forth the word of the Lord and the law of God from Jerusalem.* [Isa. 2:3]

On such things, adds this apostle, *we would have a lot to say that is difficult to explain.* It was not that it was difficult for the apostle to explain this mystery, but it was not yet time, because he was speaking to the Jews and not to the faithful, to whom he explained it without mystery. Moreover, if the apostle, this chosen vessel, is struck with astonishment at the sight of so great a mystery, and if he confesses that it is beyond his thought and conception, how much more must we, worms of the earth, confess that all our lights are only darkness, and satisfy ourselves with a glimpse of things so great and so sublime, and say that the apostle only compares two priesthoods, that of the first people (Jews) and that of the last (Gentiles), and that all his argument is to show that, before Levi and Aaron, Melchisedek had been a priest from the Gentiles of such great merit that he blesses in advance the priests of the Jews in the loins of Abraham. Whatever the apostle says next in praise of Melchizedek must be applied to Jesus Christ, whose figures have become sacraments of the Church as they have developed. All that follows in praise of Melchizedek refers to the type, Christ, by whom the sacraments of the church were instituted.

5. This I read in the Greek books. And, just as it is customary to show vast regions on a small map, I have been content to enclose within the narrow limits of a letter several different explanations. But as you consulted me on this matter with the confidence of a friend, I also want to tell you as a friend all that I know and explain to you again the opinion of the Hebrews. I will even bring you the original text so that nothing is missing to your curiosity. Here is what the Hebrew text carries. UMELCHISEDEC MELEC SALEM MOSI LEHEM VAIAIN, UHU COEN LEEL ELION: VAIBARCHEU VAIOMER BARUCH ABRAM LEEL ELION CONE SAMAIM VA ARES: UBARUCII EL ELION ESER MAGGEN SARACH BIADACH VAJETHEN LO MAASER MECCHOL

The Hebrews claim that this Melchizedek was Shem, the eldest son of Noah, and that at the birth of Abraham he was three hundred and ninety years old, of which here is the calculation. Shem, two years after the flood, being then a hundred years old, begot Arphaxad, after which he lived another five hundred years, which is six hundred years in all. Arphaxad, at the age of thirty-five, begot Salem; the latter being thirty years old gave birth to Eber, who at the age of thirty-four became the father of Peleg; and Peleg, being thirty years old, begot Cain, who at the age of thirty-two became the father of Serug. He, at thirty years old, gave birth to Nachor, who, at twenty-nine years, begot Terah; and Terah, seventy years old, begat Abraham, Nachor, and Aram. By calculating the years of all these patriarchs, we will find that it amounts to three hundred and ninety years, from the birth of Shem to that of Abraham. Now, as Abraham died at the age of one hundred and seventy-five, it is easy to judge from this number of years that Shem survived by thirty-five years to Abraham, who was his grandson of the tenth generation.

6. The Hebrews further maintain that before the establishment of the priesthood of Aaron all the elders of the race of Noah, whose genealogy they make, offered sacrifices to God as priests, and, that this was the birthright that Esau sold to his brother Jacob. They add that we should not be surprised that Melchisedek had met Abraham, returning victorious, to offer him bread and wine to refresh him and his soldiers, to bless him, as he had to do, because Abraham was his grandson; that, finally, we should not be surprised that he received from him the tithe of the booty and the fruits of his victory, or that he himself gave him the tithe of all his goods, by a dignified liberality from a father to his son. For it can be said, and according to the Hebrew text and according to the version of the Septuagint, that he received from Abraham the tithe of the booty, or that he himself gave Abraham the tithe of his property; although the apostle, in his letter to the Hebrews expressly says that Melchizedek did not give Abraham a tithe of his goods, but it was Abraham who told Melchisedek of the spoil he had taken from his enemies.

7. Moreover, the name of Jerusalem being a word composed of Greek and Hebrew,* this mixture of a foreign language sufficiently demonstrates that Salem is not the city of Jerusalem, as Josephus and all our authors claim; it is a village near Scythopolis, which is still called today Salem. We see there the palace of Melchisedek, and we judge of its ancient magnificence by the grandeur of its ruins. We also read in the last chapters of Genesis that *Jacob came to Succoth* (that is to say, 'the tents'), *and that having built there a house and pitched his tents, he then went on to Salem, which is a city of the Shechemites, in the land of Canaan.*

8. It should also be noted that Abraham, having pursued his enemies as far as Dan, today called Paneas, and returning victorious, Melchizedek went out, not from Jerusalem, but from the capital of the Shechemites, to meet him. It is from this city that it is also said in the Gospel: *John was baptizing in Ennon, near Salim, because there was much water there.* It does not matter whether one pronounces 'Salem' or 'Salim', for the Hebrews seldom use vowels in the middle of words, and they are pronounced differently, according to the diversity of the countries and the fancy of the readers.

9. This is what I have learned from the most educated of the Jews. They are so far from believing that Melchisedek was either the Holy Spirit or an angel that they take him for a man whose name was widely known. It is true that Melchisedek was one of the figures of the Saviour because the priesthood of Jesus Christ has no end; that this divine Saviour being king and priest all together, we are, by his grace, of the royal and priestly race; that he is the cornerstone which united the wall of separation, and the good shepherd who of two flocks has made one. But is it necessary for that to be attached so much to the spiritual and anagogical sense that one abandons the truth of the history as do those

* Jerome here mistakenly imagines that the name Jerusalem, transcribed in Greek as *Hierosolumma*, comes from the Greek *hieros* or 'priest'.

who say that Melchisedek was not a king, but an angel in human form?

The Hebrews, on the contrary, to prove that Melchisedek, king of Salem, was Shem, son of Noah, quote this passage, which immediately precedes that in which it is spoken of this high priest: *And the king of Sodom went out to meet him* (that is, Abraham), when he returned after the defeat of Chedorlaomer and the other kings who were with him in the valley of Savé, also called the valley of the King. *But Melchisedek, king of Salem, offered bread and wine,* etc. Then therefore that Salem was a royal city, and that scripture speaks of 'the valley,' or, as the Septuagint translated, 'of the country,' where the king dwelt, and which the inhabitants of Palestine still call today Aulon. It is clear that he who reigned both in this city and over this valley was a real man.

10. This is what I have learned and what I have read about Melchisedek. I have quoted my authors to you, it is up to you to appreciate them; if you reject them, you must also reject your mysterious interpreter who, despite his ignorance, decided to teach that Melchisedek was the Holy Spirit, and thereby verified the Greek axiom that knowledge is timid and ignorance presumptuous.

It was after a long illness that I wrote this letter with great difficulty in Lent. As I was preparing to compose another work, I wanted to devote a few days beforehand to my Commentary on Saint Matthew; and I resumed my work with such zeal that if my studies benefited, my health suffered.

Appendix 3: The sign of the 'almah who is pregnant

Isaiah's prophecy, strictly translated, is as follows: *YHVH himself will give you a sign: Behold, the 'almah is/will be pregnant and is bearing a son and you/she have/has called his name Immanuel* (God with us) (7:14). This text has been a lodestone of Jewish-Christian debate since at least the second century when Justin told Trypho the Jews had falsified the scriptures, and Trypho replied that the Christian view just didn't hold, for the prophecy refers to Hezekiah (*Dial.* 67). The interpretation of the verse is far from easy, for it has historical, literary, and prophetic contexts, and they don't all point in the same direction. Let us begin with the basic interpretational issues.

Basic interpretational issues

(1) The word *'almah.* Does it mean 'virgin' or just 'young woman'? Hebrew *'almah* is more ambiguous than the real Hebrew word for a virgin, which is *betulah.* With *'almah*, virginity is often implied, as with English 'maid'. (In English, it is implied in speaking of a young girl as a 'maid'. It is not usually implied in speaking of a chamber-maid.) Every time *'almah* appears in the Bible it refers to an unmarried young woman of marriageable age, and hence, in ancient Israel, a virgin.[1] (In ancient Israel, premarital virginity was the norm.) Yet, one can argue from the root of the word, which means 'to become whole' or 'ripe', that *'almah* really just means 'early-teenage woman' just as its masculine equivalent, *'elem*, means 'early-teenage man' (1 Sam. 17:56; 20:22). (Yes, the meaning of a word does not depend on its derivation; but derivation can help to clarify meaning.) Trypho understood Hebrew pretty well—better, I imagine, than most folk nowadays—and he accepted that *'almah* meant 'young woman'. So it is reasonable to assume that an *'almah* could already be married and so not a virgin, but simply a young woman. Indeed, it is reasonable to suppose that one called *betulah* (virgin) and *'almah* the day before her

[1] Gen 22:43. Exod. 2:8; Ps. 68:26 [married women would not dance in the streets]; Prov. 30:19; Song 1:3; 6:8.

marriage, would still be *'almah* but not *betulah* the day after.

(2) The adjective *pregnant* (Heb. *harah*). The adjective is used predicatively. This means that, while there is no verb in the Hebrew phrase, *ha-'almah harah*, a verb must be supplied in English. Usually, the sense would be present tense: 'the virgin is pregnant'. But, since there is no verb, it is not impossible to render it as past or future: 'the virgin has become/will be pregnant'.

(3) The sign. After Ahaz rejects YHVH's offer of a sign, Isaiah says he will get a sign direct from YHVH. What is this sign? And what does it signify? Isaiah offers him a sign from the height above—the word is *ma'lah*, an anagram of *'almah.*

(4) *She has called* [*his name*]. The Hebrew *qara't* means 'you (2 fem. sing.) have called'. In other words, Isaiah may be addressing the *'almah* who shall bear the child. However, that makes little sense in context. And so it is generally taken as either:

a) defective for *qara'ta,* 'you (3 m.s.) have called'. In this case it refers to Ahaz. This is how the Septuagint reads it.
b) Aramaic for 'she (3 fem. sing.) has called'. Why Isaiah should use an Aramaism is unclear. But it is not unlikely. Aramaisms do occur in classical Hebrew. This reading is implied in the NIV translation of Isa. 7:14.

Either way, the verb is perfect, indicating past tense. But the two verb tenses of classical Hebrew are notoriously fluid in terms of strict past or future. And, in particular, there is the phenomenon of the 'prophetic perfect' where the prophet speaks of future events in the past tense to emphasize the certainty of their fulfilment. Isaiah speaks this way just a few chapters before: *Therefore my people have gone into captivity* (5:13), although they have not yet gone into captivity. And a little later: *He has come to Ayath; he has passed through Migron* (10:28), although the invader is yet to come. So, although the verb is perfect, the sense could be that it is a future event which will certainly be fulfilled.

Bearing these points in mind, we can turn to the three main possible interpretations of the text.

Three contexts and three interpretations.

First, the historical context and interpretation. The prophecy of the child's birth is spoken in the time of the Syro-Ephraimitic alliance of 735 BC against Judah (Isa. 7:1–2, 4–9, 16). Isaiah says that, by the time the child to be born knows right from wrong—that is within, say, three or four years—both lands and their kings will be shattered and taken captive by Assyria (7:16). Isaiah therefore means that a young woman of marriageable age—a virgin at the time Isaiah wrote, perhaps, but not long after—will conceive and bear a prince of David's line by the normal process of human impregnation. The birth of this child will be a sign that the Syro-Ephraimitic alliance will soon be shattered. The young woman in question looks like Ahaz's bride, Avi bat Zecharyah, and the child, Hezekiah (2 Kgs 18:2), just as Trypho said. Thus the prophecy was fulfilled in the eighth century BC.

Second, the literary context and interpretation. Isaiah has spoken of Jerusalem as Daughter Zion, that is, the city compared to a young girl (1:8). He is told to take his son, Shear-Yashuv—whose name means 'a remnant will return'—to meet Ahaz. Ahaz rejects Isaiah's offer of a sign to guide him in the way of true faith and peace. As a result, divine rejection and judgement will fall on both king and people, but a faithful 'remnant will return'. The *'almah* who conceives is therefore Daughter Zion, and her son is the faithful remnant who shall return, called Immanuel, for God shall be with them. And from them shall spring the Messiah, the ultimate faithful remnant. Thus the prophecy speaks indirectly of the Messiah.[2]

Finally, the prophetic context and interpretation. The following chapters of Isaiah speak of the birth of a son, who looks like the same child as Immanuel of 7:14. In 9:1–7 he is spoken of in exalted terms as Wonder Counsellor, Mighty God, Everlasting Father, Prince of Peace. And in chapter eleven he is called the shoot from the stump of Jesse, anointed (*mashiaḥ*) with the Spirit of YHVH. Such prophecies seem to point to a divine king, and it's fair to say that the Jewish interpretation regards the words in Isaiah 9 and 11 as referring to the Messiah.

> For unto us a child is born, unto us a son is given, and he has taken the law upon himself to keep it. His name is called from eternity wonderful, the mighty God who liveth to eternity, the Messiah whose peace shall be great upon us in his days. (Targum Jonathan on Isa. 9:5)

> *And the spirit of God was hovering* (Gen. 1:2). This is the spirit of the King Messiah. And where is this taught? *And I will place upon him the spirit of Ha-Shem* (Isa. 11:2). (Genesis Rabbah 8:1)

[2] See Webb, *Isaiah*, 62–64 for this view.

> Rabbi Samuel ben Nachman, said: When Esau met Jacob he said to him, 'Jacob, my brother, let us walk together in this world as one.' Jacob replied: *Let my Lord, I pray thee, pass over before his servant* (Gen. 33:14). What is the meaning of, *I pray thee, pass over*?...He said to him: I have yet to establish the King Messiah, of whom it is said: *Unto us a child is born* (Isa. 9:5). (Deuteronomy Rabbah 1:20)

> Some say that *Wonder Counsellor, Mighty God, Everlasting Father* are names of Ha-Shem and that only *Prince of Peace* is the name of the child. But the correct interpretation in my view is that these are all names of the child. (Ibn Ezra on Isa. 9:5)

So bearing in mind the prophetic context, if one then takes *'almah* in its usual sense as unmarried woman and virgin, and takes 'is pregnant' as a present tense, then the verse says *the virgin is pregnant*, and so it points to a miraculous virgin conception. Taken this way, the Immanuel prophecy is about the virgin conception of the Messiah, and its fulfilment is yet to come.

The history of interpretation

Before trying to decide between these options, we should turn to the history of interpretation. The earliest interpretation is in the Septuagint, from the third century BC.

> Behold the virgin (*parthenos*) will have in belly (*en gastri hexei*), and will bear (*texetai*) a son and you (masc. sing.) will call his name Immanuel. (LXX Isa. 7:14)

It renders the ambiguous Hebrew word *'almah* with the unambiguous Greek word for a virgin, *parthenos.* Then it renders the Hebrew adjective *harah*, 'pregnant', with the nearest Greek equivalent, *en gastri hexei*, 'she will have in belly', and it does so in the future, not the present. Altogether, this could point to the future birth of a virgin-born Messiah. But it could also support the historicist reading: she who is a virgin, in Isaiah's time, will conceive (thus being no longer a virgin) and bear a son.

In the first century AD, Matthew mostly follows the Septuagint, but he changes 'you will call (sing.) his name' to 'they will call his name'.

> Behold the virgin (*parthenos*) will have in belly (*en gastri hexei*), and will bear (*texetai*) a son and they will call his name Immanuel. (1:23)

Given the context of his citation, he certainly takes Isaiah's words as pointing to the virgin conception of the Messiah (1:23). Clearly, he saw the sense of the verse as prophetic rather than historical. He may also be borrowing from the literary context, seeing Daughter Zion as the virgin who bears the remnant, and thus taking the life of Israel as a type of the life of the Messiah, just as when he says *Out of Egypt I called my son* (2:15; citing Hos. 11:1).

The fact that Matthew can use Isa. 7:14 as a proof-text in this way does suggest that it was widely understood as referring to the birth of the Messiah in his own time. Gabriel's words in Luke 1:31 may also allude to Isa. 7:14.

From this point on, Christian translators follow the Septuagint and Matthew. The Peshitta text of Isaiah, probably of Christian origin, translates Hebrew *'almah* as Aramaic *b'tultâ*, equivalent to Hebrew *betulah*, 'virgin'. It replaces both the adjective, 'pregnant', and the participle, 'is bearing', with perfect tense verbs: *baṭna w-yalda*, 'the virgin has conceived and bears'. The Peshitta of Matthew renders both verbs as imperfects with a future sense: *b'tultâ têbṭan w-tilad*, 'the virgin will conceive and will bear'.

Meanwhile, rabbinic translators takes the historicist line. Aquila, Symmachus, and Theodotion all translate *'almah* as Greek *neanis*, a 'young woman', just as Trypho did. And it is not an unreasonable translation. The Aramaic targums are close to the Hebrew and ambiguous. The Aramaic noun *'ulemta* is equivalent to Hebrew *'almah* and means 'young woman'. The verb 'conceive' (*t'lid*) is future, just as in LXX.

It is fair to add that these Aramaic renderings of the Hebrew adjective *harah,* 'pregnant', as verbs are defensible enough. *Harah,* though it is an adjective, can also be a contraction for the third-person feminine singular perfect verb, *haratah*, 'she conceived', just as we find it in Judges 13:5, 7. (See *e.g.,* Gen. 16:4 for the uncontracted form.) This is probably how the Aramaic translators read it. Indeed, it is likely that LXX and Matthew understood it the same way, yet as a prophetic perfect, giving rise to their future tense translations.

Deciding between the three interpretations

Deciding between these interpretations is not easy. The historical interpretation downplays the wider context of messianic prophecy in

Isaiah 7–11 and the real possibility of reading a virgin conception in the words *the ‘almah is pregnant.* The same is true of the literary interpretation. But the prophetic interpretation tends to downplay the prophecy and fulfilment of the destruction of the Syro-Ephraimitic alliance in the eighth century BC.

Justin’s reply to Trypho in this matter was to say that the promised ‘sign’ must be truly a sign (*Dial.* 84) and the natural birth of a child is no great sign. If a virgin conceives, remaining a virgin, then that is a sign indeed. But if a young woman conceives, that is no great sign. Trypho’s reply, though not recorded, would probably have been to say that the sign was a portent: the birth of the child Hezekiah would portend the destruction of the threatening Syro-Ephraimitic alliance.

Perhaps Isaiah’s appeal to a sign *in the height above* (*ma‘lah*) which will be from YHVH himself suggests that the sign to be given must be a greater sign than the one Trypho imagined. And perhaps Isaiah’s words, *Hear now, house of David. Is it not enough to try the patience of men that you also try the patience of my God?* (7:13), might just suggest a divine decision to bypass the male line of David’s house. But I’m not sure that one could be dogmatic about it.

In the end, in my view, Isaiah’s words ‘the *‘almah* is pregnant’ can be taken as pointing to a virgin conception. But the same text speaks also of the birth of eighth-century BC Hezekiah as a portent of the destruction of the Syro-Ephraimitic alliance. Hezekiah’s mother was perhaps a *betulah* at the time of Isaiah’s announcement, then an *‘almah* but not a *betulah* at the time of his conception. But the life of yet-unborn good king Hezekiah is spoken of in exalted language—in chapters 9 and 11—which points beyond Hezekiah himself to the highest conception of the messianic office of the kings of David’s line. In this way, Hezekiah is a type of the coming one. And so the possible allusion to a virgin conception in Isaiah 7:14 can be taken as pointing to the conception of the Messiah. The evidence is that it probably was taken this way by the translator of Septuagint Isaiah in the third century BC, and it was certainly understood this way by Matthew and other Israelites of his time.

It is, perhaps, not the most unambiguous Bible text about the extraordinary conception of the Messiah. But, together with the others, it adds its voice to the chorus of witnesses to the Messiah’s heavenly nature.

Glossary

amidah: the central prayer of Jewish liturgy, dating from temple times. It formerly comprised eighteen blessings, from whence it is called *Shmoneh esreh* ('The Eighteen'). The ***bet-din*** of Gamliel II added a nineteenth paragraph, the ***birkat ha-minim***. Observant Jews say it three times a day, and four on Shabbat and holy days.

amora, pl. ***amoraim***: a rabbinic teacher of c. AD 200–400.

amoraic: describing the period of the *amoraim.*

baraitha, pl. ***b'raitot***: a **tannaitic** tradition, absent from the **Mishnah**, transcribed by later sources.

Bavli: see **Talmud Bavli**.

bet: house or institution; *bet David*, house of David; *bet Shammai*, the school of Shammai.

bet-din: Jewish court of law.

birkat kohanim: the 'priestly' blessing of Numbers 6:24–26.

birkat ha-minim: the 'blessing' (curse) upon the 'heretics', added to the *Amidah* by Gamliel II.

Gaon, pl. ***geonim***: title of the heads of the academies of Pumbedita and Sura from c. 540–1040 AD.

***elohim*:** God or gods. The word is plural in form. Since there is also a duple form, *elim*, the plural must refer to at least three beings. It can refer generally to an assemblage of heavenly beings. But when used of Israel's God, the plural noun is associated with a singular verb. In such cases, it is often explained as a plural of majesty. But it is reasonable to see within it the plurality of God; that is, the greater and lesser God, spoken of by Philo, or the New Testament Trinity.

Exilarch (Gk): the ***Resh G'lutha*** (Aram. 'head of the exile') or ***Rosh Galut*** (Heb. same), the king of David's line who ruled the Israelite community in Babylon.

gemara: **Talmud** commentary on a **Mishnah** text.

gematria: biblical interpretation based on the numerical value of Hebrew words.

halakhah: the laws and ordinances, in addition to the law of Moses, that regulate Jewish life, conduct, and religious observance.

Hinneh yaskil avdi: 'Behold, my servant shall succeed'; the biblical *parshah* (section) Isaiah 52:13–53:12.

LXX: see Septuagint.

k'hunah: the status of being a *kohen*; the 'priesthood'.

kohen, pl. ***kohanim***: an Aaronite 'priest' offering temple sacrifices.

Kohen Gadol: the chief 'priest'.

k'tsatsah: 'cutting-off' ceremony, to exclude an offender from the Israelite community of Israel.

HaShem: Hebrew for 'the Name'; *i.e.*, the Tetragrammaton.

malkut: kingdom or kingship.

mamzer: a child conceived in adultery or incest.

mashiaḥ: 'anointed'; a divinely-appointed king or priest; the Messiah.

meshiḥa: Aramaic for ***mashiaḥ***.

mezuzah: lit. Heb. 'doorpost'. A piece of parchment with the words of Deut. 6:4-9 and 11:13-21 contained in a decorative case. It is fastened to the doorpost of Jewish homes as an amulet to protect against evil.

min: heretic; the term normally indicates an Israelite Christian.

minut: heresy (see above); the term normally refers to Christianity.

midrash: a rabbinic commentary on scripture or scriptural themes.

Mishnah: a collection of Israel's temple laws and oral traditions, compiled by R. Judah ha-Nasi in the latter 2nd or early 3rd century AD. Its purpose was to save Israel's national memory from extinction, following the Roman proscriptions of 135 AD.

nasi: prince.

Nazarenes: Generally, a Jewish and Rabbinic term for Hebrew followers of Jesus (cf. Acts 24:5), in distinction to 'Christian', which is Greek. Specifically, an early Torah-observant group of Hebrew Christians, spoken of by Jerome, Letter 75; Epiphanius, Panarion 29.

notzrim: Nazarenes, Christians.

paytan: the poet of a ***piyut.****

parashah, parshat (gen.): a portion or 'paragraph' of a biblical text.

Peshitta ('simple'): Early Syriac Aramaic translation of the Bible.

pesikta: a midrash on the festal cycle.

piyut: a Jewish liturgical poem.

Rav shel olam: Master of the universe.

Resh G'lutha (Aram. 'head of the exile'): The ***Rosh Galut*** (Heb.) or **Exilarch** (Gk), the king of David's line who ruled the Israelite community in Babylon.

Septuagint (LXX): Greek version of the Law, Prophets, and Writings (Old Testament), made in Alexandria in the 2nd or 3rd century BC.

shem meforash: the 'explicit name'; that is, the **Tetragrammaton**, YHVH, fully pronounced.

talmid, pl. ***talmidim***: disciple, Torah scholar.

Talmud Bavli (Babylonian Talmud): a commentary on the **Mishnah** compiled in Babylonia in the 5th century AD. It contains ancient traditions omitted from the **Mishnah** and **Tosefta**.

Talmud Yerushalmi (Jerusalem Talmud, Palestinian Talmud): a commentary on the **Mishnah** compiled in Galilee (not Jerusalem) in the 4th century. It too contains ancient traditions omitted from the **Mishnah** and **Tosefta**.

tanna, pl. ***tannaim***: a rabbinic teacher of the period 0–200 AD.

tannaitic: describing the period of the *tannaim.*

targum: Aramaic for 'translation', especially the Aramaic translations of the books of the Bible.

Tetragrammaton: the sacred personal name of Israel's God, written in the Bible as YHVH, and vocalized in the Masoretic text as Y'ho**vàh**.

Tosefta: supplement. Specifically, a collection of temple laws and oral traditions, compiled in the late 2nd century, supplementary to R. Judah's **Mishnah**. Many of its teachings date from temple times.

tosefta: supplement. Generally, a 'supplement' or 'addition' to another text, such as the marginal **tosefta** of the Codex Reuchlinianus text of the **targum** of Zechariah 12:10.

tsadik: a righteous, just, and spiritual person.

Yerushalmi: see **Talmud Yerushalmi**.

YHVH, Yehovah: the revealed personal name of Israel's God. Aharon ben Asher's 10th-century Aleppo Codex vocalizes it as Yeho**vah**. This is the likeliest pronunciation. For more, see Appendix 1 in my *Songs of Ascents.*

yeshiva: a school for the study of Jewish texts.

Zadokites: the temple priesthood of the second-temple period, who traced their descent from Zadok, the *kohen gadol* of David's time. In the New Testament, they are called Sadducees.

Abbreviations

Ancient Bible texts and translations cited

LXX	Septuagint
MT	Masoretic Text
Symm.	Symmachus
Peshitta	Syriac Peshitta
Tg	Targum
Tg Jon.	Targum Jonathan
Tg Neof.	Palestinian Targum Neofiti
Tg Onq.	Babylonian Targum Onqelos to the Pentateuch
Tg Yer.	Targum Yerushalmi (Pseudo-Jonathan) to the Pentateuch
Vg	Vulgate

Apocrypha and Pseudepigrapha

1 Enoch	1 (Ethiopic Apocalypse of) Enoch
2 Bar.	2 (Syriac) Apocalypse of Baruch
4 Ezra	4 Ezra (2 Esdras 3–14)
1 Macc.	1 Maccabees
2 Macc.	2 Maccabees
3 Macc.	3 Maccabees
4 Macc.	4 Maccabees
Pss. Sol.	Psalms of Solomon
Sib. Or.	Sibylline Oracles
Sir.	Ben Sira (Ecclesiasticus)
T12P	The Testaments of the Twelve Patriarchs
T. Jos.	The Testament of Joseph (T12P)
T. Jud.	The Testament of Judah (T12P)
T. Lev.	The Testament of Levi (T12P)
T. Naph.	The Testament of Naphtali (T12P)
T. Reub.	The Testament of Reuben (T12P)
T. Sim.	The Testament of Simeon (T12P)
T. Zeb.	The Testament of Zebulon (T12P)

Dead Sea Scrolls (omitting those referred to by reference number only)

CD	Cairo (Genizah text of the) Damascus (Document)
1QApGen	*Genesis Apocryphon*
1QH	*Hodayot* (The Hymns Scroll)
1QM	*Milḥamah* (The War Scroll)
1QS	*Serekh hayyaḥad* (The Community Rule)
1QSa	Appendix A (Rule of the Congregation) to 1QS
4Q175	Testimonia
11QMelch	Melchizedek

Mishnaic and talmudic tractates

Ber.	Berakhoth	MK	Moed Katan	Sanh.	Sanhedrin
Bik.	Bikkurim	Hag.	Hagigah	Sheb.	Shebuot
Shab.	Shabbat	Yeb.	Yebamot	Edu.	Eduyot
Erub.	Erubin	Ket.	Ketubot	AZ	Avodah Zarah
Pes.	Pesahim	Ned.	Nedarim	Abot	Abot
Shek.	Shekalim	Sot.	Sotah	Zeb.	Zebahim
Yoma	Yoma	Git.	Gittin	Hul.	Hullin
Suk.	Sukkah	Kid.	Kiddushin	Arak.	Arakhin
RH	Rosh ha-Shanah	BK	Baba Kamma	Tam.	Tamid
Ta'an.	Ta'anit	BM	Baba Mezia	Mid.	Middot
Meg.	Megillah	BB	Baba Batra	Nid.	Niddah

Other rabbinic texts and abbreviations (for Targums, see **Ancient Bible texts**)

B.	Babylonian Talmud (Talmud Bavli)
Deut. R.	Midrash Rabbah to Deuteronomy
Eccl. R.	Midrash Rabbah to Ecclesiastes
Exod. R.	Midrash Rabbah to Exodus
Gen. R.	Midrash Rabbah to Genesis
Lam. R.	Midrash Rabbah to Lamentations
Lev. R.	Midrash Rabbah to Leviticus
M.	Mishnah
MAB	Midrash Aleph Beth (ed. Sawyer 1993)
Midr. Tan.	Midrash Tanhuma
Midr. Pss.	Midrash Tehillim (Midrash on Psalms)
Midr. Vay.	Midrash Vayyosha
NRSY	Nistarot Rav Shimon ben Yoḥai
Num. R.	Midrash Rabbah to Numbers
Otot	Otot ha-Mashiah
Pes. R.	Pesikta Rabbati
Pir. M.	Pirqei Mashiaḥ
PHR	Pirkei Hekhalot Rabbati
R.	Rav, Rabbi
Sef. Z.	Sefer Zerubbabel
SER	Seder Eliyahu Rabbah
T.	Tosefta
Y.	Jerusalem Talmud (Talmud Yerushalmi)

Classical and Patristic texts

Ant.	Josephus, *Antiquities*
Dial.	Justin Martyr, *Dialogue with Trypho the Judean*
War	Josephus, *Jewish War*

Frequently-cited periodicals, reference works, serials, and other

BDB	Brown, Driver, & Briggs, *Hebrew Lexicon*
BHM	*Beth ha-Midrasch* (ed. Jellinek)
EJ	*Encyclopaedia Judaica*
ET	English Translation
GKC	Gesenius, Kautzsch, Cowley, *Gesenius' Hebrew Grammar.*
JBL	*Journal of Biblical Literature*
JETS	*Journal of Theological Studies*
JSP	*Journal for the Study of the Pseudepigrapha*
JE	*Jewish Encyclopedia* (ed. Singer, 1906)
PG	*Patrologia Graeca* (ed. Migne)
PL	*Patrologia Latina* (ed. Migne)
ZAW	*Zeitschrift für die alttestamentliche Wissenschaft*

Bibliography

Adler, M.N. (ed.)

1907 *The Itinerary of Benjamin of Tudela* (London: Frowde, 1907).

Agrell, S.

1927 'Runornas Talmystik och dess antika Förebild', in *Skrifter utgivna av Vetenskaps-Societeten i Lund* 6: 31 ff.

Allen, L. C.

1983 *Psalms 101–150* (Waco, TX: Word).

Amzallag, N.

2012 'The Identity of the Emissary of YHWH' (Scandinavian Journal of the Old Testament) 26:123–144.

Anderson, R.H.

1997 'Theophilus: A Proposal,' *Evangelical Quarterly* 69:195–215.

Aslan, R.

2013 *Zealot: The Life and Times of Jesus of Nazareth* (New York: Random House).

Avni, G.

2010 'The Persian Conquest of Jerusalem, 614 c.e. An Archaeological Assessment', *Bulletin of the American Schools of Oriental Research* 357: 35–48.

Barag, D. and D. Flusser,

1986 'The Ossuary of Yehohanah Granddaughter of the High Priest Theophilus', *Israel Exploration Journal* 36: 39–44.

Bardy, G.

1926–27 'Melchisédech dans la tradition patristique', *Revue Biblique* 35:496–509; 36:25–45.

Barker, M.

2008 'Who was Melchizedek and who was his God?' SBL 2008 http://www.margaretbarker.com/Papers/SBLMelchizedek.pdf

Bauckham, R.

2009 'The Divinity of Jesus Christ in the Epistle to the Hebrews' in R. Bauckham *et al., The Epistle to the Hebrews and Christian Theology* (Grand Rapids, MI: Eerdmans).

2006 *Jesus and the Eyewitnesses: The Gospels as Eyewitness Testimony* (Grand Rapids, MI: Eerdmans).

2004 *Jude and the Relatives of Jesus in the Early Church* (London: T. & T. Clark).

Bauer, W., F.W. Danker, W.F. Arndt, F.W. Gingrich (eds.)

2000 *A Greek-English Lexicon of the New Testament and other Early Christian Literature.* 3rd edition (Chicago: University of Chicago Press).

Bazes, M.

1976 *Jesus the Jew, The Historical Jesus: The True Story of Jesus* (Jerusalem).

Beasley-Murray, G.R.
1986 *Jesus and the Kingdom of God* (London: Paternoster).
Becker, J
1980 *Die Testament der Zwölf Patriarchen*, Jüdische Schriften aus hellenistisch–römischer Zeit III.1 (Gütersloher Verlagshaus).
Becking, B.
1992 *The Fall of Samaria: An Historical and Archaeological Study* (Leiden: Brill).
Bickerman, E. J.
1950 'The Date of the Testaments of the Twelve Patriarchs', *JBL* 69:245–60.
Bodenheimer, F. S.
1960 *Animal and Man in Bible Lands* (Leiden: Brill, 1972).
Bonwetsch, N.
1910 'Doctrina Iacobi nuper baptizati', *Abhandlungen der königlichen Gesellschaft der Wissenschaften zu Göttingen, philologisch-historische Klasse*, NF. 12/3 (1910).
Box, G.H.
1918 *The Apocalypse of Abraham* (London: SPCK).
Boyarin, D.
2019 'The Quest of the Historical Metatron: Enoch or Jesus', in D.R. Katz, N. Hacham, G. Herman, and L. Sagiv (eds.), *A Question of Identity: Social, Political, and Historical Aspects of Identity Dynamics in Jewish and Other Contexts* (Berlin: de Gruyter) 153–162.
2012 *The Jewish Gospels: The Story of the Jewish Christ* (New York: New Press).
2004 *Border Lines: The Partition of Judaeo-Christianity* (Philadelphia: University of Pennsylvania Press, 2004).
1999 *Dying for God. Martyrdom and the Making of Christianity and Judaism* (Stanford, Stanford University Press).
Braude, W.G. and I.J. Kapstein,
1975 *R. Kahana's Compilation of Discourses for Sabbaths and Festal Days* (Philadelphia: The Jewish Publication Society of America).
Brettler, M.Z.
1989 'The Book of Judges: Literature as Politics', *JBL* 108: 395–418.
Brown, R.E.
1977 *The Birth of the Messiah* (Doubleday, 1977).
Bruce, F.F.
1990 *The Epistle to the Hebrews* (Grand Rapids, MI: Eerdmans).
Buber, S.
1868 *Pesiqta de-Rav Kahana* (Lyck).
Buttenwieser, M.
1906 'Messiah' in *Jewish Encyclopaedia* 8.505–512.
Cargill, R.R.
2019 *Melchizedek, King of Sodom* (Oxford: Oxford University Press).
Carrington, P.
1957 *The Early Christian Church*, vol. I (Cambridge University Press).

Chadwick, H.
1965 *Contra Celsum* (Cambridge University Press; 1st ed. 1953).
Charles, R. H.
1913–19 *The Apocrypha and Pseudepigrapha of the Old Testament.* 2 vols. (Oxford: Clarendon).
1912 *The Book of Enoch or 1 Enoch: Translated from the Editor's Ethiopic Text* (London: Adam and Charles Black).
1908 *The Greek Versions of the Testaments of the Twelve Patriarchs* (Oxford: Clarendon).
1893 *The Book of Enoch* (Oxford: Clarendon).
Charlesworth, J.H. (ed.)
1983 *The Old Testament Pseudepigrapha.* 2 vols. (NY: Doubleday).
1991 *Jesus' Jewishness: Exploring the Place of Jesus in Early Judaism* (NY: Crossroad).
Chilton, B.
2000 *Rabbi Jesus: An Intimate Biography* (New York: Doubleday).
Cohen, S.J.D.
2013 'The ways that parted: Jews, Christians,and Jewish-Christians ca. 100-150 CE.' *Near Eastern Languages and Civilizations*, Harvard University, preprint.
Collins, J.J.
2003 'Sibylline Oracles' in Charlesworth 1983: 317–472.
Crossan, J.D.
1994 *Jesus: A Revolutionary Biography* (San Francisco: HarperCollins).
1991 *The Historical Jesus: The Life of a Mediterranean Jewish Peasant* (San Francisco: HarperCollins).
1989 *The Birth of Christianity* (San Francisco: HarperCollins).
Danker, F.W. (ed.), *see* Bauer, W.
Dagron, G. and V. Déroche,
1991 'Juifs et Chrétiens dans l'Orient du VIIe siècle' in *Travaux et Mémoires* 11, pp. 69–219.
De Bruin, T.
2015 *The Great Controversy: The Individual's Struggle Between Good and Evil in* The Testaments of the Twelve Patriarchs *and in Their Jewish and Christian Contexts* (Göttingen: Vandenhoeck & Ruprecht).
Delitzsch, Franz
1887 *Biblical Commentary on the Psalms.* 3 vols. (tr. D. Eaton) (London: Hodder and Stoughton).
Dillmann, A.
1853 *Das Buch Henoch* (Leipzig: Vogel).
Driver, S.R. and A. Neubauer
1877 *The Fifty-Third Chapter of Isaiah According To The Jewish Interpreters.* 2 vols. (Oxford: Parker–Leipzig: Weigel).
Dunn, J.D.G.
2003 *Jesus Remembered* (Eerdmans: Grand Rapids MI/Cambridge).

Dupont-Sommer, A.
1952 'Le Testament de Levi (XVII–XVIII) et la Secte Juive de l'Alliance', *Semitica* 4 : 33–53.

Edwards, J.R.
2009 *The Hebrew Gospel and the Development of the Synoptic Tradition* (Grand Rapids MI: Eerdmans).

Ehrman, B.D.
2014 *How Jesus Became God* (San Francisco: HarperOne).

Emerton, J.A.
1958 The Origin of the Son of Man Imagery', *JETS* 9: 225–242

Evans, C.A.
2009 'Jesus and the Extracanonical Works' in J.H. Charlesworth and P. Pokorny (eds.), *Jesus Research: An International Perspective. The Proceedings of the Biennial Princeton-Prague Symposium on the Current State of Studies on the Historical Jesus* (Grand Rapids: Eerdmans) 182–98.

Falk, H.
1985 *Jesus the Pharisee: A New Look at the Jewishness of Jesus* (NY: Paulist Press).

Ferguson, J.
1974 *Clement of Alexandria* (New York: Twayne).

Flowers, M.
2016 'The Two Messiahs and Melchizedek in 11QMelchizedek', *Journal of Ancient Judaism* 7 (2016): 194–227.

Flusser, D.
1997 *Jesus* (Jerusalem: Magnes).
1989 *Jewish Sources in Early Christianity* (Tel-Aviv: MOD).

Frank, C.
1924 *Deutsche Gaue* 25 (1924), 76.

Fredriksen, P.
1999 *Jesus of Nazareth, King of the Jews: A Jewish Life and the Emergence of Christianity* (New York: Knopf).

Friedmann, M.
1880 *Pesikta Rabbati: Midrasch für den Fest-Cyclus und die ausgezeichnete Shabbate* (Vienna).

Fruchtenbaum, A.G.
2010 *Jesus was a Jew* (San Antonio, TX: Ariel Ministeries).

Furuli, R.J.
2018 *The Tetragram: Its History, Its Use In The New Testament, and Its Pronunciation* (Larvik: Awatu Publishers).

Gammie, J.G.
1960 *Melchizedek: An Exegetical Study of Genesis 14 and the Psalter* (PhD Dissertation: University of Edinburgh).

Garber, Z.
2011 *The Jewish Jesus* (Purdue University).

García-Martínez, F.
1996 *The Dead Sea Scrolls Translated. The Qumran Texts in English.* 2nd edition. (Leiden: Brill, 1996).

Gerstenberger, E.
2001 *Psalms, Part 2 and Lamentations* (Grand Rapids: Eerdmans).
Goldstein, M.
1950 *Jesus in the Jewish Tradition* (NY: Macmillan).
Gordon, N.
2012 *Shattering the Conspiracy of Silence* (Jerusalem: Hilkiah).
Gordon, R.P.
2008 *Hebrews.* 2nd ed. (Sheffield: Phoenix Press).
Gottlieb, M.
2011 *Moses Mendelssohn: Writings on Judaism, Christianity, and the Bible* (Brandeis University Press).
Green, M.
1984 *The Empty Cross of Jesus* (London: Hodder and Stoughton).
Gregg, R.C.
2015 *Shared Stories, Rival Tellings: Early Encounters of Jews, Christians, and Muslims* (Oxford: University Press).
Grosser, F.
1926 'Ein neuer Vorschlag zur Deutung der Sator Formel', in *Archiv für Religionswissenschaft* 24 (1926), 165-169.
Hachlili, R.
2000 'Hebrew Names, Personal Names, Family Names, and Nicknames of Jews in the Second Temple Period' in J. W. van Henten and A. Brenner (eds.), *Families and Family Relations as Represented in Early Judaisms and Early Christianities: Texts and Fictions.* (Studies in Theology and Religion 2. Leiden: Deo), 83–115.
Haelewyck, J.-C.
2019 *The Old Syriac Versions of the Gospels. A Status Quaestionis (From 1842 to the Present Day).* BABELAO 8: 141–179.
Hanson, A.T.
1965 *Jesus Christ in the Old Testament* (London: SPCK).
Hanson, P.D.,
1992 'Messiahs and Messianic Figures in Proto-Apocalyptism,' in J.H. Charlesworth (ed.), *The Messiah: Developments in Earliest Judaism and Christianity* (Minneapolis: Fortress Press): 67–75.
Hart, M. H.
1978 *The 100: A Ranking of the Most Influential Persons in History* (New York: Hart Publishing Company).
Hayward, R.
2009 *Targums and the Transmission of Scripture into Judaism and Christianity* (Studies in the Aramaic Interpretation of Scripture 10; Leiden: Brill).
Heiser, M.
2015 *The Unseen Realm: Recovering the Supernatural Worldview of the Bible* (Bellingham, WA: Lexham Press).
Herford, R.T.
1903 *Christianity in Talmud and Midrash* (London: Williams & Norgate).

Hickes, T. D.
1924 'Roman Square Palindrome: Inscription at Cirencester', *Notes and Queries* 16: 119.

Hollander, H.W.
1985 'The Testaments of the Twelve Patriarchs' in M. de Jonge (ed.), *Outside the Old Testament* (Cambridge University Press): 71–91.

Horowitz, E.
1998 '"The Vengeance of the Jews Was Stronger Than Their Avarice": Modern Historians and the Persian Conquest of Jerusalem in 614', *Jewish Social Studies* 4: 1–39.

Howard, D.M. Jr, and A. Schmutzer (eds.),
2021 *Reading the Psalms Theologically* (Bellingham WA: Lexham Press).

Howard, G.
1986 'The Textual Nature of an Old Hebrew Version of Matthew', *JBL* 105: 49-63.

Hughes, P.E.
1977 *A Commentary on the Epistle to the Hebrews* (Grand Rapids, MI: Eerdmans).

Humphreys, C.J.
2011 *The Mystery of the Last Supper* (Cambridge: Cambridge University Press).

Ilan, T.
2002 *Lexicon of Jewish Names in Antiquity. Part 1: Palestine 330 BCE–200 CE* (Tübingen: Mohr-Siebeck).

Isaac, E.
1983 '1 Enoch' in J.H. Charlesworth 1983: 1:5–89.

Ishida, T.
1977 *The Royal Dynasties in Ancient Israel. A Study on the Formation and Development of Royal-Dynastic Ideology* (*Beihefte zur ZAW* 142; Berlin: de Gruyter).

Jacobus, H.R.
2009 'The Curse of Cainan (Jub. 8.1-5): Genealogies in Genesis 5 and Genesis 11and a Mathematical Pattern', *JSP* 18: 207–232.

Jastrow, M.
1950 *Dictionary of the Targumim, the Talmud Babli and Yerushalmi, and the Midrashic Literature* (Pardes).

Jellinek, A.
1853–77 *Bet ha-Midrash.* 6 vols. in 2. (Leipzig: Nies–Vollrath, 1853–77; photog. repr. Jerusalem: Wahrmann, 1967).

de Jonge, M.
1904 *Jeschuah, der klassische jüdische Mann* (Berlin).

de Jonge, M.
1953 *The Testaments of the Twelve Patriarchs: A Study of Their Text, Composition, and Origin* (Leiden).
1964 *Testamenta XII Patriarcharum* (Leiden: Brill).
1975 *The Testaments of the Twelve Patriarchs* (Leiden: Brill).
1991 *Jewish Eschatology, Early Christian Christology and the*

Testaments of the Twelve Patriarchs: Collected Essays of Marinus de Jonge (Leiden: Brill).

Joosten, J.

2004 'Aramaic or Hebrew behind the Greek Gospels?' *Analecta Bruxellensia* 9: 88-101.

1996 *The Syriac Language of the Peshitta and Old Syriac Versions of Matthew. Syntactic Structure, Inner-Syriac Developments and Translation Technique.* Studies in Semitic Languages and Linguistics 22 (Leiden: Brill).

Joosten, J. and M. Kister

2010 'The New Testament and Rabbinic Hebrew' in R. Bieringer, F. García Martínez, D. Pollefeyt, P. J. Tomson, eds., *The New Testament and Rabbinic Literature*, Supplements to the Journal for the Study of Judaism 136 (Leiden, Brill, 2010), 335-350.

Juster, D.C.

1977 *Jewishness and Jesus* (IVP)

Kaiser, W.

1985 *The Uses of the Old Testament in the New* (Chicago: Moody Press).

1998 The Christian and the 'Old' Testament (Pasadena CA: William Carey Library).

Kee, H.C.

1983 'Testaments of the Twelve Patriarchs' in J.H. Charlesworth (ed.), *The Old Testament Pseudepigrapha.* 2 vols. (London: Darton, Longman & Todd): I:775–828.

Kjaer-Hansen, K.

1992 'An Introduction to the Names Yehoshua/Joshua, Yeshua, Jesus and Yeshu', A paper presented at the Ninth North American Coordinating Committee Meeting of the Lausanne Consultation on Jewish Evangelism, Los Angeles, California, 23–25 March 1992.

Klausner, J.

1925 *Jesus of Nazareth* (New York: Macmillan Company, 1925).

Kloner, A.

1999 'Did a Rolling Stone Close Jesus' Tomb?', *BAR* 25: 23–29, 76.

Krauss, S.

1888 *Das Leben Jesu nach Jüdischen Quellen* (Calvary: Berlin, 1902).

Kugel, J.L.

1995 'Reuben's Sin with Bilhah in the Testament of Reuben' in D.P. Wright *et al.* (eds.), *Pomegranates and Golden Bells: Studies in Biblical, Jewish and Near Eastern Ritual, Law and Literature in Honor of Jacob Milgrom* (Winona Lake: Eisenbrauns): 525–54.

Kung, H. and P. Lapide

1977 'Jesus: a bond or a barrier', *Journal of Ecumenical Studies* 14: 466–483.

Kutscher, E.Y.

1976 *Studies in Galilean Aramaic* (Ramat-Gan, Israel: Bar-Ilan University Press).

Laato, A.
2016 'Celsus, *Toldot Yeshu* and early traces of apology for the virgin birth of Jesus' in *Jewish Studies in the Nordic Countries Today* (Scripta Instituti Donneriani Aboensis, 27; 2016) 61–80.

Lapide, P.
1983 *The Resurrection of Jesus: A Jewish Perspective* (London: SPCK).

Lauterbach, J.Z.
1951 'Jesus in the Talmud', in *Rabbinic Essays* (Cincinnati), 473-570.

Lee, B.J.
1988 *The Galilean Jewishness of Jesus* (Paulist Press)

Leibes, Y.
1987 מלאכי קול השופר וישוע שר הפנים (The Angels of the Shofar and Yeshua Sar ha-Panim) in *The Proceedings Of The First International Conference On The History Of Jewish Mysticism: Early Jewish Mysticism: Jerusalem Studies in Jewish Thought* / מחקרי ירושלים במחשבת ישראל 6 (Jerusalem: The Mandel Institute of Jewish Studies): 171–195.

Lieu, J.M.
1996 *Image and Reality: The Jews in the World of the Christians in the Second Century* (London: T & T Clark).

Lindars, B.
1976 'A Bull, a Lamb and a Word: I Enoch xc.38' *New Testament Studies* 22: 483-86: 485.

Lowe, M.
1981 'Ἰουδαῖοι of the Apocrypha: A Fresh Approach to the Gospels of James, Pseudo-Thomas, Peter and Nicodemus,' *Novum Testamentum* 23: 56–90.
1976 'Who were the Ἰουδαῖοι?' *Novum Testamentum* 18: 101–131.

Martin, F.
1906 *Le Livre d'Hénoch* (Paris: Letouzey et Ané).

Masson, J.
1982 *Jésus, Fils de David dans les Généalogies de Saint Matthieu et de Saint Luc* (Paris: Téqui, 1982).

McCaul, J.B.
1871 *The Epistle to the Hebrews* (London: Longman, Green, & Co.).

McGrath, J.F. and J. Truex,
2004 ''Two Powers' and Early Jewish and Christian Monotheism', *Journal of Biblical Studies* 4:43–71.

McNamara, M.
2000 'Melchizedek: Gen 14,17-20 in the Targums, in Rabbinic and Early Christian Literature', *Biblica* 81: 1–31.

Meier, J.P.
1991 *A Marginal Jew*. Vol. 1 (New York: Doubleday, 1991).

Milik, J.T.
1976 *The Books of Enoch: Aramaic Fragments of Qumran Cave 4* (Oxford: Clarendon, 1976).

Mishkin, D.
2015 *Jewish Scholarship on the Resurrection of Jesus* (Eugene, Oregon: Pickwick).
Mitchell, D.C.
2015 *The Songs of Ascents: Psalms 120–134 in the Worship of Jerusalem's Temples* (Newton Mearns, Glasgow: Campbell).
2016 *Messiah ben Joseph* (Newton Mearns, Glasgow: Campbell).
Moffic, E.
2016 *What Every Christian Needs to Know About the Jewishness of Jesus* (Abingdon Press).
Na'aman, N.
2010 'David's Sojourn in Keilah in Light of the Amarna Letters', *VT* 60: 87–97.
Neubauer, A.
1888 "Jewish Controversy and the 'Pugio Fidei' ", *The Expositor* 7: 24.
Neusner, J. & W.S. Green (eds.)
1996 *Dictionary of Judaism in the Biblical Period* (New York: Simon & Schuster Macmillan).
Neyrey, J.H.
1991 "'Without Beginning of Days or end of life' (Hebrews 7:3): Topos for a true Deity", *Catholic Biblical Quarterly* 53: 439–55.
Niedźwiedzki, T.
2016 'Joseph's Two Garments. The Reception of Joseph in Targum Neofiti', *Aramaic Studies* 14:147–183.
Nutzman, M.
2013 'Mary In The Protevangelium Of James' in *Greek, Roman, and Byzantine Studies* 53:551–578, esp. 556-559.
O'Neill, J.C.
1991 'The Man from Heaven: SibOr 5:256–259' in *JSP* 9: 87–102.
Orlov, A.
2000 'Melchizedek Legend of 2 (Slavonic) Enoch', *Journal for the Study of Judaism* 31:21–38.
Petrovich, D.N.
2016 *The World's Oldest Alphabet: Hebrew as the Language of the Proto-Consonantal Script* (Jerusalem: Carta).
Philonenko, M.
1958–59 'Les interpolations chrétiennes des Douze patriarches et les manuscrits de Qoumrân', *Revue d'histoire et de philosophie religieuses,* 38 (1958) 309–43, 39 (1959) 14–38.
Postell, S.D.
2020 'Messianism in Light of Literary Strategy', *Bibliotheca Sacra* 177: 329–350.
2019 'A Literary, Compositional, and Intertextual Analysis of Psalm 45', *Bibliotheca Sacra* 176: 146–164.
Prothero, S.
2003 *American Jesus: How the Son of God Became a National Icon* (New York: Farrar, Straus and Giroux).

Rabow, J.A.
2002 *50 Jewish Messiahs: The Untold Life Stories of 50 Jewish Messiahs Since Jesus and How They Changed the Jewish, Christian, and Muslim Worlds* (NY: Gefen Books).
Reich, R.
1994 'The Ancient Burial Ground in the Mamilla Neighborhood, Jerusalem', in H. Geva (ed.), *Ancient Jerusalem Revealed* (Jerusalem: Israel Exploration Society): 111–118.
Rico, C. & A. Dan (eds.),
2017 *The Library of Alexandria: A Cultural Crossroads of the Ancient World* (Jerusalem: Polis Institute Press, 2017), 79-87.
Rokeaḥ, D.
1969 'Ben Stara is Ben Pantera—Towards the Clarification of a Philological-Historical Problem / בן סטרא בן פנטירא הוא (לבירורה של בעיה פילולוגית-היסטורית)', *Tarbiz* 39: 9–18.
Ross, A.P.
2011–15 *A Commentary on the Psalms*. 3 vols. (Grand Rapids, MI: Kregel).
Rosenberg, G.
2020 'An Allusion Connecting Genesis 18:10, 14 and 2 Kings 4:16–17.' *JBL* 139.4: 701–720.
Roth, C.
1959 'The Zealots in the War of 66–73', *Journal of Semitic Studies* 4: 347–48.
Sáenz-Badillos, A.
1993 *A History of the Hebrew Language* (Cambridge: Cambridge University Press).
Savran, G.W.
2005 *Encountering the Divine; Theophany in Biblical Narrative* (London: T & T Clark).
Sawyer, D.F.
1993 *Midrash Aleph Beth* (Atlanta, Georgia: Scholars).
Schaeffer, E. & U. Middelmann
1975 *Christianity is Jewish* (Tyndale House).
Schäfer, P.
2012 *The Jewish Jesus: How Judaism and Christianity Shaped Each Other* (Princeton University Press).
2007 *Jesus in the Talmud* (Princeton University Press, 2007).
Schaff, P. (ed.)
1887 *Nicene and Post-Nicene Fathers*, First Series, Vol. 1. (Buffalo, NY: Christian Literature Publishing Company).
Schonfield, H.
1927 *An Old Hebrew Text of St. Matthew's Gospel* (Edinburgh: T&T Clark).
Schwartz, J. & P.J. Tomson
2012 'When Rabbi Eliezer was arrested for Heresy' in *Jewish Studies Internet Journal* 10: 145–181.

Schwartz, S.
1993 'John Hyrcanus I's Destruction of the Gerizim Temple and Judean-Samaritan Relations', *Jewish History* 7: 9–25.
Segal, A.
1977 *Two Powers in Heaven. Early Rabbinic Reports about Christianity and Gnosticism* (Leiden: Brill).
Simon, M.
1937 'Melchisédech dans la polémique entre juifs et chrétiens et dans la légende,' *Revue d'Histoire et de Philosophie religieuses* 17:58–93.
Skiena, S. and C.B. Ward
2014 *Who's Bigger?: Where Historical Figures Really Rank* (Cambridge University Press).
Sproul, R.C.
1990 *The Glory of Christ* (Wheaton IL: Tyndale House).
Stec, D.M.
2004 *The Targum of Psalms: Translated, with a Critical Introduction, Apparatus, and Notes* (The Aramaic Bible 16; London–New York: T&T Clark).
Strelan, R.
2008 *Luke the Priest* (Farnham, Surrey: Ashgate).
Stuckenbruck, L.
2018 'Melchizedek in Jewish Apocalyptic Literature', *Journal for the Study of the New Testament* 41: 124–138.
Thiede, C.P. and M. d'Ancona
1996 *Eyewitness to Jesus: Amazing New Manuscript Evidence About the Origin of the Gospels* (New York: Doubleday, 1996).
Thomas, J.
1969 'Aktuelles im Zeugnis der Zwölf Väter' in Walther Eltester (ed.), *Studien zu den Testamenten der zwölf Patriarchen* (Berlin: Töpelmann): 62–150.
Tiller, P.A.
1993 *A Commentary on the Animal Apocalypse of 1 Enoch* (Atlanta: Scholars).
Toepel, A.
2005 'Planetary Demons in Early Jewish Literature', *JSP* 14: 231–38.
Torrey, C.C.
1947 'The Messiah Son of Ephraim', *JBL* 66: 253–277.
1945 *The Apocryphal Literature* (New Haven: Yale University Press).
Tsahar, E.I., Izhaki, S. Lev-Yadun, G. Bar-Oz
2009 'Distribution and Extinction of Ungulates during the Holocene of the Southern Levant', PLoS ONE 4(4): e5316. doi:10.1371/journal.pone.0005316.
VanderKam, J. C.
2001 *Introduction to Early Judaism* (Grand Rapids, MI: Eerdmans).
Vermes, G.
2003 *Jesus in His Jewish Context* (Minneapolis: Fortress Press).
1993 *The Religion of Jesus the Jew* (Minneapolis, Fortress Press).

1973 *Jesus the Jew: A Historian's Reading of the Gospels* (London: Collins).

Walck, L.W.

2011 *The Son of Man in the Parables of Enoch and Matthew* (London: T.&T. Clark): 15–23.

Waltke, B.

2007 *An Old Testament Theology: An Exegetical, Canonical, and Thematic Approach* (Grand Rapids: Zondervan, 2007).

Wenham, G.J.

1987 *Genesis 1–15* (Word Biblical Commentary; Dallas, TX: Word).

Wilson, G.H.

2005 'King, Messiah, and the Reign of God: Revisiting the Royal Psalms and the Shape of the Psalter' in P.W. Flint and P.D. Miller (eds.), *The Book of Psalms: Composition and Reception* (Leiden–Boston: Brill), pp. 391-406

Witherington, B.

1995 *The Jesus Quest: The Third Search for the Jew of Nazareth* (Downers Grove: IVP).

van der Woude, A.S.

1957 *Die messianischen Vorstellungen der Gemeinde von Qumrân* (Assen: Van Gorcum).

Wünsche, A.K.

1885 *Bibliotheca Rabbinica* (Leipzig).

Young, B.H.

1995 *Jesus the Jewish Theologian* (Peabody: Hendrickson, 1995).

General Index

Made in United States
North Haven, CT
20 March 2024